Modern Music

TO ADDIE ABBOT

For Good Songs and Good Words.

Modern Music

COMPOSERS AND MUSIC
OF OUR TIME

Max Graf

PHILOSOPHICAL LIBRARY
New York

TRANSLATED BY BEATRICE R. MAIER

46 - 7085

Table of Contents

"I am one of those who admire the ancients, yet I do not, like some others, underrate certain instances of genius which our own times afford. For it is not true that nature, as if weary and effete, no longer produces, what is admirable."

THE YOUNGER PLINY.

"This epoch will constitute a special great chapter in world history. It will be recognized as a transition, a break, and a creation. The world as a whole has always proceeded and will always proceed along a line of progress, in spite of even the bitterest reaction. It is its fate, the law of its maintenance. Not only the fight for world security, but also the fight for world culture is indivisible."

DR. EDOUARD BENES,
President of Czechoslovakia.

Modern Music

1

The Twilight of the Classical Gods

I

ON OCTOBER 13, 1896 I stood among several hundred persons who had gathered in the Karlskirche in Vienna to bid Anton Bruckner a last farewell. Beneath the high cupola of the church, in whose fresco paintings the Heavens open up, Saints descend on clouds and Angels float gracefully around the gleaming monstrance, stood the catafalque onto which the coffin was lifted.

From high above the church choir sounded the funereal music of the Seventh Symphony which Bruckner had composed on the occasion of Richard Wagner's death. The mighty metal tones of Bruckner's music ascended solemnly together with the incense which the priests, in black chasubles, sent up from silver vessels. The music increased in volume, reaching its climax in the radiant sounding of the cymbals, heralding the Glory and the Honor.

Bruckner's music became as one with the baroque style of the church, for it was itself ornate baroque art, just like the church of Karl the Sixth, in which marble saints guarded the altars, angels of marble and gold hovered over the chapels and the fresco of the cupola showed the Heavens.

The composer, at whose coffin the priests were now chanting monotone prayers for the dead, had spent all his life in such baroque structures. One of them had been the Convent of St. Florian. Here, as a young musician, Bruckner had first played the organ and here he had reverently kneeled in its baroque passages when the Prelate passed by in solemn procession.

Other similar structures were the domes of Linz, Vienna, and the monastery Klosterneuburg. Here, Bruckner had sat on the organ bench and had let the church organ peal out, stronger and stronger—verily a "musician of God" and perhaps the last of his kind.

After the coffin had been consecrated according to the rites of the Catholic Church, it was carried to the hearse by students who, with drawn sabres, had stood guard around the catafalque. Then, as was his wish, Bruckner was brought to his home in Upper Austria. The autumn mists were already hovering over the fields and meadows and the crows sang their gloomy song that had always put him in a mournful mood when he traveled from the city to the country in the fall.

In the church of the St. Florian Convent, where Bruckner's coffin was brought, the "De profundis" sounded while the bier was placed under the organ that had been Anton Bruckner's organ and that had first taught him to elevate himself with music to the heavens and to the Halo of God, as heralded to the world by the radiant timbre in the finales of his symphonies.

It was but half a year later—on April 6, 1897—that we accompanied Johannes Brahms to his last resting place in the Protestant Cemetery of Vienna.

If Bruckner was familiar with the glory of Heaven, Brahms was intimate with the bitterness of death. His last composition sings movingly: "Oh, Death, how bitter art thou." His "Deutches Requiem" had preached with the gloomy tones of a funeral march: "For all flesh is like the grass." Even as a young man Brahms had intoned, strictly and austerely, the serious melody "Nun wollen wir den Leib begraben" ("Now will we bury the body").

A strong, simple, homely man was now being lowered into the earth, a man who had known the bitterness of life and whose favorite book was the Lutheran Bible. A life that had been filled with work was ended; what remained were the mighty works written by the man who now had passed on to the Great Beyond.

Both composers belonged to the Vienna in which we grew up. Going for a walk, we met Brahms and Bruckner almost daily. When we attended a concert they were both there, too. When new compositions of Brahms and Bruckner were performed, they appeared on the stage and acknowledged the applause: Brahms somewhat embarrassed, clumsily bending his heavy body; Bruckner with deep bows and throwing hand kisses.

Often we listened to Brahms playing piano in the Vienna concert halls when he accompanied artists singing his songs, or when he had new chamber music performed. Every Sunday found Bruckner sitting at the organ of the old court chapel, letting his short legs, encased in wide, baggy trousers, run over the pedals.

Occasionally we would wait for a whole hour at the small door leading to the Imperial chapel before we could enter the high, narrow room. Above its altar the old Emperor would pray in his private box, and high above the entrance ran the gallery from which the music tones descended. At other times we listened to Bruckner improvising at the organ of the Stephanskirche or in the church at Klosterneuburg.

Of an evening, Brahms and Bruckner would sit in one of those cozy inns in Vienna where the tables in the low-ceilinged rooms were covered with white cloths and the beer came up from the cellar light, cool and fresh, with the frothy head they both appreciated. Here one could hear Brahms hissing sharp and sometimes poisonous words in his North German dialect, while Bruckner conversed with his friends and pupils in the Upper Austrian peasant dialect.

On Sundays both composers took walks through the Vienna woods. Brahms loved the woods in the southern district of Vienna where Beethoven had stormed through forests of beech and fir trees, where Schubert sat beneath the linden "Am Brunnen vor dem Tore." We, too, rested under that tree after wandering through the woods, but without ever getting the inspiration for such a lovely melody. Bruckner on the other hand liked to ride out to the North of Vienna where the green cupola of Klosterneuburg arch over the gardens; where apple and peach trees blossom out near the Danube in the spring and where low yellow houses string along to the river.

At that time neither Johannes Brahms nor Anton Bruckner belonged to music history, but rather to life and to their era. Their music did not yet bear the scholars' seal of approval. In the large concert hall where we went evenings, the hissing with which the Brahms Fourth Symphony was met still clung to the caryatides of the loges and to the chandeliers suspended from the ceiling, from which the nine Muses looked down upon the hissing audience in wonderment. The music of Anton Bruckner even caused concert goers to flee.

Only a handful of young musicians who later achieved fame as conductors—among them Arthur Nikisch, Ferdinand Loewe and Franz Schalk—recognized the genius in Bruckner.

Vienna's conservative society agreed with the authoritative music critics who considered Bruckner a foolish Wagnerian. In their parlors Hanslick cracked jokes about modern music, and Brahms growled like an old poodle. But Brahms as well as Bruckner still stood among the praetorian guards who spoke their critical opinions in the music markets; and Praetor Hanslick and Deputy Praetor Kalbeck and the other magistrates were severe judges, in possession of all the law books of classical music, omniscient as God Himself and infallible as the Pope, the representative of God on earth. Brahms and Bruckner were poor sinners who, like all other composing sinners, had to appear before a tribunal where hung the marble tablets inscribed with the laws of art.

Johannes Brahms had come to Vienna from the gloomy North in 1862, and had stayed there. Life was sunnier than in the North, where the ocean's storms blew through Hamburg's streets; the people were gayer, life easier and the women more sensual.

Six years after Brahms, Bruckner arrived in Vienna (1868) to teach harmony, counterpoint and organ at the conservatory. Since that time all important works of the two composers had been written in Vienna and belonged to the music life of Vienna. Since Brahms had settled permanently in Vienna and had started work on his "Deutsches Requiem" here, one of his new compositions appeared each year on the programs of the Viennese concert halls.

With the exception of the First Symphony, composed in Linz, all of Anton Bruckner's symphonies were written in Vienna: beginning with the Schubert-like Second—mockingly called the "Symphony of Pauses"—all the way through to the Ninth Symphony, the finale of which Bruckner sketched almost illegibly on his deathbed. An ostentatious funeral ceremony was the last gift of the musician city to the two great composers before Brahms was laid to rest in the earth that harbored Beethoven and Schubert and in which Mozart had disappeared somewhere, and before Bruckner was brought to St. Florian.

Those of us who had been present at both funeral services felt for the first time that with these two composers a great music era had ended. As long as Brahms and Bruckner could be seen in Vienna's streets, that idea never really occurred to us. Their music, on which the ink had barely dried, belonged to the living world together with so much other great music: with Goldmark's luxuriant orchestra timbre; with Johann Strauss' new waltzes; with Hugo Wolf's new songs; with Verdi's philosophically smiling "Falstaff"; with Humperdinck's fairy opera "Haensel and Gretel"; with the new operas of Massenet and Mascagni.

The whole era, Vienna and the rest of the world were full of new music. Everywhere there were battles about music—a sure sign that it was living music.

How difficult things had been for Brahms, when he came to Vienna with his first compositions! How gray and misty, how Nordic and heavy had the new Brahm's Music at first been considered in the sensuous Vienna of that time; how colorless it appeared to be in the era of Wagner, Liszt and Berlioz. Bruckner was fought with sarcasm and mockery, Hugo Wolf with silence.

All music was still in the present, full of fight, contrast and argument. Even the controversy over Wagner's art had just ended victoriously the previous day, and the older generation submitted resentfully to the yoke of the tyrannical musician.

But standing at the grave of Brahms and at the catafalque on which rested Bruckner's coffin, we realized that a whole music epoch had gone, not merely two great musicians, and we knew that the events we had witnessed were a part of music history. Our enthusiasm, our battles, our controversies, our excitement had become a piece of the past that would wither just like the wreaths that had been placed on the biers of Brahms and Bruckner. Brahms and Bruckner now belonged to History. Their era had become one of the important historical eras of all time.

II

With the arrival in 1740 of Joseph Haydn, who came to Vienna at the age of eight to sing with the choir of the old Stephan Cathedral, the great classical era had begun that was lowered into the earth with Brahms and Bruckner.

An unseen force drew musicians from all ends of the world to Vienna, and the Gothic tower of the Stephanskirche looked down on the city that has been acclaimed by the whole universe as a City of Music. In 1791 Mozart left the service of the Archbishop of Salzburg and remained in Vienna, where he created his biggest works and vanished in its earth. In 1792, 22-year-old Beethoven came from the Rhine and from then on Vienna became a Beethoven City. When Brahms and Bruckner came to Vienna, whose brown walls encircled the Imperial Palace, old castles, churches and tall merchant buildings, there were still many people living in that fortress city, who had watched the demon-like maestro walk through its narrow streets, or who had played in orchestras, when his compositions had first been performed. As yet, the houses, landscape, palaces, concert halls and the people themselves belonged to Beethoven.

Brahms remained in Vienna because it was the city of music classics, and above all, because it was Beethoven's City. Shortly before coming to Vienna, he had taken the turn from the romantic Storm and Stress period and from fantastic music forms to the severity of the classical form in his Serenade Opus 11. With this music he had consciously become a classicist. The Beethoven tone is apparent throughout this music. Its second movement is a Beethoven scherzo.

Almost during the same period, in his D-Minor Piano Concerto, Brahms had tragic, Beethoven-like storms raging. Like a mighty waterfall, the dismal-passionate trills cascade at the start of the concerto and no listener can fail to think immediately of the beginning of Beethoven's Ninth Symphony when the first mournful D-Minor triad is struck. Brahms came to Vienna as a Beethoven musician, as a Beethoven heir. The pathos of Anton Bruckner, too, is Beethoven pathos and in later times only Bruckner could write the great Beethoven Adagio that rises to Heaven like a prayer.

For Brahms, as well as for Bruckner, the symphony is above everything else the Beethoven Symphony. From Haydn to Bruckner and Brahms the symphony is the center of all musical creation. It constitutes the greatest form. In it are unfolded the largest riches of thoughts, the greatest art of forming. The symphony represents in music the same as the novel does in fiction: a world picture comprised of many personalities and events.

However, it was not merely the Beethoven form that made Brahms and Bruckner Beethoven's heirs, but the Beethoven spirit of the symphony as well, which lived for the last time in their music. Even the symphony of the romanticists before Brahms and Bruckner had become something else than a Beethoven symphony had been. The two greatest Mendelssohn symphonies: the "Scotch Symphony" and the "Italian Symphony" are landscapes and impressive aquarells. They are seen through the eyes of an educated wanderer, who always carries his sketchbook with him and with a light hand sketches all the peculiarities of a strange landscape.

As a musician, Mendelssohn was the first to compose impressionistic music with the fantasy of a painter. Drawing the mists of the Scotch Hebrides, the gray, windblown waves, Mendelssohn is just as much the impressionist painter as when he reproduces the spook of "A Midsummer Night's Dream" with colorful dabs and speckles, with dancing colors and with sparkling lights. These are already realistic landscape paintings, no longer the ideal scenery of Beethoven.

On the other hand, Schumann's symphonies are novelistic inventions. They are romantic stories, filled with wanderlust, spring magic, recollections of youthful dreams; with chorals sounding from the churchtower, and with fanciful love singing its songs in all forms of nature—in the magic of the forest and on dewy meadows, in the flowers and in the breeze of Spring.

How far Schumann withdrew from the Beethoven symphony becomes apparent from the fact that in none of his symphonies did he compose an adagio with an enlarged melodic line. All his slow movements are short ones, containing the mood of a dreamy hour but never the intensity of a prayer. The colorful frescoes of Berlioz, bold and subjective as Lord Byron's poems, glowing in color like paintings by Delacroix; and the pathetic symphonic poems of Franz Liszt, declamatory music comparable to Lamartine's Periods, music with grand dramatic gestures have nothing in common with the spirit of Beethoven's symphonic music. They belong to the French romantic period. They are painting and theatre, not philosophy.

But then, none of the great symphonies written after Brahms and Bruckner are Beethovenish in spirit. The noble D-Minor symphony of César Franck, the symphonies of Russian composers, from Tschaikowsky and Borodin and to Shostakovich, the lyric symphonies of Dvorak, the Nordic symphonic bardic lays by Sibelius are all personal, gripping music, but romantic music, not classic. In their music the scenery is characteristic, the subjective feeling strong, the form rich and artistic, the orchestra colorful, but in none of these symphonies does the landscape approach a simile, a symbol, a portrayal of God as in Beethoven's works. None of these composers possessed, as did Beethoven, a cosmic sense when he communes with Nature, when he listens to the brook murmuring, the birds singing and, particularly, to the raging storms which Beethoven, like all ancient peoples, interprets as the thundering voice of God.

How little does the romantic subjectivism of such musicians have in common with the heroical and metaphysical might of Beethoven! How far apart are the spiritual battles of Tschaikowsky from the Faust-like struggles of Beethoven; how elegant are the fanciful laments of César Franck, how playful the virtuosity of Shostakovich, how primitive Dvorak's lyric compared to the Titanism of Beethoven!

What Brahms and Bruckner actually did accomplish in the romantic period was the resurrection of the spirit of the Beethoven symphony in their music, not merely of the form of this symphony. In the biggest moments of their creative lives they both wrote Beethoven music again. Their music contains the tone, the soulful magnificence, the spiritual background of the Beethoven symphony, and reaches into the metaphysical depths which Beethoven presents to the world with the chorus of the Ninth Symphony: "Ahnest Du den Schoepfer, Welt?"

The dark tragic tone, or the hard belligerent timbre that had been missing in the romantic symphony make their first reappearance in the works of Johannes Brahms. With the start of his D-Minor Piano Concerto Brahms produces the genuine sound of tragic passion. Again, the first movement of the Brahms Symphony in C-Minor is filled with man's struggles against unknown forces of the soul. The musicians of the Romantic era had completely forgotten that music was capable of expressing the spiritual battles of mankind by employing tone and melody, and that there had been created such works as the "Eroica," and the Fifth and Ninth Symphonies.

Mendelssohn's gentle melancholia and Schumann's dreamy sadness constitute the borderline at which the German romanticists in music penetrated the sphere of darkness.

But Brahms again finds himself in the center of night and storm, and he fights it. The Beethoven rhythm reappears in the Brahms Piano Sonata No. 1, and the festive victory march at the close of his First Symphony is pronouncedly reminiscent of the joyful hymn in Beethoven's Ninth. Thus one comes across the Beethoven symphony in all of Brahms' instrumental music, and after Beethoven's era it was Brahms who first brought to mind that music can contain dark storm clouds.

The romanticists depict lovely summer nights punctuated by glow worms flashing through the green; meadows shining silvery in the moonlight; gray mists rising from the fields; even foreign countries. But they know nothing of heavy clouds massing for a storm, or of thunder and lightning. In Schubert's music a dark cloud may occasionally disturb the serene scenery of the Vienna Woods, but it passes quickly. Brahms, however, more often than not saw the skies gray. He is the exponent of autumnal scenery, described so beautifully in his Fourth Symphony. In the first movement of this composition one can almost see the leaves falling from the trees. Everything here is dark and fallow, reminding the listener of death and sorrow, of the grave and the instability of life. The slow movement is funereal, and the variations of the final movement a danse macabre as Holbein painted it.

Brahms' attitude towards life is that of a pessimist, not heroic like Beethoven's. Nevertheless, the fact that he knew the dark side of life and the depths of passion, and that he perpetuated this knowledge in his music is responsible for bringing him closer to Beethoven than the romantic composers ever were.

III

Despite the great difference in personalities—Brahms was bourgeois, Beethoven demonic—the classicism of Brahms gave his music the last Beethoven touch. This classicism is a composite product. By no means is it to be taken for granted, since the classic form represents a work of art to the modern musician. To Haydn, Mozart and Beethoven the symphonic form had been their natural means of expression, but certainly for a musician like Brahms the classic mold was not natural and self-understood. All around him it began to transform itself, to dissolve into poetic moods, literature and paintings. The spiritual strength that had held the classic form together had disappeared. The romantic fancy was too colored, too subjective, too arbitrary to be able to construct musical thoughts into great arcs in which was contained an eternal law.

As a matter of fact Brahms started out as a romantic musician. We can only imagine the storms raging within him when, like a true romanticist, he wandered through the Spring nights in company of the violinist Remenyi. When he played his early compositions for Schumann, the latter found in him a "kindred soul" who was at home in "magic romantic circles, close to a waterfall supporting a rainbow, with butterflies swarming around and accompanied by nightingales." Thus he proclaims jubilantly in his essay "Neue Bahnen."

Much of the music composed by the youthful Brahms is written in free romantic form. Much of it was later destroyed by Brahms for this very reason. One of these romantic works—the

Piano Trio in B-Minor, which he composed as early as 1854, Brahms altered in 1891 when he was a mature composer. In its original form the Trio was romantic style. Not until he reshaped it did it show any classic style. Brahms himself admitted having written at least twenty string quartettes before he could master the perfect classical form contained in the two string quartettes which he published in 1873. Even the D-Minor Piano Concerto whose dark romantic passion and tragedy was considered too modern by the Leipzig conservatives at its first performance, did not receive its classic form until later.

As is found to be the case in all romantic music, programmatic allusions play a big part in the works of the young composer Brahms. He quotes folk songs in the FiFrst Piano Sonata—or the stanzas of a poem in the slow movement of the F-Minor Piano Sonata, or a musical theme: A-G-A-H (B)-E. These musical letters call out the name of the woman he was enamored of: Agathe von Sternheim in Goettingen. Schumann, too, favored such themes in his piano music.

As a young musician Brahms belonged heart and soul to the romantic style. He came from a romantic city in which the storms and mists of the North Sea had created as early as the eighteenth century a seascape romanticism that differed greatly from the landscape romance of Middle Germany. There is a serious romantic mood to be found on the Heath near Hamburg, too, and the desolate quiet of the brown, barren country makes the inhabitants austere and taciturn, even melancholy. One such man of the Heath was Storm, Brahms' favorite poet.

This northern romance, clinging to the landscape like the fogs of that region, was the romance of Brahms. It is to be found all through his music. The sadness and gloominess of the song "Am Kirchhof" is a part of it; likewise the elegy of the Intermezzo in E-Flat Minor in which the wind blows across the Heath. The ballad-like storms of his Piano Rhapsodies belong to it, as does the autumnal desolation of the Fourth Symphony. All of this music is filled with moods of death and instability, moods created in the awkward, incommunicative, passionate inhabitants of the northern regions by the dismal surroundings.

That is the kind of man Brahms was, and the romantic music of his youth was of such a dark, gloomy, stormy nature.

When in 1860 Brahms emerged from several years' retirement with the lithographed score of his D-Major Serenade, he was a changed man. He had abjured his romantic youth. The Serenade was an imitation of the classics with many reminders of Beethoven's music. There is something deliberate and artificial in this Serenade in which Brahms barricades his romanticism behind classic forms.

To Brahms the new form signified a restraint of his romantic passion. The classic, Beethoven form provides protection for him against all the storm, gloom and pathos of his nature; in other words, against everything that Brahms had inherited from his northern habitat and that, heritage of his ancestors, stirred his blood. It was an escape to self-control, to lucidity and to moderation. To him, the classic form was a fortress in which he barricaded himself. He makes use of these forms, which were employed by the classic fantasy to attain its greatest freedom, for the purpose of repressing the natural inspirations of his romantic fancy.

From that time dated the attitude that was to characterize Brahms. His emotional being remained romantic, but hid behind classical forms. This self-negation is one of the most striking traits in Brahms, and is also to be found in the personal life of the artist. Brahms liked to cloak the gentle side of his nature with gruff remarks, conceal his soft-heartedness behind biting sarcasm. He could be kind and tender with children, but to the world in general he showed his thorny side. When he committed a kind act, he preferred to keep it a secret. Similarly, in his music he often covered up its free spirit with a network of rhythms, like a protective fence around his true self.

His scherzos are never free play of his spirit as they are in the music of Haydn and Beethoven. They are either an expression of a crude sense of humor, as represented in the Fourth Symphony; or they are reflective, meditative like in the Symphony Number II; or muted merriness as in the First Symphony. The expression of full, brightly gleaming jubilation that proclaims victory in Beethoven's music; the hilarity of a festive hour, or the elation of a triumphal procession is missing altogether in Brahms' compositions. The victory music towards the finale of the C-Minor Symphony borrows its jubilant tones from Beethoven; the "Triumphal Song" that is to glorify the German victories is, in its entirety, an imitation of Haendel.

Brahms gives vent to his feelings more freely in the intimate forms of chambermusic and song, not in the large structures of orchestral and choral music. His songs often contain a wonderful gentleness and warmth, but in his symphonies he appears to be ashamed of such tendeeness. An adagio in which emotion might unfold in broad singing tones—a prayer adagio such as Beethoven wrote so often—was never composed by Brahms.

The conflict between a passionate Ego and the law of objectivity which played a fundamental part in the lives of so many artists and which in Goethe was represented in great epics such as "Iphigenia" or "Tasso"—this conflict in Brahms, the energetic man, found its outlet in his music. The law of objectivity to him was the Beethoven form, and to that form he surrendered his passionate strength. In it he saw mainly the force of logic in musical shape, and the energy in the concentration of thoughts. No other musician is as close to this construction energy of Beethoven as Brahms. Nor could any other symphonic music attain creative energy comparable to that which constitutes Beethoven's greatness, with the exception of the first movement of the Brahms Symphony Number One. This work surpasses in logical strength every music creation of modern times. Here everything is crowded together, the clouds of passion condensed, the world of shapelessness and agitation controlled by spiritual power.

Thus we find in Brahms a complicated and, as such, a modern personality, just as his relation to the classic form is complicated. The classic music forms are for Brahms not merely "form"—that is the outer shape of an emotional and artistic core; rather they are dams that repress this emotional and artistic core. They are historic forms, not the natural patterns of artistic imagination. Brahms is a romanticist who uses the classic form to suppress his romanticism. Brahms the classicist holds Brahms the romanticist a prisoner who becomes visible behind iron bars.

Brahms fights his romanticism as Goethe struggled against his

Werther moods. When Goethe was once asked whether his "Werther" were a true story, he replied "there were two persons in one. One of them had perished while the other remained alive in order to write the story of the first." He quotes the Book of Job which says: "Lord, your sheep and slaves have all been slain. I alone have escaped to bring you the news." Brahms the classicist also proclaims the news that sheep and slaves have been slain. He alone has survived, a strong and severe man, hiding his dismal, tempestuous, melancholy romanticism behind a classic wall.

IV

It was not to the strict form of the Beethoven symphony that Anton Bruckner turned with his nine symphonies, but rather to its idealistic value. The form presented no problem to the naïve and unsophisticated Bruckner. It was a natural gift. He accepted this form from his teacher, Simon Sechter, as a school lesson whose perpetual validity was not to be doubted. Thousands of composers before him had made use of this mold and had poured into it music which, if not beautiful, at least had been correct. Thousands more would avail themselves of it. Like the alphabet and like the Lord's Prayer, it was unchangeable.

Standing at his lecturing desk in the University of Vienna, Anton Bruckner taught us young students the form which he in turn had learned from Simon Sechter. Always interspersing his lectures with comical similitudes from everyday life, he led us to the peasants of his Upper Austrian homeland and to its houses. Standing thus he was the old schoolmaster with hundreds of wrinkles lining his old face, who instructed his pupils how to write and figure. "The substantive rules the sentence." "Two and two equals four." Those were time-established rules. And so, for Bruckner, was the classic form.

The classic structure became a model for Bruckner, a stencil that he employed in all his symphonies. It was the mold into which he poured the fiery metal of his musical fantasy. For this reason all nine of Bruckner's symphonies are of the same construction; just as all the churches in which Bruckner attended services—

whether in Linz, in Vienna or in St. Florian—had the same fundamental structure: the arched nave, the pillars, the altar at the east
side, the organ atop the church gallery at the west. While the form
is fluid at the hands of the classicists, it becomes fixed and unchangeable for Bruckner. He appears to consider form not so much
the exterior surrounding the core and the shape of artistic ideas
as he believes it to be something independent, self-sufficient, an
unalterable shell for his great imagination.

Bruckner did not share at all Brahms' conviction that form is
a moral law that must control passion and that subjects the fantastic and the excessive to the power of thought. His nature
resembles Schubert's, and his symphony is a lyric song. His music
flows along like the Danube flows past villages, forests, shrines
and convents in his own Upper Austrian region. The music pours
out in a broad stream, and no musician of modern times invented
music in such great patterns as did Bruckner in his Adagios. Here
the music sings its melodies in wide arcs, the enhancements are
like a climb to high mountain peaks. Bruckner is hardly a musician
for modern people who find no time either for their sentiments
or their thoughts and who do not know what it means to possess
serenity and depth of soul.

To Bruckner music is comparable with religious services. His
symphonies could sooner be considered Masses in symphonic form
instead of actual secular music. His adagios are supplications to
God in whom he believed as devoutly as a mediaeval saint. His
entire pure, child-like nature was more closely related to the
nature of the great saints of the thirteenth century than to the
nature of modern humans.

His countenance, refulgent with celestial bliss and radiating
the kindness within him bears a marked resemblance to the faces
pictured by Giotto and other Italian painters of the Middle Ages.
In their portrayals of the Assumption of the Blessed Virgin the
Apostles, gazing reverently and devotedly after the vanishing
image, bear the same facial expression. We had accompanied
Bruckner often enough during his walks to realize that the busy
life of the big city was, and always would be, strange to him.
Only when Bruckner sat at the church organ and let the tones

peal out broad and mighty, when the church filled with the radiance of his music—then he was in a world of his own: a man of prayer in the House of God, for whom time stood still as it did for the Almighty.

Anton Bruckner does not sound Beethoven-like in his symphonies merely because he uses the classical form as a foundation. More than that, he has captured the Beethoven spirit as no later musician has done. His symphonies, like those of the titanic maestro, are not simply music in which an individual sings of his joy or sorrow. They are not just personal musical expression of his passions, or moods of his inner life, of his battles and his victories.

Again like the Beethoven symphonies, those of Bruckner are divided into three sections. In the foreground is visible only the individual, with his individual moods and his own particular adventures; the song of the individual soul, the prayer of the individual personality, the joy and sorrow of the individual human. In the background the great world looms like a second and larger stage: Nature, absorbing all moods of man, fortifies them and blends them with everyday life. Humanity, with the voice of the individual chiming in with its chorus. And above all this an eternal sphere for all great and profound humans, whence the life of the individual, and life in general, derive their purpose.

Only a symphony of this kind can rightfully be called a Beethoven symphony, and even as great a composer as Schubert never penetrated further than the second world: Nature.

In comparing Bruckner's symphonies to those of Schubert, one thinks of the many scenic pictures and moods surrounding Bruckner's music. In his symphonies the Upper Austrian home of Bruckner comes to life. One can hear the rustle of the forests in this piece of land; in his Fourth Symphony the thrush sounds its call, the hunters' horns peal through the green woods and "Michel" (Bruckner's symbol for his people) dreams at the forest's edge. The broad river of the Bruckner countryside; the dance floor and the spinning room; school room and meadow—all are contained in this music which, just like Schubert's music, is itself a piece of nature and just as colorful.

The symphonic composers of Russia, whose works rarely omit the Russian landscape, progressed that far too. So did Dvorak, in whose symphonies the Czech village and the Czech forest appear, and wherein the Czech folk dance. Likewise Sibelius when he translated the Finnish lakes and mountains into music. In all European countries romanticism evoked an interest in national life, and in the landscape, the peoples and their sagas.

But Bruckner goes further. As a religious being he knows that the life of the individual, life in general, man and world have their significance in a higher sphere. There is not one symphony of Anton Bruckner's that does not seek the way to Heaven. This Heaven is for Anton Bruckner the Catholic Heaven with God Father, Son and Holy Ghost; with saints, martyrs and confessors, and with hosts of angels. It was Heaven as he saw it in altar pieces at church, and as it was portrayed on the Trinity Posts standing in every village square of his homeland.

When Bruckner heightened the themes of his symphonies to chorals, he purported to symbolize the descent of the Holy Spirit to the carnal world. Towards the end of the Fifth Symphony, when the brass section sounds its glorious choral, all Heaven opens up; and the Ninth Symphony was dedicated to the "Dear Lord."

This faith in God lends a certain solemnity to every theme of Bruckner's symphonies, intensity to every enhancement, and pomp and splendor to every finale.

It is wrong to call Bruckner a Wagnerian musician. He is a Baroque musician and, like all Baroque adherents, he pays homage to "Ecclesia Triumphans." The radiance of his symphonies is equal to that of the colors in which Rubens let the Heavens shine, and the arcs of his symphonies are the arched cupolas of Fonatana's and Borromini's churches.

Bruckner became acquainted with Baroque in his home country. Upper Austria is crowded with memorials in the Baroque style. The churches in St. Florian and in Linz in which he developed as an organist are Baroque structures, and the services at which he played the organ were Baroque services.

Anybody hearing Bruckner play his instrument knew that the timbre of his symphonies, their crescendos and triumphant mass expansion are as much sacred music as his organ improvisations had been.

In Bruckner's symphonies we find for the last time in the modern era the combination of man, world and Heaven, as we find it in the great art of the Middle Ages and the Renaissance, and (on a philosophical basis) in the classic art and philosophy of modern times.

Music obtains its purport, its goal, its value from a Beyond. In it, as in every great art, there is a joining of the physical and spiritual, mind and matter, sound and ideal. After Bruckner's time this association gets lost or becomes problematic. Such was the case in Gustav Mahler's symphony which, during a crisis of mental and spiritual strife in the new era tried with extraordinary energy to rescue Bruckner's idea; that symphonic music is universal interpretation like all great art, like every great tragedy, every great painting, every great structure that purports to express eternity. Anton Bruckner was the last great idealistic musician with such naïve and religious world sentiment. As such he influenced his pupil, Gustav Mahler, when the latter Ahasuerus-like, sought Heaven.

What Bruckner learned from the Beethoven symphony was the idealism of artistic conception. With it he brings to a close the great epoch of idealistic art that had started with the musical classicists, with Schiller and with Goethe, and which, in Goethe's "Faust" and Beethoven's Ninth Symphony had attained giant peaks.

There is still an influx of this metaphysical spirit of Beethoven's music into the symphonies of Brahms and Bruckner. They did not learn it out of scientific books. They did not absorb it consciously at all. Nevertheless, it lived within them: in Brahms' great logical form and his spiritual energy; in Bruckner's broad background and his reverence of God and Eternity. While Brahms inherited Beethoven's idealistic style, Bruckner became heir to his impetus towards the distant Beyond. Brahms adopted Beethoven's courage in emotion struggles; Bruckner learned from his intensity of prayer. Of the Beethoven realm, earth belongs to Brahms; to Bruckner, Heaven.

V

To be sure, the world in which Brahms and Bruckner wrote their symphonies was no longer the world of the musical classics, the world of Beethoven. Since the death of Beethoven the social and spiritual foundations of the classic epoch began to change. Romanticism became aware of its contrast to classic art. The romantic artists considered themselves representatives of a modern "Weltanschauung," a new society, a new philosophy, even though they did not, as their French contemporaries, fight classical art as revolutionaries.

The new spiritual and artistic movement pervaded all Europe, and everywhere it became the expression of a new era which made the European nations aware of their specific traits. Music, too, became expression for nationalism; it was endowed with a landscape, a special atmosphere, personal coloring. No longer was music at home in the idealistic landscape as it was during the classic period; now it belonged in a national landscape.

Even more than by the romantic era the foundations of spiritual life were changed by the new scientific-technical age which was also the age of industrial development and capitalism. For this reason the symphonic form of Beethoven as used by Brahms and Bruckner, is neither fluid nor fully alive. Brahms develops a discord between his romantic fantasy and the classic form which not even his virile genius nor the steel girders of his logic could bridge.

The symphonic form of Bruckner has fissures that any skilled laborer could have cemented with ease. Bruckner was unable to do it because his was a genius that would always sense the contrast between his musical imagination and a rigid antiquated form. Only great artists find artistic problems in the form, never the artisan or the craftsman. Brahms and Bruckner would not have been geniuses had they not found a problem in the relationship of their personalities to traditional music patterns, to contemporary art and to the forms of ancient art. The solutions that Brahms and Bruckner found for their form bear testimony to their genius; that which remained imperfect in these solutions is evidence of the idiosyncrasies of their individual personalities.

Both Brahms and Bruckner were modern artists as well as modern personalities. They lived and created at a time when social and spiritual forces no longer formed an absolute whole that was reflected in great, bound art patterns. There was no philosophical unity in the reasoning of that era. Religious faith was feeble and undermined by scientific thoughts. The social, scientific and religious world picture that had been a unit in the classic era, had begun to disintegrate.

The new tasks of the period demanded new methods of thinking; the new problems of society and administration required new solutions. Every art was in a state of fermentation. In the music world every one strived for new forms, new tones, new harmonies. It was pervaded by a strong subjectivity, by a detachment of tone from the forms, and the infiltration of philosophical or poetical ideas into the music proper. The picturesque predominated.

All this commotion undermined the foundation of the symphonic form. The greatness of Brahms and Bruckner lies in the fact that, in the midst of ever changing times, they strived for the majestic style of symphonic creation. They formed the last link between the new century of science, machinery and social upheaval and the great humanistic age of classic art. Their music was the last music of great classical form and classical spirit during an age that fought as much for reorganization of life as for new music forms.

Stepping from the high portal on which the names: Johannes Brahms and Anton Bruckner are inscribed in big gold lettering, one finds oneself in a new era in which political, social and spiritual struggles shake the universe and, simultaneously, the classic forms of music.

2

The Crisis of the Times

Toward the close of the nineteenth century this new era gave in-
dications of a crisis. Unrest was in the air. There was subdued
grumbling under the surface. Political and social conflicts were
increasing. Contrasts developed all over Europe that could not be
adjusted. And inasmuch as all agitation that cannot be controlled
intellectually turns to nervousness, obscure fear and uncertainty,
nervous unrest grew.

At the time of Brahms' and Bruckner's demise Europe spoke of
all those phenomena that emerged from a turbulent age, like steam
out of a cauldron, as "Fin de Siècle." Fin de siècle was everything
that was sickly, and everything that was opaque and unintelligible
and new to the times. "Fin de siècle" was the rising hysteria in life.
"Fin de siècle" was naturalism in art which was considered ugly
and repulsive. "Fin de siècle" was socialism and anarchism and "fin
de siècle" was clarification of the Unconscious by Freud.

One of the most widely read authors of that time, Max Nordau,
published a book in 1891 entitled "Entartung" (Degeneration)
which pictured as degenerate all products of contemporary art
from Richard Wagner to Henrik Ibsen. In France one spoke of
"décadence." Verlaine wrote his sonnet: "Je suis l'empire a la fin de
la décadence," and Stephen Mallarmé wrote: "La chair est triste
et j'ai lu tous les livres."

In his essay on Baudelaire Theophile Gautier defined
"décadence" as the style of an art that had reached that point of
extreme maturity where aging civilizations cease to be. Pessimism
was spreading, and Schopenhauer became the Philosopher of the
Day.

21

On March 17, 1887, Friedrich Nietzsche had compiled in a sketch the thoughts that were to be the nucleus of his new book "The Will to Power." All during the summer and fall of that year he composed similar sketches. In 1901 a selection of these ideas was printed.

In his book the modern philosopher analyses all phenomena of his time, which he calls the age of "European nihilism." That word implied the decline, the ruin and deterioration of life, morbidity and exhaustion; for "disintegration, *i.e.*, insecurity, is peculiar to this age; nothing has a firm footing nor faith in itself; one lives for tomorrow, for the day after tomorrow is questionable."

Truly prophetic, Nietzsche proclaims in the preface of his book: "Our entire European culture has been moving for a long time already with a tortured tension that is growing from decade to decade, as though prepared to meet catastrophe; restless, violent, precipitate, it resembles a river rushing to reach the ocean."

Nietzsche had been a disciple of the great historian Jacob Burckhardt. The latter, during the years 1868, 1870 and 1871, delivered his lectures at the university of Basle in which he pictured the character of "historic crises." He also spoke of his era as a time of crisis in which "there is a constant threat of involving the present crisis with violent international wars."

When, in 1914, one such international war did break out, Oswald Spengler coincidently published his book that prophesied the "Downfall of the Occident."

What was it that caused these crises as early as the close of the 19th century? What had robbed the time of its firm self-confidence, what created insecurity, discontent and even fear of the future?

The reasons were many, and one must understand them in order to fully comprehend the evolution of the arts in the years between 1890 and the present time. Art is not created in a sphere of isolation; it is influenced by all the intellectual powers of an epoch.

Art—if it be real art, not merely commercial trade, business, or a form of entertainment or industry—is interpretation and formation of life. All great classic musicians were allied with the social, spiritual, industrial and political trends of their time.

Certainly Haydn was a simple enough man, who neither reasoned nor read much. Yet he was deeply affected by the spirit of the humanistic era in which he lived. The popularity of his symphony and the rational purity of its structure; the moral profundity of his adagios and the free flow of emotion in his music—all this, like Schiller's lustre and Goethe's perspicuity, belong to the intellectual forces that shaped the entire eighteenth century. Without the democratic, civil movement of the eighteenth century, without Rousseau's glorification of nature and emotion, without the deism of that period, without the ethical probing of Shaftesbury and Kant, they would have been unthinkable.

In his "Magic Flute" Mozart already indicates how strong were his ties with the humanism of his era, and his great symphonies prove that he was aware of the storm and stress of his time. Beethoven's great symphonies contain all this and in addition the pathos of Mirabeau's and Siyes' discourses that enraptured the Assembly in the ball court of Versailles.

When the national movements at the start of the nineteenth century opposed the humanistic ideals stemming from the time of the French Revolution; and when rationalism gave way to the mystic and religious ideas of romanticism, the symphonic pattern lost its intrinsic strength. The new purport of romanticism demanded a new form that was less lucid and distinct, less dialectical.

Underlying all intellectual agitation is a foundation of social and economic forms that carries and supports the spiritual system. Music, being the most sensitive of arts, and of itself vibration, is influenced by all these social and economic forces. And the personality of great musicians manifests itself in their ability to distinguish and digest essential and non-essential, permanency and transitoriness. They hear, as Bismarck demanded that all great politicians must hear, "the step of God in the universe."

This step of God was very perceptible at the close of the nineteenth century. During the nineteenth century national movements in Europe had begun to swell, and had been reinforced by the motion of independence brought on by the revolutions of 1830 and 1848. In the eighteenth century humanistic ideas had been proclaimed with a nigh-sacred solemnity and with the thought of eternal peace; in Saint Pierre and Kant those ideas reached their culmination with the dream of a league of nations that should insure permanent peace for all humanity. Yet these ideas had to retreat before national ideas.

In Germany the national idea gained strength from 1848 on, and the wars of 1864, 1866 and 1871 made the unification of Germany a reality. Thirty-nine German states united to form Bismarck's "Deutsches Reich," and on January 18, 1871 King Wilhelm I placed the German imperial crown on his head in the hall of mirrors at Versailles.

One year previously Victor Emmanuel had united all Italy under his royal regime.

The humiliation of defeat produced increasing nationalism in France, and in Russia Slavic nationalism waxed stronger. The Nordic countries and Czechoslovakia, Poland, Hungary and the Balkan States were all affected by the wave of romantic nationalism that swept through Europe; and with the intensified consciousness of the individuality of nations and national states, tension within Europe itself began to heighten.

During this same period modern development of industry had begun to change the shape of the earth. England had been a great industrial country since the close of the eighteenth century, and France followed this development from the start of the nineteenth century on. By 1835 England was already producing 60% of all cotton in the world while France still produced 16% and the United States of America 7%.

By 1845 as much as 34,000,000 tons of coal were mined in England with which the factories were heated; during the same period France hauled 5,000,000 tons out of its mines. Since Darbys and Cort had invented methods for using coal instead of charcoal, England's smelting furnaces and forges were heated with coal that blackened the countryside. The manufacture of pig-iron in new factories in England between 1788 and 1838 grew from 68,000 to over one and three-quarter million tons.

The manufacture of cotton was no longer undertaken with water-power but with steam which Watt had enslaved for the benefit of mankind, and which had to propel factories, ships and trains.

The textile industry took giant strides since the invention of the flying shuttle and the rolling spinning-jenny. In England's factories machines spun the fragile muslin that women in India had woven with delicate fingers. The period around 1820 brought the inception of the most important innovation produced by Watt's discovery—the manufacture of machinery by machines.

In 1838 the first steam hammer had been invented by Nasmyth; 1856 brought the Bessemer procedure. In 1866 the Siemens Brothers, and in 1879 Snelu, had reorganized modern steel production methods. In every great industrial country, one of which was Germany since the middle of the nineteenth century, the factories were smoking, the great steel forges droned, wheels turned and armies of workers streamed into subterranean passageways, factories and workshops.

With the beginning of the steel era, men and merchandise were shipped by rail and steamship. Georges Stephenson became engineer on the Stockton and Darlington railway and drove his train "Rocket" at a speed of forty-five miles, filling the onlookers with panic.

In 1830 the Liverpool and Manchester railroad, steam-powered, began its run on steel rails, and by 1848 almost 5,000 miles of railway lines had been built in England. A net of steel rails spread all over the world on which trains whizzed by day and night, on highways and high above rivers, through mountain passes and across the desert.

In 1819 the first steamboat, the "Savannah," crossed the Atlantic. Krebs designed the first Panhard automobile in 1894, and on December 17, 1903 Wright rose into the ether for the first time with a heavier-than-air machine. The skies started to fill up with aeroplanes which, like giant birds, flew above land and sea, high above the tallest mountain peaks, faster than the speediest train and higher than the highest clouds. The globe grew smaller and smaller and the space shrank into which the merchandise poured out of the factories of the world.

A new power was placed in the service of humanity when, following the discoveries of Volta, Galvani and Faraday, electricity was subjugated to the mind of man. In 1835 the electric telegraph first transmitted news across space by transforming it into atomic vibrations.

The first cable connecting France and England was laid in 1851. In Boston, Mass., A. G. Bell invented the telephone and in 1878 the first switchboard was installed in New Haven, thus utilizing the telephone for commercial purposes. Conversations were held across vast expanses and the conception of distance lost its meaning.

During the years 1878 to 1880 Thomas A. Edison created the electric bulbs, and in every city in the world the carbon threads in the lamps began to glow and to brighten rooms, squares and streets. Electric power began to drive machines, dig oil wells, melt copper in smelting furnaces, to hammer, drill and solder since 1858 when an unknown invented the dynamo to propel trolleys and trains.

In Boston in 1880 St. E. Field demonstrated how to operate electric trains with current emanating from a generator and runing through cables to the locomotive. With that the electric motor, which until then had produced the current on a small carriage, became obsolete. The magic cabinet of a modern Doctor Faustus that accomplished all this work consisted of dynamo-electric machines and transformers; and the magic wand was a switchboard with levers and dial-plates from which the energy of the electro-magnetic force could be read off like the time from a clock.

The century had become an industrial and mechanical age, and likewise a scientific one. New metals such as nickel and aluminum were scientific discoveries; chemistry invented artificial soil fertilization, and the artificial colors into which coke was converted. New powers of nature were found in the laboratories of the scientists. In a small laboratory in Wuerzburg Professor Roentgen discovered new rays in 1895. In Paris, around 1898, the Curies discovered radium.

In 1895 Marconi had begun experimenting with electro-magnetic waves in his father's house in Italy. By 1889 he employed these waves to send signals across the English Channel, and in 1918 the first wireless messages flew like spectres from England to Australia. The wireless telephone evolved into the technique of sending out electric waves in all directions (1912–1914) and with that, broadcasting was born. Another "first" was marked by the English radio when, in 1922, it broadcast music and entertainment into space via electric waves. The start of the twentieth century witnessed, in amazement, the first motion pictures, and 1928 brought the first talking picture.

Science and technics dominated the universe as never before. Mankind would have had every reason to feel proud and content.

The earth yielded more produce. Houses were more comfortable and cleaner. Health was no longer menaced by so many incurable diseases. International commerce brought commodities from all over the world to the most obscure villages. The middle classes of society had become more prosperous. The laborer earned higher wages and lived better. Education of the people had advanced, for during the second half of the nineteenth century general schooling had been introduced all over western Europe, and inexpensive newspapers acquainted everyone with world events, with the latest inventions and with new political and social ideas.

What had happened to intensify uneasiness, discontent and anxiety at the turn of the nineteenth century? What caused pride and security to give way to fear and awe? Had not living become easier, healthier and more convenient? Waterpipes brought healthy water into the houses of the poorest in the new big cities where thousands converged to earn a livelihood in offices or in factories. Electric lights illuminated the smallest apartments. Workers in large European countries were given social security, provision against age, sickness and unemployment.

Children were attending good new schools. Even the minor citizen and laborer were better dressed, better nourished and in better health. Large labor parties sprang up in all big states of Europe and furnished the working man with increased self-respect. Unions protected him and fought for higher wages.

There were universities and newspapers for the laborer, and

cultural institutions in many European countries. Germany in particular was exemplary as far as protection of the working class and national education was concerned.

What, then, had happened to shake the foundation on which society stood, and to weaken the earth so it could no longer carry the society system?

One of the main reasons was to be found in the fact that the industrial revolution of the nineteenth century led to social and economic and political crises that could no longer be controlled. The revolution itself was the result of inventions, progress in science and increased technical skill which made possible the production of more, and less expensive, merchandise and which tried to manufacture and sell goods en masse.

This increase of production first drove the big European states to colonial expansion in Asia and Africa. Colonial possessions meant markets. Colonies also meant new raw material to feed new factories; copper and gold, cotton and rubber. The new steel boats brought cheap wool from Australia or from Egypt, diamonds from South Africa, rubber from the Congo.

War was waged in Asia and Africa for the purpose of enlarging colonial possessions or to augment trading possibilities. Within half a century, almost all Africa was divided up by 1900. In Egypt and in the Transvaal, in Indian and China wars were fought. A fleet of English, Dutch, French and American ships appeared at Kyoto in 1865 and enforced the opening of Japan for world trade. Such colonial conquests created political tension among the countries and aroused avarice in Germany and Italy to emulate the old colonial powers. Ambition and rivalry caused a land unrest in Africa and Asia that communicated itself to Europe.

In Europe proper the unleashed production procedures created crises that threatened the security of the working man. Market congestions threw thousands of laborers out of employment. Larger markets meant fights for rising wages and strikes. The insecurity of the workman's existence seemed to be inseparably tied to the magnificent development of the industrial apparatus; to the technical perfection of production procedure; to the formation of ever new industries; to the scientific exploitation of materials, machines and methods; to the growing concentration of capital and to the establishment of powerful concerns and cartels.

Contrasts in society deepened. In France Saint Simon, Bazard and Pecqueur taught socialism and class conflict. In England Hodgkins and Thompson criticized and accused capitalism. In 1858 a book by Engels appeared: "The Position of the Working Class in England" in which were portrayed, in an accusing manner, the contrasts between the swelling wealth of the manufacturers and dealers and the uncertain economic position of the factory and home proletariat.

In 1848 Marx and Engels released their communistic manifesto that called upon the proletariat to fight for its elevation to the ruling class. In every European country political labor parties formed and united. Carrying the Marx-Engels appeal: "Proletarians of all countries, unite" on their red flag, they formed the "International." Speakers such as Jaurès in France, Bebel and Liebknecht in Germany, or Huysmanns in Belgium became leaders of labor in parliament. Persecution of labor parties, as for instance in Bismarck's German Reich, could not stem their growth. Meanwhile the great industrialists strengthened their political might all over, and the remnants of the old feudal system joined these new bigwigs of industry to take over the political leadership in their states.

However, the peak of unrest was reached in the big European countries when they tried to protect their industries and markets with a customs-union. Everywhere merchandise poured out of the factories, but all over Europe transportation of the goods was checked.

The alienation of the states, their differences and rivalries waxed larger due to the economic barricades. All these economic differences joined forces with nationalism which had taken possession of the states. The masters of the new industrial society, the big steel and coal magnates, the princes of the chemical and electrical industries fed the nationalism that was separating countries. The factory owners in the Ruhr, proprietors of ore mines in Lorraine, cotton kings from Manchester and Birmingham and their retinues of steel, wool, color and electric industries had become Europe's masters, and economic interests waged war to the same extent as during the middle ages religious interests had waged wars.

These tensions and differences, hiding behind national colors, had increased menacingly at the close of the nineteenth century. National differences, contrasts in society and in the economic structure created ever deeper rifts in Europe. The industrial age that had produced such wonders was unable to cope with the forces that governed production and sales, trade and economy, concentration of capital and distribution of national wealth. The daily increasing process of production found no balance in a similarly planned process of merchandise distribution.

The industrial era was like a locomotive without an engineer, riding out into the night. That is how Zola described it in his war novel "Le Débacle," as a symbol of the times which daily were coming closer to big wars.

What significance did this whole development, already critical near the end of the nineteenth century, have for the music that went along with it? One of the most important phases of this age and its agitation, its many differences and battles, its cleavage and its critical acceleration of development was the fact that contemporary composers no longer lived and created in a uniformly intellectual world. They were no longer united by an absolute world-philosophy. Each of them stood by himself in the midst of whirls of ideas.

The new era was an age of rationalism, governed by science and scientific thinking. Physics and chemistry, based upon observation and analysis, were the leading sciences, instead of spiritual sciences that are founded on ideas.

Since the days of August Comte philosophy had been replaced by sociology, which studied society and history with scientific methods, and Stuart Mill and Herbert Spencer were the leading scholars of the time.

However, alongside of the rationalism of that period irrational forces were fighting. One of these forces was nationalism which was increasing daily. Old and new, romanticism and realism were fighting to gain control. Schematic formation of life, society and economy fought against the mighty powers that had ruled life in the past; political catholicism had been one of them. Democracy, the society system of modern time, that divided society into equivalent units, battled with the old feudal system that classified society in superior and subordinate ranks.

Capitalistic economy, built on a mathematical and scientific foundation, had to establish itself in a world penetrated everywhere by the remains of old systems—systems that were based upon irrational ideas, religious conceptions and metaphysical thoughts.

The new technical inventions with which the rational thinking of science had enriched the world caused Europe and indeed the whole globe to grow smaller day by day. Railroad and steamer, telegraph and telephone, automobile and aeroplane eliminated distances. World economy and commerce united the most distant countries. But nationalism, the tariff walls between Europe's countries, trade rivalries among the states split even this smaller world. They, too, were contrasts that could not be reconciled in a uniform world-philosophy.

In art, however, in music, uniform world-philosophy means: great artistic form. The classic symphony had come forth from such spiritual unity, and the faculty for creating great artistic and great musical forms hinges on just such uniformity of world philosophy. Nobody saw more clearly the connection between great art forms and the philosophical thinking of an era than did a French art historian, Elie Fauré. In his "Histoire de l'art" Fauré writes: "When an artist desires to compose works of art on a grand scale, his aspiration of a certainty corresponds to that general desire which was formerly called religious or metaphysical aspiration. The composition, the subordination of all parts under the idea of one rhythm and arrangement is nothing external that is dependent upon an individual mood or a transitory vogue. The mystic feeling of a common creation that demands to be done, inundates the individual being."

In the nineteenth century this force of cohesion, extension and organization became weaker, and the more contrasts and conflicts created rifts in life, the weaker grew the force that shapes the great pattern of the symphony. At the start of the nineteenth century already there began a disintegration of the elements within the classic symphony form of romantic music. And as the crises of the twentieth century approached, this disintegration and weakening were increasing.

The symphonic form became smaller. The classic harmonies were split; they crumbled; they loosed their logical lawfulness. Tone became independent of forms. Interest was shifted from the purely musical to the literary and the picturesque. Music became a pompous or mood-inspiring decoration. Musical art production was no longer an ideal world transformed into sound, no longer a world of pure forms standing high above the material world.

From Mendelssohn and Weber to Berlioz, from Chopin to Debussy, from Liszt to Richard Strauss, from Schumann to Reger, music took on more and more timbre and color magic, more portrayal and more hue. A new Baroque style originated in music, ostentatious, luxurious, a wealth of colors with all the glowing tints of a sunset.

However, the organisatory faculty of thinking and shaping in great idealistic forms diminished more and more. The supporting and regulating harmonic props under the large arcs of music became ever weaker, and the pillars that had carried the high vaults and gables of the classic symphony began to lose their supporting strength and to collapse.

This had been an historical development. There was nothing arbitrary about it. Great artistic and intellectual powers participated in this evolution. Musicians, poets and painters considered themselves a unit, and literature and music, as well as painting and music, were reciprocally influenced.

Musicians were men of intellect, familiar with all artistic trends of the time, and the history of modern music is unthinkable without the history of modern poetry and painting. Music became an integral part of the collective production of the modern era, a part of its struggles, a part of its crises and a part of its fight for a new phase of life.

3

Romantic Music

I

In 1896, the year of Anton Bruckner's death, Richard Strauss gave the first performance of "Thus Spake Zarathustra." Gustav Mahler was writing his third symphony. In Paris "L'Après-midi d'un faune" and the String Quartette had made the name of Claude Debussy famous. Max Reger had just begun writing his organ compositions, in which the most modern chromatics are molded into the Bach form.

Thus, at the end of the nineteenth century we find the old and the new era at a crossroad—like two highways leading in different directions. Bruckner had left this world, followed one year later by Brahms; but a new generation of young musicians had started to attract the attention of musical audiences. All these composers were young men. All of them belonged to a new age that gave evidence of a strong stimulus in literature and art, in the theatre and in architecture, in the ways of life and in its intellectual interests.

In the music of these new composers romantic art found its last and greatest enhancement. The pattern of their compositions was the romantic form. The symphonic epics of Richard Strauss were descendants of symphonic poems by Franz Liszt. They were "program music" as Liszt had written it. The symphonies of Gustav Mahler were derived from Bruckner and Hector Berlioz. Mahler adopted Bruckner's metaphysical and religious interpretation of the symphony, the great dimensions, the solemnity of the chorals in the great transfigurations of the finales; Hector Berlioz taught him the color finesse of the giant orchestra. The chromatic harmonies of

Max Reger are an intensification of the Hugo Wolff chromatics; the tone is Brahms', the structure of the organ music the Bach form.

Claude Debussy right from the start was more influenced by painters and poets than by musicians. His "Damoiselle Elue" with its spirited, gentle lines and its ethereal tones emulates pictures by English pre-Raphaelites, and its lyrics are taken from a poem by Dante Gabriel Rossetti.

"L'Après-midi d'un faune" was originally meant to be a triptychon and is one of those mythological fairy tales that French painters such as Gustave Moreau and Puvis de Chavannes depicted so often. When Debussy's music was first heard it was immediately compared with painting. In Paris "Damoiselle Elue" was called a "symphonic church window of Fra Angelico Debussy," and after the first performance of "L'Après-midi d'un faune" in Brussels it was characterized by Maurice Kufferath as music "of the new school of Pointillism."

Paul Verlaine influenced Debussy's form more than musicians did, and the verses of Paul Verlaine:

> "De la musique avant toute chose
> et pour cela prefere l'Impaire
> plus vague et plus soluble dans l'air
> sans rien en lui, qui pèse et pose"

are of greater import to Debussy's musical style than all previous music. But all this poetry belonged to romantic art. It is the last improvement of the romantic fancy and its last transformation into symbolic forms, just as Debussy's music was the last to show decomposition of romanticism into colorful atmosphere.

The epoch of romantic music which had followed the era of classical music, and which dominated the whole nineteenth century, was the greatest period of color and colorific fantasy the world has ever known. From the time of Weber and Schubert, Mendelssohn and Chopin to Hector Berlioz, and Franz Liszt, from Richard Wagner to Richard Strauss, Gustav Mahler and Claude Debussy, streams of musical color gushed out into the world.

In Weber's music the German forest begins to rustle, in the "Wolfschlucht" eerie ghostly voices terrify; in "Oberon" the latter's magic horn resounds, the mermaids sing and the Orient shines in varied colors.

Mendelssohn lets the elves and goblins dance in Shakespeare's glistening magic forest, with the moon throwing its light on trees and bushes. Out of the mists rises the Scotch royal palace. The wind whistles across the gray North Sea, while the sprites play around in the water. Italy's sun shines down upon brightly garbed couples dancing a tarantella.

In the music of Hector Berlioz will-o-the-wisps scamper across the moors, sylphs dance, hosts of witches flock to the Blocksberg. Wagner portrays in large pictures all the phenomena of nature: the Rhine flows broad and majestic, storms rage, a rainbow forms an arc above the clouds.

His music contains the colors of sunrise and sunset, the rustling of the forest and the hissing of the flaming fire. The moon throws its silver rays upon the gabled roofs of Nuremberg. The flower beds start to glitter when the Good Friday sun shines down upon them.

Never had the world experienced such a glittering array of colors as rose up from the romantic orchestra. Growing ever larger, it employed more instruments in increasingly artistic combinations. Now it would disperse the colors, now spread them out upon broad tone surfaces, then again amass them. Only in the history of painting had there been a similar spectacle. That was after the great age of classical paintings, in the seventeenth century, when the tints and hues of Caravaggio, and Tiepolo offered a feast for the eye. Here, too, the classic age had been succeeded by an era that delighted in color and light.

II

The colorful world of romanticism was the world in which Richard Strauss, Gustav Mahler and Debussy grew up. Their orchestra is the color orchestra that was enhanced to its greatest lustre by Berlioz, Liszt and Wagner and was finally enlarged to giant proportions by Richard Strauss and Gustav Mahler. Both Arnold Schoenberg and Stravinsky as young composers took their cue from this romantic orchestra, and Dukas and Ravel, Scriabin and Rimsky-Korsakoff adopted it for their work.

It was the romantic tone with its magic powers that described air and sun, colors and atmosphere of foreign landscapes. In his "Turandot" overture Weber discovered the Orient. Felicien David portrayed the African desert in musical tones and started an evolution that led to Verdi's "Aida," Goldmark's "Queen of Sheba" and Puccini's "Turandot." Bizet's music uncovered Spain, the Spanish sun, Spains motley array of colors, its wine taverns and the bull-fight arena. This development culminated in Debussy's "Iberia."

Wagner revived old Nuremberg, with the sun streaming through the Gothic windows of its churches, with its crooked lanes, with its fairgrounds in front of the old gates.

Japan was brought to the stage in Puccini's opera "Madame Butterfly." By virtue of the romantic tone, music came into possession of new interpretative means. The sceneries of the world, foreign peoples, past ages of history, strange attires were expressed by tone which transformed itself into color, light and air. It was the invention of "local color" that finally made possible such musical works as Richard Strauss' "Salome." This colorful music depicts the moribund Roman Empire and the blooming of Christianity with all the conglomerations of the Orient and all the cunning of aging culture. It is spiced with oriental dances, shrieking Jews, Christian sermons and the sensuous lusts of a decaying civilization.

Similarly, "Elektra" paints in alternately gloomy and brash colors the bloody, barbaric Greece of the earliest epoch, while "Der Rosenkavalier" portrays the sensual-graceful Vienna of the eighteenth century. Richard Strauss brings to a close a period that had begun with Karl Maria von Weber. Tone color is the great magician that summons the whole world, near and far, all places and all times, to be at its beck and call.

Thus it happened that color, which in classical music had been slave to the idea, began to detach itself from the spiritual structure of art works. From a servant and helper it grew into an independent master, a real sovereign and king of music who, within his newly acquired kingdom has granted full liberty to all the forces of musical fancy.

Simultaneously with color, harmony began grasping for freedom. In classical music the harmonies stayed in line according to strict laws, and they unfolded and developed by the same strict laws. One and the same fundamental harmony unified all harmonies, and the most liberal harmonies and boldest absurdities were rays emanating from this harmony basis. The most fantastic classical music had its harmonic center, and the sun and planets of these harmonies circled around that center.

In romantic music the classic harmonies began to loosen. The chromatic harmonies invaded more and more the orderly laws of the triad harmony. In the "Manfred" overture by Robert Schumann, and in his piano compositions chromatics began to change the triads from the core, to fill them with dramatic life and to accentuate their expression. Into the place of classic clarity stepped romantic twilight, oftentimes refracted light, gradations of color.

Louis Spohr used chromatics as an expression of romantic sentiment. According to Schumann "a peculiar, eerie spirit" flows from the last movement of Chopin's Piano Sonata in B-Minor, "which holds in check with superior force anything that would fight against it." In this work the harmony is already impressionistic, dismal color and sinister mood, no longer pensive but picturesque.

In 1865 Munich witnessed the first performance of Richard Wagner's "Tristan and Isolde" where nostalgic love and the quest for death are played to the hilt in chromatic harmonies: the classic work of the new chromatic harmony. Another magnificent climax of this development is reached in 1909 with "Elektra" by Richard Strauss, in which even more liberal chromatics transform themselves into realistic expression and color.

While Wagner's genius in "Tristan and Isolde" arbitrated between modern chromatics and classic harmonics, and his music moves exactly in the middle between the classic harmony system and the new chromatics, Richard Strauss advanced to the extreme limit of the classic system in "Elektra." One step further and one is already in the sphere of the so-called "atonal music," based entirely upon the chromatic system.

This whole evolution stretches over a period of a hundred years. It is the result of romanticism in music, and Johannes Brahms and Anton Bruckner were the only composers to oppose this development without being able to arrest it. The chromatic stream flowed past their house that was built on a foundation of classic harmonies: a strong burgher house with solid walls was that of Brahms, a tall church Bruckner's.

III

The relation between form, tone and harmony had changed in romantic music. The sensuous forces of music had been strengthened while, at the same time, the spiritual and idealistic powers had weakened. Beethoven could still be called a philosophical musician who established musical thought structures equal in their stability to a work by Kant. All his music culminated in great ethical emotions; in the glorification of man, love, freedom humanity and adoration of God, much as the philosophy of Kant and Fichte culminates in moral and ethical ideas.

The melody of the musical classics was not only beautiful, clear and noble—whether it be in Haydn's adagios, in Mozart's symphonies or in Beethoven's chorals of "Fidelio" and the Ninth Symphony. It also possessed ethical sentiment. The greatest intensification of a classic melody in the music of Haydn, Mozart and Beethoven leads to a religious melody. The Haydn melody that most impressed itself on Mozart and Beethoven was the aria in "Creation" which solemnly describes the appearance of man on earth: "Mit Wuerd' und Hoheit angethan." Dignity and majesty, nobility and humanity were the symbols of classical music. This soulful substance molded the clear, distinct, nobly organized classic form.

In romantic music the evolution of ideas was replaced by portrayal of moods, the fantastic took the place of the lucid, the irrational of a dream, of subjective passions and fantasies assumed the place of rationality. Thus the romantic form was bound to change.

The lesser forms of the piano poem took the place of the broadly constructed sonatas as the main creations of romantic imagination. As early as Schubert's time the piano sonatas, blossoming forth in tone but allowing the musical form to grow broad and leisurely, were overshadowed by the smaller piano poems: the "Impromptus," the "Moments musicaux" and the dances.

Schumann's fantasy is at its best in "Carnival" and "Novelettes," in "Kreisleriana" and "Davidsbuendler Dances"; Chopin's fantasy most peculiar in ballad form and in dances. The grand sonata style of Schumann as well as of Chopin is oppressed by the abundance of romantic ideas, but in the small forms both are great, personal, like Mendelssohn in his "Songs without Words."

Franz Liszt wrote but a single piano sonata, and among twenty-three piano compositions of Brahms, only three are sonatas, all of them written in his youth. Debussy constructs his small piano poem, his preludes and images, his estampes and epigraphs with the finest genius; yet he lacks completely the sonata form which requires not so much intellect in the grasping of moods and not so much nervous sensitivity as strength of thought.

There is an astounding wealth of romantic piano music in moods, diaries, personal confessions, in sketches and nature scenes, in rhapsodic avowals, in fleeting colorful dreams, in whimsical notions, in witty apercues.

A most peculiar poetic and artistic world developed in the nineteenth century, poetry in its most individual form that stands on a pedestal alongside of the poems of Novalis and Tieck, of Musset and Theophile Gautier, of Baudelaire and Verlaine and of romantic and impressionistic landscapes.

The power of mind to organize on a grand scale, such as the one which, in classic sonatas, joined form to form, figure to figure and welded four movements to one great unit—this power had weakened. It was not poetic strength, not wealth of momentary moods, not esprit nor peculiarity of fantasy—all of which play such a big part in all music of the nineteenth century.

IV

The construction of the romantic symphony—so rich in fancy and color, in spirit and in soul, in natural scenery and representation of the outer world, grows smaller too. The "symphonic poem" in romanticism takes the place held by the symphony in the creative work of the classics.

Mendelssohn's overtures: the "Hebrides," "Tale of beautiful Melusine," and "Meeresstille und glueckliche Fahrt" as well as the overture to "A Midsummer Night's Dream" are already true symphonic poems. As such they exercised a deep influence on all symphonic music of the nineteenth century, from Berlioz to Debussy. Franz Liszt devoted the full riches of his cultural interests to this symphonic poetry and sheltered in a noble musical heart all great poetry and all great thoughts from Dante and Tasso to Lamartine and Goethe.

Richard Strauss provides the symphonic poem with the realistic coloring of a virtuoso, and running the gamut from "Till Eulenspiegel" to "Alpensinfonie," his symphonic poetry assumes more and brighter colors.

For the time being the four-movement symphony continues alongside of these symphonic poems: as a landscape painting in Mendelssohn's music, as a romantic legend in Schumann's works, a fantastic dream with Berlioz, a tragic melody of passion for Tschaikowsky; in the music of Sibelius, a Nordic epos, and in many other personal transformations. However, in the symphonic poem the historical evolution is more uniform and more complete.

In this development everything presses towards a musical form that either consists of only one movement or that brings the four movements of a symphony closer and unites them. These four movements of the symphony blend without a pause as early as Mendelssohn's Scotch Symphony. Schumann intertwines the various movements with themes, and in the "Symphony Phantastique" by Berlioz the "idée fixe" makes its appearance in all the movements.

This romantic unification was adopted by the symphonic composers of Russia. The most decisive step had been taken by Franz Liszt in his Fantasia quasi Sonata "Après une lecture de Dante" and, in 1853, in his B-Minor Piano Sonata when, in a single form he joined the four movements of the classical sonata to a unit.

It was this Liszt form which Scriabine let swell to huge mystic shapes. And it was this same Liszt form that Richard Strauss spread out in his giant symphonic tableaux. Beginning with "Thus Spake Zarathustra" down the line to his "Sinfonia Domestica" he makes use of the new Liszt form that develops the symphony out of uniform theme material. As a matter of fact this Liszt form of the symphony is discernible in operas like "Salome" and "Elektra." Towards the close of the romantic era Arnold Schoenberg still constructed his symphonic poem "Pelleas and Melisande" and his D-Minor String Quartette in the Liszt style.

A secondary form of Liszt's is the structure of the symphony in two parts with contrasting moods. Examples of such partition are to be found in "Prometheus": mourning and transfiguration; in "Ce qu'on entend sur la montagne": nature and humanity; in "Tasso": lament and triumph; in "Mazeppa": martyrdom and victory. This form, too, was adopted by Richard Strauss in its entirety when he composed "Death and Transfiguration."

Although they went about it in different ways, the romantic composers all had one goal: to shape the classical symphony form into a uniform picture of psychological, poetic or artistic representation. The classic symphony had been a large structure consisting of four movements that carried and support one another. Each of these movements was a unit in itself, and all of them together formed a superior unit. Each one was clear and distinctly isolated like the parts of a Greek temple, and all together they were a single structure.

The symphonies contained not merely the greatest wealth of thoughts and the most profound sentiments and moods but the most artistic organization of thoughts as well. To achieve such a form was only possible by an affiliation of the strongest musical fantasy with the most intense power of shaping and organizing. Romantic fantasy leaned towards mysticism; therefore it allied itself with moods of nature and fairy tales, with myths and ancient history and no longer possessed such a powerful core of thought concentration. Its strength consisted in sentiment, poetic mood, a sense for color and the picturesque, in the brightness of its dreams. That is why it changed the large symphonic pattern and sought its artistic unity elsewhere: in poetry, in the uniformity of a colorful atmosphere, in descriptions and in psychological development.

V

During that Romantic period "evolution" had become the chief notion of romantic philosophy. Hegel, Fichte and Schelling saw the world motivated by spiritual forces that filled all nature, from stones and moss upwards to man. Everywhere there was a Divine Spirit that unfolded in nature as well as in human life and in history. The voices of spirits spoke out of inanimate nature, out of the forest and the mountains, out of rocks and plants. The world had changed into a large sphere of spirits. Every figure on earth had come to be a symbol, and religion, philosophy and art interpreted these symbols.

Out of this perception, which was a new mysticism, the tone in music developed into something spiritual, into color and mood. Music painting and poetry were intertwined. Like dreams, poetry became a performance of pictures; music a different kind of poetry or painting. Religion and philosophy mingled with pure art. Everywhere firm boundaries vanished, as did clear patterns. Forms loosened.

The music of Richard Wagner—who at the height of this romantic evolution comprises all romantic ideas (the "total work of art") becomes a mighty symphonic stream. Its waters carry pictures, scenery, colors, sentiment and passion and increase in power. The melody loses its organized form, no longer is it akin to the crystal: an erection of mental and spiritual forces around an axis, it no longer breathes regularly. It becomes an "endless melody" that expands into the universe like every romantic emotion does.

Descendants of this romantic music are Richard Strauss, Gustav Mahler and Claude Debussy. Together with Max Reger, Hans Pfitzner, Franz Schrecker, Scriabine and Sibelius they were the last champions of romanticism in our time. That grand, colorful, brilliant epoch of artistic fantasy ends with them. Longer than any other music style of modern times, longer even than the classic style, romanticism had dominated the artistic mind. Only the era of Baroque music, so similar to romantic music in technical imagination, display of lavishness and which was so important to the whole music life of Europe, lasted some thirty years longer than the romantic period.

The entire nineteenth century belongs to romantic music, which originated in France and Germany, swept over all Europe and engulfed to equal extents ancient music countries like Italy and new ones like Russia, the Nordic states and Czechoslovakia.

Russia first developed into a modern music land by virtue of romantic poets like Puschkin and Turgenjieff, and with the help of romantic composers such as Glinka and Borodin, Rimsky-Korsakoff and Cui. Among the Nordic countries in the romantic era Denmark was led to musical production in grand style by Niels Gade; Norway by Edvard Grieg and Finland by Sibelius. In Czechoslovakia the romantic operas and romantic symphonies of Smetana and Dvorak respectively elevated music from the standard of the folk song and church music to the peak of European music production.

Everywhere music was awakened by romantic imagination, and romantic sentiment, romantic tone and romantic harmony, romantic mood and romantic spirit. In the works of Richard Strauss, Gustav Mahler and Claude Debussy romantic music is for the last time in possession of its full radiance. The color glows from the orchestra. Music becomes allied with poetry and painting; in Mahler's works with philosophy, in Debussy's with mysticism. The harmonies free themselves, become independently tone and expression. Descriptions of natural phenomena fill their scores.

At the age of 22, Richard Strauss began describing the Italian landscape in musical tones, giving the impression almost of a new Felix Mendelssohn-Bartholdy. The last of his symphonic works to be composed was the "Alpensinfonie," that had all the appearance of a plastic panorama as it is shown to a gaping audience in the tent of a wandering show.

In the "Third Symphony" Gustav Mahler paints the whole sequence of the world, beginning with inanimate nature through

flora and fauna to the angels and God,—a romantic philosopher.
Debussy paints impressionistic pictures, landscapes and seascapes.

In opera Richard Strauss starts his career with an imitation
of "Parsifal." Mahler begins his by composing songs from "Des
Knaben Wunderhorn," the main work of romantic lyric poetry,
and Debussy starts with songs by Paul Verlaine and Beaudelaire.
Gustav Mahler as a young composer is captivated by old German
fairy tales which the romanticists were the first to collect (Grimms
Fairy Tales were published 1812 and 1815).

A fairy tale—Pelleas and Melisande—becomes Debussy's masterpiece. A figure out of German folk lore, "Till Eulenspiegel" is
used by Richard Strauss for his mightiest symphonic poem.

In the creative work of all three modern composers the dominating trait is solidarity with romanticism. Without romantic
fantasy these three great musicians would have been less great,
poorer in color, and there would be no Strauss and no Mahler
orchestra, and no Debussy harmonics. Neither would we have any
descriptive symphonic poems such as Richard Strauss created, nor
revelry in dreams of world and Divinity, death and resurrection as
contained in Mahler's symphonies. It is just as unlikely that there
would be a sad legend such as "Pelleas and Melisande" in opera, or
play of colors and light and scenic pictures like "La Mer" in the
symphony. There would be no songs by Strauss and Mahler, and
no piano poems comparable to Debussy's. All of this is romantic
in fantasy, technique, in harmony and sound, in emotion and in
the conception of nature and world.

To be sure, the greatness of Strauss, Mahler and Debussy consists in their having combined romanticism with other modern
ideologies. It is the realism of Richard Strauss that illuminates
romantic opalescence and romantic lyrics with clear sharp daylight.
"Salome" and "Elektra" are a concentration of naturalistic expression and description which made them masterpieces of opera
in the first half of the twentieth century. Debussy emerges as the
greatest impressionistic composer in the nervous era of Paul
Verlaine and Huysmann, Mallarmé and Maeterlinck, the philosopher Bergson and Doctor Freud.

Mahler, most intensely at home in the romantic world, knows

satanic emotions to the same extent as August Strindberg, possesses hysterical twists in his soul as much as Dostojewsky, and is aware of all the discord and torture of modern humans.

In the music of these composers romanticism is transplanted to a new era that was essentially unromantic.

However, the inner contrasts were overcome by the musical genius and the personal greatness of the composers who live, not in a past age, but in a new age.

4

From Romanticism to Realism

I

WHEN, IN 1827 the leader of the Romantic School in France, Victor Hugo, appealed to the romantic artists: "Let us shatter with a hammer theories, poetics and systems," the first great epoch of the new industrial and technical age in France had dawned.

Big factories were founded. The Rothschilds and the banks were amassing capital in their respective coffers. Railroads were being constructed and the public at large was urged to subscribe to shares. Fortunes were won and lost on the Paris exchange. Side by side with the proud names of feudal aristocracy one found the nouvelle riche bourgeoisie sitting in the theatre boxes, radiating their enjoyment of Meyerbeer and Italian operas. They were at the race tracks trying to relax from the strain of market speculations, and they possessed houses, country homes and expensive mistresses. Augier described this society in his stage plays: the coquettes, the big speculators, the corruptible journalists and the sneering aristocrats. Ingres painted them.

There existed a contrast between the new era of materialism and romanticism that influenced the entire evolution of art in the nineteenth century. The time was realistic, technical, a time of calculation and scientific analysis. Romantic art was a product of glowing fantasy. Life in the new industrial age was sober and colorless; Art was overflowing with colors. The minds of the men in industry, commerce and at the stock exchange, who had succeeded the generation of Napoleonic wars in world domination, these minds were always calculating and were interested only in facts and realities.

"Enrichissez vous," France's prime minister, Guizot, had called to bourgeois society and they obeyed his call, cold and relentless in speculations and enterprises. Romantic art, though, was fantastic. Victor Hugo's words revelled in emotions. The pictures of Delacroix, Delaroche and Guericault were steeped in glaring colors that flowed across the canvas like rivers of fire. The music of Berlioz flashed across the sky in irregular orbits like a glowing comet. Art was an escape from the prosaic routine of the dealers and speculators, manufacturers and politicians.

Artists fled from the present time to the past. The French romantic painters portrayed historic scenes. Delacroix painted the death of the Bishop of Liège after Walter Scott, whose novels were being devoured, and the death of the Doge Marini Faliero, adapted from Dante. Delaroche painted Cromwell and the children of Edward the Seventh. Victor Hugo in the "Hunchback of Notre Dame" reconstructed ancient Paris with its old nooks, gothic houses and dark narrow streets. Mostly the romantic artists of France sought escape from a colorless, insipid Paris in the glaring colors of Spain or in the sun of the Orient, just as Lord Byron had fled England and gone to the south: to Italy, Spain, Greece and the Orient because a passionate soul like his required sun, colors, freedom and adventure.

Theophile Gautier, the romantic poet, described his trip to Spain in his book "Voyage en Espagne," the first of the French romanticists to wander to Spain before Prosper Mérimée brought back his "Carmen" novel from that country. Chateaubriand had traveled to the Orient as early as 1806; in 1835 Lamartine migrated to the Orient which Victor Hugo had depicted in 1827 in his "Orientales" with extravagant colors, with words that glow like rubies and impart a fragrance like some exotic perfume.

Gerard de Nerval traveled to Cairo, Syria and Constantinople where he composed his "Queen of Sheba" as a libretto for Meyerbeer who wanted to write an oriental opera. It was this same material that later motivated Carl Goldmark's tonal fancy, in the same year in which Verdi's "Aida" caused the sun of Egypt to shine on its melodies.

Delacroix the painter went to Morocco; here he portrayed

Oriental women in a harem, and the wedding of Moroccan Jews. Prosper Marilhat visited the Orient from 1842 to 1846 and painted pictures of Arabs, a Moorish funeral and hawking in Algiers; it was here that Eugene Fromentine painted his Herodias. Alexander Decamps crossed the Oriental desert with a caravan and painted Oriental sun and Oriental colors.

In 1844 the composer Felicien David got his inspiration for the symphonic ode "The Desert" from the Orient. In this work almas dance and the muezzin sings his praise of God and the Prophet Mohammed in an original Arabian melody.

What all these romanticists were seeking in the Orient was a landscape with brilliant tints, a life that was more colorful than the civilization of the day; glowing dreams and fantasy in its full glory.

For the young people growing up in the Paris of bankers and industrialists, jejune citizens, merchants and money-changers this materialistic generation was an enemy. There was profound dissatisfaction in these romantic youngsters. They were pale, saturated with Byronic "weltschmerz," and as though in protest against the colorless time, they dressed eccentrically. Some of these youthful romanticists wore Rubens hats, others vests of Chinese satin in glaring colors, still others braided coats.

At the premiere of Victor Hugo's "Ernani," on February 25, 1830, the romantic poet Gautier stood aggressively in the pit, his hair as long as Albrecht Duerer wore it and garbed in a burning red waistcoat that could have been used for the muleta of a torero, while the old dandies stared at him through their lorgnettes and the women giggled.

At the premieres of romantic writers the two factions—the young romanticists and the bourgeoisie—clashed. At the premiere of Victor Hugo's "Ernani," in which the noble chivalrous brigand-chief recited his blazing tirades one became first aware of the two camps: the young folks in the galleries dressed in gayly-colored costumes, the burghers in the pit and in the boxes.

The hero of Alfred de Vigny's play "Chatterton" is a poet who comes in conflict with the world and poisons himself with opium. At the first performance of this play in 1835 at the Theatre Francais, the excited young people looked with contempt upon the burghers who considered the whole thing very eccentric.

During the premiere of "Antony" by Alexander Dumas in the Porte St Martin theatre, there was sobbing, weeping and shrieking by the pale young folks in conspicuous costume and long hair. It was an excitable, tempestuous passionate generation.

Hector Berlioz, who at performances of Shakespeare plays, Beethoven symphonies and Gluck operas would weep and rave, belonged to this young generation; and this was the generation that hated the contented, indulging new bourgeoisie whose nouveaux riches sat fat and all-important in the round armchairs of their offices, for all the world like kings on a throne.

This hate can be read out of Hector Berlioz' memoirs and in the diary of Delacroix. The older generation that had taken possession of the riches of the earth, did not understand the younger generation, and vice versa. They were like two worlds, two civilizations, two armies. The age of industry on one side; romantic art on the other. Here, reality; there, escape from reality and protest against reality; dreams and fantasy, blazing colors and glowing words, brilliant tones and foreign lands.

II

In Germany this contrast between romantic art and the industrial era did not flare up until much later. Germany around 1830 had not progressed as far as England and France in the development of modern technics. As yet Germany was not a large industrial country, and her big cities still possessed a distinctly rural character. Even in the Weimar of Goethe's time the cows were led to pasture in the morning through the streets, and the cow-herd blew his horn.

It was not the citizen who governed, but the old party of the past, the noblemen, the officials, court society. Reaction was stifling free ideas, liberalism; and the federal diet in Frankfurt saw to it that liberal ideas did not spread. Heinrich Heine was forced to flee to France from the stuffy narrowminded Germany of that period, and dissemination of his writings were prohibited by the diet.

Germany had seen no revolution comparable to the one that had created modern France. The greatest of all German poets, Goethe, wore the uniform and breeches, buckled shoes and sword befitting the rank of a high official at a small German court and saw only the destruction brought on by the French Revolution.

Neither could Germany boast of an epopee such as the Napoleonic era had meant to the French nation, with its campaigns, its expedition to Egypt, the march across the Alps and through Italy, the conquest of Europe and the emperor's coronation. It had never experienced the rise and decline of a mighty power, the tragedy of a general who has risen from the ranks and perishes in the snowy plains of Russia.

Germany had but one great moment during this period: the battle of Leipzig that destroyed Napoleon. But the German nation that had fought this battle side by side with the Russians and Austrians soon found itself oppressed again, and their desire for a modern constitution, for spiritual and political freedom went unheeded.

There was no July revolution in the Germany of 1830 like in France, where liberals and laborers led the fight; no street battles for free thoughts as Delacroix had glorified in one of his most flaming pictures. The revolution of 1848 collapsed.

Thus German romanticism lacked the impetus, tension and great pathos of French romanticism. Although it, too, sought refuge in dreams, in the past, in the far distance, still it was governed by quiet minds who fled unsatisfactory reality. The German romanticists were not as comfortable in glaring sunlight and among burning colors as they were in the night, which Novalis celebrated in wonderful hymns; or in the twilight of the forests. The towns they love are quiet little hamlets in lovely woodland surroundings such as Heidelberg; or ancient cities full of dreamy nooks and old houses and churches like Bamberg and Nuremberg. The most important journal edited by romantic writers was entitled "Zeitung der Einsiedler"—the hermits' newspaper.

The romanticists collected old German poems, legends and fairy tales—"Die Deutschen Volksbuecher" (The German Folk Books) edited by Goerres in 1807; "German Legends" published by the Grimm brothers 1816–1818; "German Mythology" by Jacob Grimm in 1835.

Tieck elaborated on ancient German love songs. The Grimm brothers collected fairy tales for children and home (1812–1815). The ancient epic of the "Nibelungen" is revived. In 1801 Tieck is busy with the Nibelungen; in 1807 they are revised by Hagen.

The romanticists escape to the middle ages, to the past, to mythology and to the fairy tale as they escape to twilight and night. Here the imagination can dream. The urge toward mysticism, inherent in all romanticists, also leads them to the past and the legend. They create new legendary figures of their own. Lorelei is not an image out of folk lore but was invented by Clemens Brentano in 1802. "Undine," the mermaid, is the creation of another romantic poet: De La Motte Fouqué.

Contrary to the romantic age in France, romanticism in Germany is not an era of great paintings, lumps of color, fantasies of light, but an era of music. Out of the romantic forests the French horn sounds its dreamy note. Brentano, the poet, plays the guitar, and a romantic young lady, daughter of the Prussian court conductor Reichardt, enjoyed sitting in the woods like a fairy and playing her harp there.

The tones of the Aeolian harp aroused poetic emotions in Novalis. A musician is the fanciful hero of a novel by Wackenroder: "Herzensergiessungen eines kunstliebenden Klosterbruders" (Heart effusions of an art-loving monk). Musical mysticists like Palestrina, and later Bach, were re-introduced to present-day life by the German romanticists.

The gothic style was re-discovered as a mystic art by the romanticists. In 1808 Boisserée surveyed the Cologne Cathedral where Friedrich Schlegel and his wife were converted to Catholicism, and which one can visualize in Schumann's songs and in his "Rhenish Symphony."

Another leading romanticist, Tieck, turned Catholic in Rome; his sister-in-law, Maria Alberti, was converted and entered a convent. Karl von Hardenberg, younger brother of the poet Novalis, turned Catholic when he saw his brother die serene. In glorifying the mysticism of the Catholic Last Supper in "Parsifal" Richard Wagner gave evidence of his romantic heritage; likewise in the fiction of the "Flying Dutchman" which he found among Heine's works, and in "Tannhaeuser" which he adopted from Th. A. Hoffmann, and which Brentano had already composed as a libretto for Th. A. Hoffmann. The "Nibelungen" offered the chief theatrical material of romantic fiction ever since De La Motte Fouqué had first brought it to the stage.

The desire for distant places, journeys to foreign countries, the longing for primitive and colorful civilizations are some of the characteristics of German romanticism too. They assume different forms than in France. The German romanticists do not roam actually, only in the imagination. They are explorers in the realm of intellect. From the desk of a poet or a man of learning they roam through all lands, European countries and the Orient. Only two of the German romanticists really travelled: Alexander von Humboldt who visited America in 1799, and George Forster who joined Cook's second world tour.

The rest remained in their simple studies lined with book shelves and let their fantasy journey to distant peoples and foreign countries.

No generation could surpass the romanticists in the art of translating. From 1799 to 1801 Wilhelm Schlegel translated 16 plays of Shakespeare and made a German poet out of him. He translated Spanish and Italian poets with equal artistry. In 1799 Tieck translated "Don Quixote." Gries translated Tasso, Ariost and Calderon. Streckfuss translated Dante. Joseph Hammer translated Persian, Arabian and Turk poets (1814 and 1815); Friedrich Rueckert Hindustan, Hebrew and Chinese literature.

Friedrich Schlegel began to study Hindustani and Persian in Paris, and in 1808 he published his book: "Language and Wisdom of the Indians," which introduced the study of Sanskrit in Germany.

Wilhelm von Humboldt, minister and statesman, studied the grammatical structure of idioms starting with the Greek and ancient Indian to the malayan and polynesian idioms.

The romantic poet Uhland was also a great scholar of the French moyen age; together with Wilhelm Schlegel he founded Romanic philology in Germany. Historians and linguists and philologists were on the faculty of the newly established university in Berlin (1809) where Fichte, the philosopher, became the second rector and where Hegel lectured. These, and jurists like Savigny, historians like Niebuhr, Raumer and Ranke, philologists such as Fr. A. Wolf, Boeckh, Lachmann, and the Grimm brothers—all of them universal geniuses, extended their research across all time and all space.

Sparks from this light also fall upon music. Here too we have the discovery of foreign countries during that period. Weber discovered Spain in the music to "Preciosa," China in his "Turandot" and the Orient in "Oberon." Schumann loved the local color of Spain, and in many of his "lieder" one hears the Hidalgos strumming their guitars. This Spanish tone is still captivating in Hugo Wolf's compositions and lends the coloring of the country, of heavy wines and proud women to his "Spanish Song Book," his opera "The Corregidor" and his "Spanish Serenade."

Since Weber's time German music is unthinkable without the Orient. It is to be found in the "Barber of Bagdad" by Peter Cornelius and in Carl Goldmark's "Queen of Sheba," colorful and shining. Wagner's "Tannhaeuser" and "Lohengrin" would never have been imbued with the genuine colors of the chivalrous middle ages, nor the "Meistersinger of Nuremberg" with those of the urban moyen age had not Wagner animated his imagination with the stories of romantic poets and the research of romantic scholars and historians. It is impossible to imagine the "Ring of the Nibelungen" without romantic research in mysticism. In the romantic era art and science are a unit. In those days they are both creations of fantasy. Both love distant spheres, ancient times and foreign lands.

To what extent romantic learning in Germany soars into space on wings of romantic fantasy becomes apparent from the insignificance of physical science in those days. In France during that period Lavoisier had produced modern chemistry. In romantic Germany the fantastic poetry of natural philosophy predominated.

The universe was a formation of mental powers, motivated by intellectual minds and joined to a unit by genius.

The natural pholosophy of Hegel, Fichte and Schelling, romantic philosophers all, was governed by the pantheism of Spinoza, who made thinking and being attributes of God; by the mysticism of Plotin who represented all phenomena of the universe as resulting from God; and by the fantastic philosophy of Jakob Boehme.

Johann Christian Reil, a physician, had taught the unity of organic and inorganic nature; Heinrich Steffens, the naturalist, the unity of all natural evolution and occurrences of life. Ritter found galvanism in anorganic nature too. Everywhere in nature mysterious forces, the ethereal, animation of nature were enhanced to the degree of the fabulous and the mythical. Finally Fichte, the romantic philosopher, deprived nature of all reality.

Romantic imagination was being irresistibly drawn to the mysterious apparitions of spiritual life, in which superior forces manifested themselves. From 1818 to 1824 Clemens Brentano sat at the sick-bed of the stigmatized nun, Anna Katherina Emmerich, and in 1833 published his book: "The bitter suffering of our Lord Jesus Christ. From observations of the sainted Anna Katherina Emmerich."

The belief in animal magnetism, which was supposed to explain all the obscure phenomena of spiritual life, was wide-spread. Romantic fantasy thought itself in possession of the key to the world. Methodical research, based on calculations and figures, seemed a poor thing indeed to the romanticists, and the mathematical genius of Gauss remained an enigma for a long time. Escape from reality is noticeable everywhere in romantic science too.

III

As industrial and technical development in Germany progressed, the breach between reality and fantasy must become more apparent, and the contrast between society of the industrial age and romantic art more profound.

In Germany the evolution to an industrial country begins

around the middle of the nineteenth century and increases to the Franco-Prussian war of 1871. Cities are growing. Industry is drawing the people from rural districts into the towns. The grand bourgeoisie of manufacturers and bankers, industrialists and speculators takes its place next to Germany's old feudal society. After 1871 Berlin becomes the capital of a great empire, the industries of which compare favorably with those of older industrial states such as England and France, and even surpass some of them.

The first great musician in Germany in the nineteenth century to sense the contrast between his romantic art ideals and the materialism and realism of the times, was Richard Wagner. In 1848 the inner contrast to his time made him a revolutionary who, at a meeting in Dresden demanded general suffrage, abolition of nobility and the standing army, and the transformation of the Kingdom of Saxony into a republic. When the revolution broke out in May 1848 in Dresden and barricades were erected from behind which the insurgents shot at the soldiers, Richard Wagner was among the insurgents, a comrade of the Russian revolutionist Bakunin.

Following his flight from Dresden, Wagner published his "Art and Revolution" which contains all his thoughts on the position of the artist to the problems of his time. These ideas were later promulgated in "Music of the Future" and "Opera and Drama." Art, which fills all civilization, is: "Industry; its moral purpose the acquisition of money, its aesthetic pretense the entertainment of the bored. Our art absorbs its vital power from the heart of our modern society, from the center of its circling motion and money speculation on a grand scale." Theatre is: "Impoverished caricature." Operas: "Gutter platitudes." Only a great revolution of humanity would be able to change this condition.

Towards such conditions a genuine artist cannot be conservative, only revolutionary. "We consider real art revolutionary because it exists solely in the contrast to valid generality."

Like Wagner, Franz Liszt takes the attitude of the artist who stands opposed to his era. When revolution broke out in Paris in July 1830, he sketched a "Revolution Symphony" that was meant to be the victory hymn of humanity.

He is a steady guest of the Saint Simonists, enthuses about human rights and general charity, and absorbs the Simonistic doctrine about the homogeneity of art and religion. Abbé Lammenais became his friend and advisor. Lammenais' pamphlet "Paroles d'un croyant" affected him deeply, and in a small essay he presented his ideas on the religious significance of art—ideas which were those of Lammenais.

That Liszt renounced the career of a virtuoso just when he was at the peak of his fame was by way of protest against the times which made an exhibit of the artist. Another expression of Liszt's protest against his era was that, at the age of 55, he took the small vows. With his black abbé robe he took leave of a world turned materialistic, as Wagner did when he dressed in velvets and silks and donned a beret reminiscent of the middle ages.

The romantic artists lived in a world different from that of the burghers. Their life often resembled a fantastic novel more than it did reality. Relations of romantic artists to women are unconventional. The 23 year old poet Novalis, consumed with longing for his adored Sophie after that lovely and interesting girl had died at the age of 13, follows her in death. The Jewish woman around whom the circle of romanticists revolve in Berlin are all novel-like figures: Henriette Herz, adored by both the Humboldts and by the philosopher Schleiermacher; Rahel Levin, to whom the statesman Gentz paid homage; Dorothea Veit who leaves her husband for Friedrich Schlegel. Chopin's infatuation for George Sand could be a tragic novel or a motion picture play. The relations of Liszt to Countess D'Agoult and to Karoline von Wittgenstein would be a credit to a Balzac.

The women surrounding Richard Wagner: Mathilde von Wesendonck, Jessie Laussot, Cosima Buelow, and the fates of Wagner's love, the infatuations and catastrophes, could not have been invented even by the combined imaginations of Balzac, Flaubert and D'Annunzio. This whole world of love and passion, of free relations and unconventionality is beyond the limits of all reality with its ties, its barriers and codes.

Romanticism and reality were growing further and further apart. Towards the middle of the nineteenth century, when life grew stronger and fuller, technical wonders more perfect, and the big cities became larger yet; when national education and enlightenment increased, the masses gained in political importance and social value: then it was that apprehension increased and realization that romantic raving, living in dreams and fancy, emphasis of subjectivism no longer corresponded to the spirit of the time, which had turned rational.

Science, guided by natural sciences, governed life. Every progress of the time was a product of scientific thinking. It was a French philosopher of that period, Auguste Comte who set forth in his books (Course of Positive Philosophy, 1830–1842; System of Positive Polity, 1851–1854) that a religious era, as the middle ages had been, and an era of philosophical and general conceptions such as the age of enlightenment, were bound to be followed by a positivistic age.

This positivistic era of mathematical thinking that animated all sciences had dawned on Europe in the middle of the nineteenth century. Even phenomena of social life, mass agitation, could be defined mathematically. Religion and spiritual learning, even the arts, appeared to be a kind of superstructure above the social and economic fermentation, its finest radiation and subject to its laws.

Karl Marx turns from Hegel's romantic philosophy, and in 1843, in his "Introduction to the critique of Hegel's law philosophy" he developed the idea that it is the duty of history: "since the Beyond of truth has vanished, to establish the truth of Here." Saint Simon's ideas that: "all real forces of society are incorporated in industry" and the tenet of Auguste Comte that ideas: "are the historic transitory products of industry" culminate in the Marxian materialism which transplants scientific thinking to history and spiritual life.

IV

The struggle against romanticism, out of which all modern music developed, had its inception in France in 1856. In that year Hyppolite Taine published his book on the French philosophers of the nineteenth century which was the heaviest attack upon romanticism, Victor Hugo and Lamartine who "kept their distance from youth," "remnants of an era that had once been great but that no longer existed."

During that same period Francisque Sarcey, the critic, published an article in "Figaro" that closed with the following words: "Forwards, my friends! Down with romanticism."

In 1865 Sainte-Beuve wrote in a letter to the minister of education, Duruy: "If I had a motto, it would be, the genuine, and the genuine all alone—let the beautiful and the good get out of it as best they can." In the preface to the naturalistic novel "Les Frères Zemganno," Jules Goncourt declared: "If an ugly, actually repulsive, subject had been treated in a beautiful and kindly spirit, with pure humanity, with poetic chastity, then that piece of art is beautiful even if your servant girl and your mistress find it obnoxious."

In 1856 the first great masterpiece of French naturalism made its appearance, Flaubert's "Madame Bovary." The public prosecutor accused Flaubert of immoral tendencies, so crass was the realistic presentation considered that depicts with cold objectivity the love passions of a small provincial girl. Later Flaubert confessed in a letter to Taine that, after describing the poisoning of Emma Bovary, he had the taste of arsenic in his mouth for two days.

Therefore he was not as cold-blooded as the book wants to be in its descriptions; in its details are reproduced not the effect of sympathy and feeling, but the exact observations of a physician or a naturalist.

In 1851 Courbet painted seriously and realistically, like a factual report, his "Stone Cutter," unlike Delacroix who was theatrical and pathetic; in 1853 he created his "Funeral in Ornans" with the rough hands of the rustic men, the women in old-fashioned dresses, the grave digger and the dog. The cold daylight makes the black dresses appear blacker and the outlines harder. Upon the planked shack in which he gave his first showing, in 1855, the superscription read: "Le Réalism G. Courbet."

In France, too, the great era of realism had dawned. The realistic period had found its great artists, and the spirit of scientific thinking: rigid observation, portrayal of life without embellishment, faithful reproduction of social facts—also gained a hold on art.

When, in his "Salammbô," Flaubert wanted to describe the Orient, Carthage and life in Carthage, it was no longer the Orient of the romanticists where the imagination had looked for glowing colors. Flaubert studied the Orient much as a scientist would do; he perused 100 volumes of ancient and modern literature and traveled to Tunis to gather facts. Likewise, for the purpose of writing 30 lines about agriculture in "Bouvard and Pechuchet," he studied 107 books. The excerpts and collections of material for this work are contained in five octavo volumes.

In preparing his novel "L'Education Sentimentale," wherein he had to describe Paris of the Forties, Flaubert studied old paintings, old plans of the city, several thousand newspapers with reports on street life and street brawls. In order to properly describe the costumes, he studied old engravings. Wanting to describe a literary gypsy who delighted in puns and witticisms, Hussonet by name, he read every issue of the "Charivari" in order to study the style of puns fashionable during the reign of Louis Philippe.

In his book "Le roman experimental" Zola calls the novelists "moral experimentalists." "Why should not literature too become a science and avail itself of experimental methods inasmuch as medicine, which was originally an art, grew to be a science?"

In 1867 Zola prefaced his novel with this sentence by Taine: "Virtue and vice are products like vitriolic acid and sugar." His novel cycle "Les Rougon-Macquart" is prefaced with the phrase: "Heritage has its laws just like gravity does." In accumulating "Documents Humains" in a giant epic of modern life within the cycle "Rougon-Macquart," Zola turned the poet into a brother of the naturalist.

The greatness of Richard Strauss as a musician is to be found in the fact that he combined this modern realism with the romantic music form, with the romantic symphony and the romantic orchestra. The basic feeling of his musicianship is still romantic, but his means of performance are realistic. Seen from the idealistic and romantic era in which Brahms and Bruckner created, the force of his realism, his bold advance and proud steps into a new age are

quite appreciable. Looking back to him from the age of Schoenberg and Stravinsky, one can sense his ties with romanticism.

Like many important composers he stands between two epochs
linking old and new, romanticism and realism; grandson of Wagner's, Berlioz' and Liszt's romanticism, and son of the realistic era,
he absorbs its intellectual movements with active mind. Side by
side with Gerhart Hauptmann, the poet, he is the representative
of modernism in Germany between 1890 and 1920, and its strongest spiritual power.

Unlike romantic musicians, Richard Strauss did not flee the life
of his epoch. He accepted the good and the evil of his time with
equal sense of security. The ideas of realistic art, Nietzsche and
Oscar Wilde, modern conception of Hellenism, psychological
analysis, Freud and Bergson, symbolism and aestheticism—all of
them left their mark in his work. Still, he is also in league with
the industrialism of his time, with its materialism, its sense of the
commercial, its advertising and propaganda. He had no hesitation
about pushing his grand new music ahead on sails of sensation.

Richard Strauss is no dreamer, not an unworldly, fantastic musician as romantic artists had been. Anyone having seen Richard
Strauss in the homes of bankers, speculators and stock holders
which he liked to frequent, disdainfully appraising the business-
men with a cool glance of his blue eyes, knew that his sense of
security in this company was equal to his feeling of superiority.
He was not without business sense either when it came to earning
money for his family.

When he conducted Beethoven's Ninth Symphony in Wana-
maker's department store in New York—a symphony that to us
was like divine services and did not belong in the halls of the
dealers, I attacked him in an article that began: "In the masterful
instrumentation art of Richard Strauss the advertising trumpet is
not lacking," and I reproached him for having profaned a sacred
work of humanity for the sake of money.

His reply, "it is no disgrace to make money for wife and
child" is typical of a worthy little burgher who won't be denied
the right of making a profit on the merchandise in his store, and
who just cannot seem to understand the question of whether the

Ninth Symphony should be placed on sale like suspenders and toothpaste.

This trend of thought was certainly not romantic, but good bourgeois; the idea of a person who has compromised with the mercantile character of the modern age.

Visiting Strauss in Garmisch once, I found the score of a new composition on the table which he had written by commission of a wealthy pianist. It was the Piano Concerto "Panathenaeenzug." "The best thing about this music is the fee I am getting for it" said the composer with a smirk.

Richard Strauss' mode of living is bourgeois, not romantic. In his life there is nothing of the dramatic unrest that the romanticists knew, nothing surprising and nothing out of the ordinary. His is a family life, consisting of wife and child. Proof that Strauss found happiness in such a life, in the scoldings of his wife, the child's crying and in the chatter of relatives, is contained in his "Sinfonia Domestica" wherein, with great enjoyment he gives a musical description of bedroom and nursery, conventional marriage-bed and domestic strife.

To Strauss wife was not so much an elementary being of a child-like or demonic nature, or proud mistress or an iridescent mixture of sensuality and spirit, the way so many romantic musicians considered her; rather she was the motherly woman protecting her young like a brooding hen. The Salomes and Elektras are creations of his imagination that is guarded by domesticity.

Richard Strauss needed this domesticity because it provided him with the counterpoise for the spiritual tension and the audacity of his fantasy. The ease of mind, security and peace that other great musicians gained in their contact with nature apparently came to Richard Strauss out of domesticity. It was a limitation of the romance within him, just as the office of councillor at the court of Weimar provided Goethe with a limitation of the demonic restlessness of his soul.

To be certain, there came the time in Goethe's life too when, driven by the demon in him, he escaped to Italy and to freedom from the danger of suffocating in Weimar.

Strauss never experienced such irrational emotions. When he

traveled, it was for the purpose of propagating his works or to earn money as conductor or to restore his health, as was the case with his trip to Egypt after a serious illness in his youth. All these are simple motives for traveling. There is no urge for freedom or a more colorful world, no longing for the unusual or adventure, no violent impulse to flee limited surroundings, no storm and stress to drive Richard Strauss abroad.

Thus we find in Richard Strauss a new type of artist, an anti-romanticist, who feels at home in the world, in life and in domesticity. He is a realist, cool, sure of himself, guided by his great intelligence, and practical. As a composer, too, Strauss is clear and distinct even when his artistic imagination roves ever so far and enters ever so new courses.

Even in "Elektra" which unleashes so much wildness, barbarism and glare, Strauss is capable of constructing great arcs and clear forms, and of transforming in to distinct art patterns, according to his design, the boiling hissing lava masses of tones, the most naturalistic outbursts of primitive passion, the streams of blood and pus.

This Strauss intelligence is a modern intelligence, very conscious, the intelligence of builders of steel bridges who calculate and test coolly until finally the most beautiful structure emerges as the result of their figuring.

So one accompanies Strauss from the romantic time into a new realistic world that faces life unafraid, a world that wants to fashion life conscious and rationalistic.

Science leaves its spiritual isolation and allies itself with the present time, its life and its work. The old powers of religion and philosophy are forced to retreat. The mysticism that was predominant in the philosophy of the romantic era vanished before clarity of thought that figures and calculates, analyses and construes; that studies chemical elements and explains in mathematical formulas all phenomena from the motion of earthly substances to the vibrations of the ether.

Even movements of the masses and social groups, fluctuations in commerce, production and consumption are represented as legitimate by statistics. The realm of ideas hovering above the universe, in which the romanticists believed, dissolves in mist and in dreams of fancy.

Only the real world, the earth upon which humans live and work, has permanency. Around 1850 there are no more religious thinkers of great style as the romanticists Chateaubriand and, in Germany, Schleiermacher had been; no metaphysicians like the great romantic philosophers had been.

Schopenhauer was the last idealistic philosopher in Germany to whom romantic philosophy and Indian philosophy, which had been discovered by the romanticists, was something alive; but during that same period Germany already has a great realistic thinker in Ludwig Feuerbach. And out of Schopenhauer's romanticism there developed a destroyer of idealistic values in the person of Friedrich Nietzsche.

Marx, John Stuart Mill, Herbert Spencer, Hippolyte Taine, Ernst Mach are the thinkers of that time. Great chemists and physicists, naturalists, like Darwin, doctors like Claude Bernard, Liebault, Charcot, and Koch come to the foreground. Free thinking; to be free of religious or similar prejudices, that was the pride of the educated, just as it was the pride of Richard Strauss to be a free thinker.

The strong Protestant faith of a Brahms and the Catholic devoutness of Bruckner seemed to be a thing of the past as far as art was concerned. The Parsifal piety of Wagner was ridiculed by Nietzsche. The music of Richard Strauss shows a modern trait in not containing a Beyond and ulterior values as the idealistic music of the classics and romantic music had. His music is all ornamental exterior, an art in its description and presentation of reality, with brilliant array of colors and faithful reproduction of all events. It is masterly art in its vivacity, intuitiveness, authenticity, in its enjoyment of colorful figures.

It is no coincidence that this masterful art of description by Strauss first comes to light in the portrayal of the street hubbub in a metropolis. Strauss was the first great composer (unlike many romanticists who sought their inspiration in the dreamy quiet of the forests) to draw artistic inspiration from the tumult of a big city.

5

Richard Strauss, The Realist

I

STRAUSS REALISM first pierces the romanticism of the youthful Strauss in the fourth movement of the symphonic fantasy "Aus Italien." Strauss was twenty-two years old when he traveled from Munich to Italy and glimpsed Rome, Naples and Sorrento.

In the four movements of his symphony he employs the impressions gathered during this trip, much as Mendelssohn had done in his masterpiece. The first three movements of his composition are music within a classic frame. The orchestra is colorful, the scenery pictured gracefully. The slow movement describing a walk along the ocean front at Sorrento is filled with clean, fresh air and bright light; the waves break over the beach in white foam, and the musician is a gentle lyricist singing in the manner of Mendelssohn.

But how different is the final movement! The description of Naples is no longer academic. It is full of life itself. It yells and screams, roars and cries. Anybody who has ever passed through the narrow streets of the old section in Naples can imagine himself transplanted back into the noisy city as soon as he hears this music. He can visualize life pulsing through these streets like a whirling stream, women yelling from the balconies of the tall houses; naked children whining, goats being herded through the traffic, dealers offering their merchandise.

The picture of Naples, unlike the ocean scenery of Sorrento, is not an aquarelle with graceful lines. It is painted in speckled colors, in broad outlines, entirely impressionistic. Garish spots are the "Funiculi Funicula" song that puts in an appearance every so

64

often amidst all the noise; phrases of the melody spring up from the tumult of life, colored shreds that hang from the windows like laundry on a line, loud colors like the sound of the grinding organ.

When this music had its first performance at a concert in Munich—the date was March 2, 1887—this particular movement immediately provoked the opposition generally encountered by new and unfamiliar things. Richard Strauss described the performance: "The playing of my fantasia on Italy has caused great excitement here,—general astonishment and rage for having started to go my own way, create my own style and for giving the lazy people a headache. The first three movements received a fair amount of applause; the last theme, Neapolitan National Life, which is really a bit mad (but then, life in Naples is plenty colorful) evoked, in addition to lively applause, quite a bit of hissing. All of which, of course, I enjoyed immensely."

Similarly he writes in a letter to Buelow: "After the last movement there was loud hissing that was gradually drowned out by applause. It was a lot of fun for me, though! My first step towards independence!"

The realistic genius of Richard Strauss showed strong and fresh in the musical reproduction of Naples' streets. Under different circumstances it could have developed independently, but that would have resulted in a different Richard Strauss. His greatness lies in his ability to join realistic description with romantic melody, as well as in his lyricism, and the loftiness of his melodic structure.

His entire development is accompanied by songs in which he cultivates his melodic wealth in every direction. Some of these melodies, like the Cradle Song, are merely pleasing, some sublime and hymn-like, some graceful, others sentimental. Most of them were written down with a light hand, obviously lesser works of his imagination. Not one song can compare with the intensity of Brahms' lyricism and its dark passion, its virility and nobility.

No Strauss song equals the concentrated amorous power of the Brahms lied: "Wie bist Du meine Koenigin" or the nocturnal solemnity of the "Ode to Sappho"; none the profound pathos of "Ernste Gesaenge." Even the songs of Hugo Wolf cause the

Strauss lyrics to appear superficial for Wolf imbued his lieder with visionary force, with the profundity of his pastoral mood, with humor and strength of expression. Not once did Richard Strauss attempt a song as deeply mystic as those of the "Spanish Songbook" by Hugo Wolf.

Strauss belongs entirely to this world, his melody has no background and no depth, albeit esprit and color, rhythm and effectual gradation.

However, unlike great lyricists such as Schumann and Schubert, Brahms and Hugo Wolf, Richard Strauss did not intend his songs to be a portrayal of all human emotions and expressions of nature, nor did he attempt to join the two in the song. Rather, Strauss employs his pen in all his songs for the purpose of providing his lyric melody with a personal touch.

It is this "lieder" melody that, at the height of its enhancement develops into the arias of Salome and Elektra, sings out in "Rosenkavalier" and in "Ariadne on Naxos" and finally puts the crowning touch on all his operatic works. It is the Strauss melody which allows all realistic narratives to dissolve into the romantic, and enhances them to romanticism.

In the symphonic fantasy "Aus Italien" Strauss melody and Strauss realism were still distributed among different parts of the composition. In subsequent symphonic poems, "Don Juan" and "Death and Transfiguration," romanticism and realism unite.

In "Don Juan" realism is not confined to individual episodes, to the musical description of the women whom Don Juan sets out to conquer, or to embracing and pleasure. It is felt in the general mood of the music. The erotic is not supersensuous romantic longing, it is bold conquest, intoxication of the senses. With the first phrase the music plunges into the full of life, the erotic becomes ravenous, flares up like a torch and dissipates energy.

This work is but the first of many erotic narratives created by Strauss. It was soon to be followed by a still bolder realistic description and glorification of an amorous night in the opera "Feuersnoth."

The singing in "Don Juan" unfolds in great beauty and youthful glamor. The melody is full of the Strauss rhythm, the Strauss enhancements leading to a brilliant climax. In "Don Juan" Strauss polyphony makes its first appearance, embracing many ringing melodies, and using one melody to propel the other, condensing the tone.

Counterpoint, in contrast to the junction of opposite thoughts which it represented in the classical era, portrays tone, sensuousness, fullness of singing. Naturalistic description and melody, characteristic tone and melodic glamor are united in this music. At that time Strauss complained in a letter: "If I could only once eradicate that cursed euphony!"

The combination of naturalistic description and romantic tone is even more perfected in "Death and Transfiguration." Illness, the tortures of fever and nightmares are reproduced with a naturalism hitherto unknown. Strauss had experienced these phases of sickness when a serious case of pneumonia hospitalized him in Weimar. The orchestra moans and groans, writhes in pain, breathes heavily and feverishly. All that is reality, not just imagination.

Nevertheless this whole naturalistic narrative, that could be called pathological, rings out in broad melody that shines and beams, in singing that rises higher and higher.

Stronger yet is the realism of "Till Eulenspiegel." All details are plainly described. The clattering pots of the women vendors can be heard when Till rides across the village square. The monks mumble their prayers. The judges pronounce "Death" in trumpet tones. Till trembles and begins to feel fright. One can see him ascending the ladder to the gallows, and hear the last whistling breath of the hanged man.

The Till Eulenspiegel theme draws a caricature, a grinning face sticking out its tongue. Not until the epilogue is reached does the face that laughed and mocked all during the composition, receive a symbolic transfiguration.

The descriptions in the merry scherzo that is "Till Eulenspiegel" indicate that this work was originally planned as an opera. It was succeeded by the giant tableau of "Thus Spake Zarathustra." Here the Strauss melody for the first time assumes the character of a dance tune—in other words, the lightest, most graceful and mobile form of melody. From here this dance melody goes on to invade the "Rosenkavalier" and "Ariadne on Naxos." The most masterful realism shows itself in "Don Quixote," the greatest masterpiece among Strauss' symphonic poems. Don Quixote and Sancho Panza are pictured most realistically, as is the battle with the wind mills, the bleating sheep herds, the water dripping off the clothes of the knight who had fallen into the water, and the litany of the little monks.

Even here, however, the melody winds its way among all the details, to broaden out in emotion and warmth towards the end.

"Heldenleben" culminates in the most realistic battle narrative ever found in music, reproducing the noise and dust of battle, the clash of masses, tumultuous yelling and the hero. His proudly rising theme alternately appears in the dense crowd, vanishes, rushes forward once more and ends the fight victoriously.

Rubens painted such battle scenes in which soldiers on foot and on horseback are tangled in a heap, lances and flags flash out of the dark clouds of the fight; combatants plunge from high bridges into the river and the bodies of horses, men and weapons appear as clusters of color.

The Strauss melody unfolds particularly rich and full in this music, and in the motif "Des Heldens Friedenswerke" the melody of the "Dream in the Twilight" rises through the dusk from the many singing voices that are replete with Strauss music.

Another altogether realistic work is the "Sinfonia Domestica" which sings of domestic happiness, of the nursery and the connubial bed, of wife and family, quarrel and argument and atonement. This composition is the counterpart of "Heldenleben"; a hero's life in houserobe and slippers, with the coffee pot steaming on the breakfast table.

The Strauss melody that rises up so proudly and nobly with wings spread, changes to a philistine cheerfulness. Still, this domestic or bourgeois melody is a part of German romanticism that was at home in the clean parlors of the burgher.

The orchestral creation of Richard Strauss in which the orchestra art of the romanticists is augmented and enhanced closes with

"Alpensinfonie." In this colorful panorama Strauss depicted nature with all the virtuosity that was his. The waterfall sparkles, the forest rustles, at the mountain tops the alpine peaks are visible through the ice, the sun throws its rays across snow-covered fields, storms rage, the rain streams down, night and fog close in.

Truly the art of a virtuoso makes itself felt in the perceptibility of the narrative, the diversity of colors as well as in the construction that describes ascent and descent. Realistic presentation had become a giant tableau that satisfied even the lust for sensation.

Strauss himself felt that he had reached a borderline. Ever since "Don Juan" and "Death and Transfiguration" Strauss had augmented to the point of exorbitance the media of the orchestra. Each work, serving as a realistic painting discovered new color nuances and new mixtures. In a world grown materialistic these compositions reached artistic peaks in color array, in technical esprit, in masterly control and enhancement of the orchestra's media.

Here romanticism had changed to a new Baroque style in which was renewed the fresco art of the Caracci brothers, of Giulio Romano and of Tiepolo. It matched theirs in virtuosity, splendor and luxury of color and light. However, that was the end of the road.

For a while Richard Strauss experimented with the small, improved chamber orchestra, resulting in the sparkling music to Moliere's "Bourgeois Gentilhomme." This music too deals wittily with realistic descriptions, but it is also art of a virtuoso: romantic music within a crystal ball.

It was never publicly known that during his stay in Vienna Richard Strauss wrote a symphony in the old style. He told me one day that he was working on such a symphony and he must have shared my professed skepticism, for he never showed that composition to anyone, nor did he publish it. Thus his "Alpensinfonie" was destined to be the last of his orchestral works. It was a pompous giant tableau that possessed decorative glamor rather than depth: a "machine" as painters would call it. It was the highest degree of romanticism that had grown to virtuosity.

II

In opera Richard Strauss had taken his cue from the music drama of Richard Wagner. The romance of "Parsifal" and "Lohengrin" lends the solemn high-flown style to the opera "Guntram" which he composed in his youth. Here too there is a knightage similar to the knights of the Holy Grail. The hero, Guntram, is a pure fool in silver armor who turns down Freihild's love because it appears to him to be an inner foe and he wants to become a saint.

A Freud would opine that in this libretto a repression complex develops into an opera. In the next opera, "Feuersnoth," which consisted of only one act, this repression complex is thoroughly spent. Strauss realism makes this a lively opera. With vigorous humor he depicts old Munich and its good burghers; laborers, citizens spending their evening with a glass of black beer, chattering in their Bavarian dialect; Munich's young girls laughing and joking. The huge choruses of the opera, in which everyday life in Munich is transformed into music, are lively, reminiscent of street scenes in paintings by Breughel.

Into this world of philistines steps the artist Konrad with whom Richard Strauss identified himself as successor to Richard Wagner. He reproaches the inhabitants of Munich for their sins and finally, finding that Diemut will not give in to him, he extinguishes all the lights in town. In a big symphonic theme Richard Strauss describes the reunion of Konrad with Diemut who has received him in her bed; the embraces and kisses, the flame of passion, the progress of erotic to the climax, at which point the lights of Munich go on again. The citizens of Munich are full of glee and the young girls who sang charming trios in the opera join in the general jubilation. All Parsifal holiness has disappeared. Sex and Eros triumph.

A Wagner epigone had grown into an artist who plunges into life and grasps it with force and humor. At the time of his writing "Feuersnoth" which so shocked the bourgeoisie of Munich, Strauss had come in contact with modern poetry. He began working with new lyricists, a young generation of poets who turned free sensuality into free rhythms: J. H. Mackay, K. Henckell, H. Hart, C. Busse, G. Falke, R. Dehmel, the strongest German lyricist of the realistic era who also had at his disposal a strong social pathos; Detlev von Lilienkron was another. A former cavalry officer, he now galloped across the field of poetry with drawn reins leaving a hail of stones in his wake. Yet another was J. O. Bierbaum.

Among other things Bierbaum gave him the text of "Traum durch die Daemmerung." H. Hart wrote the verses of "Caecilie" with erotic passion flowing through its melody; Mackay had written "Heimliche Aufforderung" (Secret Invitation) and "Morgen," Henckell the glowing "Liebeshymnus." Among the lyrics of Dehmel (who in later years inspired young Schoenberg for his "Verklaerte Nacht") is "Der Arbeitsmann," in the verses of which the red banner is raised. In Richard Strauss modern poetry of the period before 1900 found the modern musician.

The greatest poet, whom young Strauss met in Munich, was Frank Wedekind. Wedekind had just completed his "Fruehlings Erwachen" which portrays in short scenes laden with erotic storms the tragedy of sex awakening in children.

Like a demon out of hell Wedekind broke in on German bourgeoisie that sat content and placid in its parlors. He grinned and mocked, destroyed and poisoned, poured vitriolic acid over the tables and beds of the citizens. Like a "Danse Macabre" of bourgeois society he parades his poetic figures: insolent swindlers, criminals, circus performers, prostitutes, Lesbians, thrill murderers, and the child-wife Lulu, a cold queen ruling this world, swinging her whip over the men, smiling, seductive, luring new lovers by elementary means, while the old lovers kill themselves by shooting.

Oscar Wilde's Salome, set to music by Richard Strauss, is just such a child-wife as Lulu, in historical guise. Wilde's belief that "ugliness was the only reality" and that "raw argument, the den of loathsomeness, the rough violence of disorganized life, the depravity of the common thief and the scum of society . . . was more vivid in the intense reality of impression than the dreamy shadows of a song"—this belief was also the credo of Frank Wedekind.

This demonic poet wrote a ballet for Richard Strauss about a flea that hops under a lady's hoop-skirt. Strauss went to work on it in 1896 or 1898. It was a far cry from the knighthood days of Guntram.

There had also been a change in the Munich of old where fat citizens spent their early mornings in the Hofbrauhaus eating sausages at long tables and drinking their beer out of tall, heavy tankards. Munich had entered into opposition against Berlin and Kaiser Wilhelm II. In every tavern there was ranting against the "Saupreussen"—the Prussian swine who disturbed the peace of Bavaria. At every corner of the city hung posters of Germany's best satirical weekly, the "Simplicissimus": a red pug-dog with bared fangs.

In drawings by Thoma, this weekly magazine derided the Prussian officers, the fat nouveaux riches of Berlin, the clique of bank speculators and industrialists, nobility and junkers who reigned supreme in Berlin. Thoeny sketched the women of this society, women who visited officers' quarters, girls who drank champagne in taverns in the company of fat burghers and exposed their legs. Saucy erotic liberty was the rule in this weekly.

Munich, city of artists, with a wealth of new painters and poets, had come to life. Richard Strauss felt at home in its fresh air in which his realism gathered strength, his erotic poesy became more sensual and his mind keener. He had grown with each composition. His orchestral art had enriched its timbre, his musical powers had become more intense, his melody more rhythmic, larger in its ties.

The beginning of "Don Juan" sweeps aloft like a falcon. His love melodies—sensual in "Don Juan," affectionate in "Till Eulenspiegel," passionate, dionysic or gentle in songs, glowing in "Feuersnoth"—were rich and gripping. More and more declamation and harmonics become the medium of expression.

Strauss had come closer to the spirit of the present; he read Nietzsche and Stirner and modern writers. In composing his "Feuersnoth" he had withdrawn from the romanticism of Wagner and turned to real life. It was not long after that he stood upon a larger stage, in the midst of all spiritual, social and artistic trends of the time whose foremost leader he was to become.

III

In 1898 Richard Strauss went to Berlin in the capacity of a conductor of the Prussian court.

Following the Franco-Prussian War Berlin had developed into a modern city in which were concentrated the political life of the new German Reich, economic life and intellectual life. The new era of mechanics and industry found its core in the metropolis that afforded opportunities for the propagation of social and political uprisings.

The nouveaux riches built luxurious country homes. Factory suburbs shot up out of the ground. The new electric industries reconverted whole suburban sections into factory districts. Subways, streetcars and buses served the rushing crowds. In the royal palace dwelled Kaiser Wilhelm II. A romanticist, he had entered Jerusalem dressed in the white burnoose of the Arabs; he held parades in the barracks, sent his warships to Tangier and traveled the North Sea on a man o' war.

But Berlin was not romantic. The city in whose Reichstag the labor party was gaining power was realistic with many American traits. It could boast of daringly modern journalists: in the "Berliner Tageblatt," one of the best liberal papers in the world; and in "Die Zukunft," one of the best political weeklies of the time, by means of which Maximilian Harden battled the Kaiser and his court.

Modern art made Berlin one of its European capitals. Germany's greatest realistic painter lived in Berlin: Adolf Menzel. It was he who first painted the modern factory, its caldrons filled with red-hot masses of molten ore, its steel wheels and cranes, with the light penetrating the steam.

In Berlin Max Liebermann painted seascapes in natural sunlight; gardens with the light streaming through the tree leaves and breaking into a hundred reflections. With the realism of old Dutch painters he portrayed women mending fish nets and spinning linen. In Berlin, too, Max Slevogt painted with broad strokes of his brush under which the colors flowed as from a boiling pot.

In Berlin modern architects were at work. In 1896 Alfred Messel built the modern department store Wertheim. Peter Behrens erected factories, Van der Velde and Gropius villas. The new practical style matched the cool realistic spirit of the city, and even its historic buildings could not hem or burden life in the present era. The air was clear and keen in this city. New thoughts could breathe and grow here. Einstein and Max Planck exploded the old physical world theory in Berlin.

Berlin was the meeting point of the new European naturalism that flowed towards Central Europe from the North, from France in the West and Russia in the East. In the north, Henrik Ibsen had turned from the romantic dramas of his youth that had reached their peak in the "Crown Pretenders." In 1877 he had written his first society drama, "Pillars of Society." In these plays men and women of the bourgeoisie were brought to the stage and discussed the problems of that society.

Henrik Ibsen had tapped the walls in the houses of the era, and many spots sounded hollow. He accused, appealed to the peoples' conscience for self-examination, pointed out the ancestral sins, fought for the liberty of women, for truth and responsibility to oneself.

The first plays by Ibsen appeared on the German stage in the Seventies, but even at that time the ending of "Nora" was considered so coarse that at its performance in Hamburg the play was given a conciliatory ending. It was not until 1880, in Munich, that Nora was permitted to forsake her husband and children.

There was a battle royal of the theatre in Berlin when, in 1887, there was a performance of the "Ghosts" at the Residenztheater. The police, worried about the spiritual welfare of their subjects had, as a precautionary measure, permitted but a single performance by invitation only. "An Enemy of the People" was first given in a suburban theatre. Ibsen's "The Wild Duck" caused indignation.

Around 1890 there came another representative of the north: Strindberg. He brought to the stage the battle of the sexes and analyzed the struggle between man and woman with dialectic force that was whetted by hate, and bored deep into the dark recesses of the human soul.

Russia was represented by naturalistic novels, the greatest epics of the present era. Dostojewsky's portrayal of suffering, torn, unhappy souls aroused his readers, as did his great Slavic compassion that saw in criminals only unfortunate humans. In "Anna Karenina" Tolstoi had presented passionate love in grand pictures that were filled with reality and the whole wealth of life.

Dostojewsky's Russian mysticism and Tolstoi's Christ sermon were voices that poured out of their realistic fiction into a materialistic world like organ and trumpet tones. The chapter in which the murderer Raskolnikow reads the Bible with the prostitute and kneels down before her, not only surpassed every other novel in realistic presentation of the lowness of society, but it also preached a new Christianity. Tolstoi's "Kreutzersonate" was not merely a magnificent naturalistic novel, it was also a sermon against passion and sin as it had not been heard any stronger in the early days of Christianity.

In this very same Russia Stanislawsky founded his "Art Theatre" for naturalistic art in 1898. At the start of the twentieth century plays by Tschechov and Maxim Gorki reached Berlin and Paris from there, plays crowded with naturalistic soul analyses and with the portrayal of unhappy, fallen humans living in darkness and misery; apathetic souls that suffered, and hearts filled with fear, compassion and love.

The first theatre to present naturalistic art opened its doors in Paris in 1887. It had been founded by a minor employe of the gas company, Andre Antoine, in a small hall off the northern boulevards, and later transferred to Montparnasse and the Boulevard Strasbourg. This theatre achieved its first great success with a proletarian play by Emile Zola, "Jacques Damour," which was performed with a cast of amateurs. In 1898 Tolstoi's "Power of Darkness" appeared there, with its Russian peasants, poor creatures who are a piece of the good earth itself; with old Akim who can only stammer incoherently but who possesses the soul of a divine child; drunken Nikita who inters the new-born baby; good Marina and other primitive souls who live in misery, in dismal shacks where oil lamps burn in front of Icons, brandy bottles can be seen and the compassion of God is at home.

Ibsen and Gerhart Hauptmann were presented here, too, and

Zola fought for the naturalistic theatre with courage and consistency in articles that were collected in two volumes of his works and published.

The Theatre Antoine found competition two years later in Berlin when Theodor Wolff, the journalist—later editor-in-chief of the "Berliner Tageblatt"—together with Maximilian Harden and the Hart brothers established the "Freie Buehne." Their opening play was Ibsen's "Ghosts." Bjoernson, Strindberg, Tolstoi's "Power of Darkness," and the Goncourt brothers were included in the repertoire of the "Freie Buehne." In 1889 a German naturalistic writer, Gerhart Hauptmann, was met with hissing, indignation and derision when his first stage work "Before Sunrise" was premiered. "The Weavers" followed in 1893, and became the biggest work of the German naturalistic theatre. A presentation of the masses, and a social accusation, it was a revolution that wallows its way from the depths into the homes of the manufacturers.

Ordinarily the stage of the royal theatre resounded with the clatter of armor-plated knights and Wildenbruch brought Prussian kings to the footlights and plenty of flag waving, but even the royal theatre of Kaiser Wilhelm II opened its doors to Ibsen's "The Lady from the Sea" and Gerhart Hauptmann's "Hannele." This latter play deals with a poor proletarian child who, in a feverish dream, visualizes Heaven with Christ and the Angels who receive her in glory and in splendor.

It was not long, though, before the indignation of court society swept this play out of the house of high-hatted Berlin society; its proletarian setting just did not seem to fit into Kaiser Wilhelm's art palace.

However, in 1884 Otto Brahm opened up his "Deutsches Theater" with Schiller's "Kabale und Liebe" (Intrigue and Love) which was given as a naturalistic play. A group of the best German actors of that time performed here, playing their modern realistic parts in a new unemotional style. Among them were Kainz, Albert Bassermann, Else Lehmann, Oscar Sauer, Kayssler. Within a period of ten years the "Deutsches Theater" presented ten plays by Henrik Ibsen and twelve by Gerhart Hauptmann.

This was the theatre where Max Reinhardt had started as a

minor actor. In 1901 this same man took over as director of a small theatre in Berlin in which he presented Strindberg and Oscar Wilde, Wedekind and Gorki, and everyone knew at once that a new master of the theatre had arrived. In 1903 he moved to larger quarters, the "Neues Theater" where he produced Maeterlinck's "Pelléas and Mélisande" and Hofmannsthal's "Elektra." Here it was that he first undertook to crowd the forest of "A Midsummer Night's Dream" with birch and bush, elves and goblins.

In 1905 he made another theatre, the "Deutsches Theater," the showplace of his theatrical fancy which, in its gayness of colors, kept Berlin breathless. The decorations were painted by great artists. Famous actors presented classical works in modern form.

Into this Berlin, whose industry and politics, science and art were propelled by modern powers of the present, stepped Richard Strauss as the musician for whom the vivacious city seemed to have been waiting. He was possessed of freshness, courage, modernism, mental agility and an ambition to make himself and his music the focal point of the new era.

His "Till Eulenspiegel" and his "Feuersnoth" had shown him to be a free mind, imbued with self-esteem and superior wit, sense of humor and aggressiveness. He was no dreamer but a very conscious musician, brilliant, bold in his technique, all his senses expended on the present that made itself felt all over the big city; he was like a fresh clear breeze that swept through the streets and the minds. Max Reinhardt's theatre was the source of his greatest inspirations, without which his next works would have been unthinkable. This was where Strauss had first seen Oscar Wilde's "Salome" and Hofmannsthal's "Elektra." The color array, esprit, the fantasy and modernism of the performances were reflected in the music to "Elektra" and "Salome."

Richard Strauss let his fantasy run free in the poetry of Oscar Wilde, written by the English poet for Sarah Bernhardt's French Theatre. His symphonic music glitters and shines, dissolves into delicate colors and recoups its strength in rich coloring. It weaves its motives like a colorful silken rug; it mixes all the cunning tints of the Orient and its polished, over-ripe and diseased civilization. This music is exotic, iridescent, crass, picturesque and passionate.

Never is Strauss realism more audacious than in the scherzo of the arguing, shrieking, jargon-babbling Jews, in the characterization of the paralytic Herod; and in the ensuing sounds—moaning and groaning, when the black executioner climbs into the cistern with the silver basin and curved sword in order to decapitate John.

The romantic melody of Richard Strauss contains the greatest melodic ties to indicate voluptuous desire, Salome's unnatural craze for the naked body of the desert preacher and the sensual orgy of Salome kissing John's bloody head. A romantic hue is contained in the oriental "Dance of the Seven Veils." The recitation is naturalistic and the transitions from declamatory precision to melodic flow are rich and varied.

The contrast between the aging Orient, its empty splendour, its senile lasciviousness, its perverted sensuousness, and the pure Christian Faith is worked out keenly, although the Christian sermon is bourgeois in its sentimentality.

All the details are welded together to form one great portrait with glowing colors. Nowhere is there a gap, and painting and lyrics, expression and description, symphony and drama, beauty and ugliness, cruelty, passion and greed, colors and moods are carried away by the current of the symphony that originates in Richard Wagner's heroic country and wends it way to the new continent where the aesthetic art of Oscar Wilde, the pictorial glory of D'Annunzio and the realistic narratives of Flaubert are at home.

In "Salome" Richard Strauss had allied himself with modernism. He grasped the good that the new times brought along with the same power as he did the evil. The heroine of his opera, daughter of the cruel, sensual Herodias, is the sort of "femme fatale" that was first glorified by Edgar Allan Poe, Baudelaire and Flaubert; a vampire in female shape, a she-devil with a child-like laugh. The action of the opera is the "poema di sangue" of which D'Annunzio dreamed.

As far as style is concerned, the Salome of Strauss certainly is of that "décadence" which Theophile Gautier, in his essay on Baudelaire, identifies with the spirit of modern life. It is the decadence of which Mallarmée wrote: "I love everything that can be encompassed in the word 'chute' (decline)."

It was impossible to be more "up to date" in 1905 than Richard Strauss was with his "Salome."

He was equally up to date in his "Elektra" in 1909. Friedrich Nietzsche had been first to describe the dark abyss of barbarism, hysteria and savagery, across which arched Homer's bright Olympus. Strauss the musician descended into the abyss. Out of this dark gorge he brought forth his "Elektra" music; the piercing yells, the clots of blood and pus, the hissing snakes of Medusa, the bleating of the sacrificial animals, the stamping of wild dances.

From here he brought a hollow-eyed Queen Clytemnestra, bedecked with amulets, whose slaves rush in like bats at her cries for help. From here he took murder and barbaric sacrificial and victory dances, rhythmically savage marching and the intoxication of ecstatic body rotations. And here he found declamation, the hissing and spitting, shrieking and moaning, the cramp-like quivering of the harmonies, the blaring tones foaming at the mouth.

Just a few years previously Sigmund Freud had been the first to peer into the dark of the "unconscious" where frustration and erotic desires transform themselves into psychalgia. That is what Richard Strauss set to music in "Elektra." Like Freud he was able to say of himself: "Acheronta movebo" (I will move Hades), that being the motto of Freud's "dream interpretation."

Elektra thrusts into the underworld of the soul sensual love, desire for a man's embrace, and womanly emotion, and out of these depths come hate, savageness and hysteria.

Only when Elektra recognizes her brother does an infinite affection and softness, hitherto buried under hate, pour from her ravaged soul. The poetry of this beautiful moment was created by Strauss, not by his librettist.

In this work the naturalism of Strauss reaches the limits of the possible. The musical descriptions of barbarism in early Greece are as naturalistic as the expression which, from a scream to a flowing melody is always equally gripping. Everywhere the great melodies step out of the naturalism of music that wades through streams of blood, and in no other work did Strauss came so close to a genuinely tragic frame of mind as in this, his greatest creation.

In a letter to Ricordi dated February 2, 1908, Puccini relates the following characteristic incident: "At rehearsals (of Elektra) in Naples, Strauss was attempting to rouse the orchestra to a brutal, stormy performance. He said: 'Gentlemen, here we are not concerned with music but with the creation of noise. Blow into your instruments!' "

"Salome" had been an ornamental picture—colorful surface and masterful description. "Elektra" in its biggest moments descends to the depths inhabited by tragic forces that throw their shadows across human lives—such moments as the gloomy monologue of Elektra, and the recognition scene between brother and sister, and the final Dionysian dance.

The Greek tragedy of a naturalistic era, so far removed from the noble humanism of Goethe's "Iphigenia" nevertheless possesses its greatness of soul and its great form. Never again did Richard Strauss arch a melody as boldly as the one in this work which spans every abyss of terror. The symphonic line curves upward like a stone tossed high.

The Elektra harmonies belong as much to history as the harmonies of "Tristan and Isolde." They move freely in harmonic space, are filled with an inner tension and with expression; the structure of triads is exploded, discords become harsher yet and harmonics are driven to the boundary where the sphere of classical and romantic harmony meets the realm of atonal harmony. This was the territory into which Arnold Schoenberg ventured at that time, similar to an explorer invading an unknown stretch of desert.

Returning to Garmisch from a modern music festival, Richard Strauss expressed his dislike of the music by Hindemith and other modernistic composers. "Dr. Strauss," I told him, "don't you criticize! You were the one that started to write such music in 'Elektra.' " He replied, laughing: "I know I originated that filth."

In the big recognition scene of "Elektra" the different keys precipitate like houses during an earthquake. At many points in the music the keys are compressed and condensed. Discords are em-

ployed to represent color specks. In the scene in which Clytemnestra's maids burst in holding torches, the harmonies vibrate like
dancing lights.

Naturalistic tone clusters become the crack of the whip, the
hollow sound of digging the earth, stamping, shrieking, the bellow-
ing of sacrificial animals. They become a shapeless mass; the undulating stream of discords boils and hisses like molten ore in the
furnace.

In this tumult of discords the triads rise like the brass shields in
the battles for Troy. The menacing Agamemnon motif projects
out of the night in D-minor, and Chrysothemis sings in triad
waltzes of her banal desire for a husband and children.

Therein lies the greatness of Richard Strauss: that he is equally
well versed in the old as in the new harmonics, and that he is
capable of fitting the two halves together—the dark and the light,
the new and the old—to form a globe.

The orchestra contains the same artistic union of tradition and
novelty. The basis of the "Elektra" orchestra is still the romantic
symphony orchestra of Richard Wagner. All the naturalistic or
modern tones hover around the nucleus of the grand, pompous
Wagnerian orchestra as a glowing atmosphere surrounds a fixed
heavenly body.

The period during which the two greatest works of Richard
Strauss were created was already crammed with the tensions that
were to burst out in a tempest five years after "Elektra." The year
of Richard Strauss' arrival in Berlin had marked the death of
Bismarck, creator of the new German Reich. It had been very
small and quiet compared to the new Germany. Now the cities
were increasing in population, factories, smelting furnaces and
laboratories were working day and night. Giant ships were being
built and science and mechanics joined forces for the purpose of
enriching life and industry.

However, beside the new and the great, danger made itself felt.
Daily the innermost contrasts loomed larger between nationalism
and modern age, between the feudalism of Germany's reigning
society and the democratic and parliamentary patterns, between
gigantically increasing capitalism and the proletariat, between

ancient religious conceptions and modern science, between the narrowminded isolationist states and cosmopolitanism.

These tensions and contrasts are also noticeable in "Salome" and "Elektra," considered the greatest works of art in the epoch of Kaiser Wilhelm II. Their technical courage is a part of the general technical invention trend of the time. Their realism belongs to the main traits of the rationalistic age. Even the materialistic gleam of these works, their polished sensuality, belong entirely in the age of materialism. Their nervousness, the perversity of "Salome," the masochism and sadism of "Elektra" are also a part of the intensified nervousness of that period.

Of course, equally strong is the association with romanticism which belongs to the moribund forces of the new millennium. The aesthetics of both operas; all that which is "art pour art" in them, and "décadence": refined, cunning intellect, technique that often detaches itself from the mind and goes its own way; the super-abundance of coloring, of the unusual, of the artistic; the sultry perfume in "Salome," the odor of blood in "Elektra"—they all separate the new artistic music of these operas from the powerful drifts of life.

Perhaps while composing "Salome" Richard Strauss did not consciously appreciate the similarity of the age in which its action takes place with the present: downfall of an old epoch in civilization and the inception of a new era; decay of the decadent old world and prophesy of a new world of faith.

Nevertheless this contrast between two eras is contained in "Salome"—on the one hand colorfully gleaming materialism, on the other a new spiritualism.

The Oriental royal court in shining gala robes, with artistically designed gold vessels, with bronzed soldier torsos, with a blacka-moor executioner, with nude women, and the desert preacher—all this becomes ornamental splendor that stimulates the senses, rather than tragic poetry. Genuine tragedy and ethics are stronger in individual scenes of "Elektra," yet wild barbarism predominates in the music, stirring up an era of nerves, and the dissonant unrest of a tortured, not a strong age.

IV

As though he had sensed this, Richard Strauss appeared in 1911 with his gay "Rosenkavalier." He had fled from the barbaric pre-historic age of Elektra to Viennese rococo; from the wild passions of mythical Greece that built Cyclopean walls and paid homage to animal gods, he turned to the amorous games of refined society in gold-inlaid canopied beds; from blood and murder to dainty chatting at the breakfast table where hot chocolate is served in painted porcelain cups.

In "Rosenkavalier" Strauss applied his realism to comedy. He created the new prattling tone of conversation in his work, a new realistic buffo recitation. Realistic, too, is the picturization of every kind of situation, the hustle and bustle at the "levée" of a great lady, the noise of the tavern scenes, the presentation of the silver rose.

Every bit as realistic as Flaubert depicted the Paris of old from pictures and copperplate engravings, old Vienna is brought back to life with waltz music. Psychological description and psychological development are also realistic.

The scene in which the aging marshal's wife detaches herself from her youthful lover after a night of passion and mourns about the instability of beauty would not have been possible before Turgenjeff's time. The psychological narrative in the final scene, too, its delicate hither and thither: the stammering embarrassment of Sophie, the majesty of the resigning Marschallin, the empty arrogance of Fanninal, the stupefaction of Ochs von Lerchenau, the uncertainty of Refrano—all this is representative of a new realistic comedy style.

One of the founders of German naturalism, Arno Holz, char-acterized this new style as a "style of seconds." An author wishing to describe a falling leaf must describe the changes in the appear-ance of the leaf from one second to another. Similarly Richard Strauss describes in "Rosenkavalier" situations and psychological developments.

Another "style of seconds" are the many fine differentiations of conversation, its variations from prosaic speech to melodies, the transition from the free to the solid form.

No previous opera had contained a scene such as shown in the first act of "Rosenkavalier": the dialogue between the marshal's wife and her boy with its melancholy note; her sorrow on discovering the first gray hair; her rejection and aggressiveness; her renunciation, her passionate ebullition, and the noble resignation of the finale.

Ranging from the sounds of everyday life to brilliant melody, that scene possesses all forms of musical expression. One emotional display follows another. The scene breathes and lives, and the music breathes and lives in unison.

A similar wealth is to be found in the ensembles. Beginning with the naturalistic tumult, indicated by a medley of voices, to the melodic duets and trios, all forms of multiple voice singing are employed. In the singing of the women's trio, the music rises at the end to perfect beauty ascending higher and higher, growing more and more radiant and is followed by the broadly singing orchestra, the delicate love duets and the scherzando of the orchestra. With the flute passages and drum beats of this scherzando the opera fades out.

The same Wagnerian symphony orchestra that had been the nucleus of "Salome" and "Elektra" was retained in "Rosenkavalier." It elaborates on the musical motifs and enhances them as in a symphony. On its silvery swells it carries realistic conversations, singing, waltzes and ensembles; it describes and portrays, causes the silver rose to sparkle and send forth its fragrance, and the lights in the tavern to flicker. At intimate points a select chamber orchestra lifts itself from out of the big orchestra, and the lustre of the masterly orchestra is reflected in hundreds of facets. The Richard Strauss symphony is directed entirely to comedy here.

Despite all the beauty of its melody, "Rosenkavalier" is a realistic opera in which the Vienna of Empress Maria Theresa is as vivid as in the pictures of Canaletto. The next following opera by Richard Strauss, the chamber opera "Ariadne on Naxos," is in its entirety pure fantasia. Just the prelude, sketched by Richard Strauss

with a light hand for the Vienna performance, is a realistic miniature opera with Viennese figures, lively motion and flying dialogue
that, towards the end, spreads its bright wings of melody and soars
aloft.

The opera itself is a mythological fairy tale; a play involving
figures of the Greek sagas in which are entwined the dances and
songs of the Italian Masks from "Commedia del'arte." In eighteenth
century Venice such operas had been written by Cesti and Cavalli.
Greek mythology and antics of Italian folk comedy were blended
in these Italian Baroque operas, and this was the form that Hugo
von Hofmannsthal revived for Richard Strauss.

Richard Strauss fled from the struggles and dangers of that era
—this was two years before the outbreak of World War I—into
the ornamental world of light and splendour. His melody was never
happier, his wit never more brilliant. During that same period
Arnold Schoenberg composed his "Pierrot Lunaire" which was
crowded with painfully agitated recitation and imaginary pictures
of agony and fantastic tortures. Richard Strauss, on the other
hand, created a colorful, festive decoration which combines color
and spirit, playful fancy and figures from many lands and many
ages to form one great total—much as the painted ceilings of
Tiepolo in the palace at Wuerzburg.

"Ariadne must emerge as a serious playwork," Hofmannsthal
wrote to Strauss; and it did, in the heroic scenes with Bacchus and
Ariadne and in the comic scenes that surround the serious scenes
with banter like golden cupids around a picture frame. True, the
contrast between Ariadne, the woman who can love but one man,
and Zerbinetta, the woman who loves hundreds of them, involves
a modern problem of womankind but on the whole, as art production "Ariadne on Naxos" is wit, lustre and play.

A second work that also turned out to be a revelry of ornamental
fantasy is the ballet "Die Josefslegende," created by Richard "Il
Magnifico" during the same period, 1912. Strauss composed this
ballet for Diaghileff's Ballet Russe, and created the part of the
chaste Josef for Nijinsky whom he described in a letter as "the
most extraordinary person the present-day stage possesses."

"Die Josefslegende" is a ballet of lavish gold display "in the spirit of Paolo Veronese," according to the composer; a genuine Baroque ballet, a tableau of silk gowns, lace and pearls, of rosy female bodies and the black torsos of Negroes and mulattoes, of colorful veils barely covering virginal breasts; of golden receptacles and of warriors, of fruit bowls and heavy rugs. Everything is color and ornament, intoxicating and voluptuous.

The peak of this evolution to a new romanticism that fairly flaunted its sensuality and splendor was attained by Richard Strauss during the war in his fairy tale opera "Die Frau ohne Schatten" (The Woman without a Shadow). In the libretto Hugo von Hofmannsthal intermingled motifs and legends of the Orient to weave a colorful carpet upon which mysterious symbols shine. The most elaborate apparatus of the magic fairy opera is exerted. Fish are singing in the kettle, the air is filled with the voices of unborn children and towards the end there is singing by choruses of sainted spirits.

This opera is a kind of "Magic Flute" in which two couples— one exalted, the other lowly—are separated and subjected to trials. Finally, purified and expiated, they become reunited upon a golden bridge suspended over a waterfall sparkling like crystals.

The symphonic music of Richard Strauss combines all the melodies, harmonies and new tones that he found in "Salome" and "Elektra," in "Rosenkavalier" and in "Ariadne on Naxos." It is more or less a compendium of Strauss art and an enhancement of his motif work, his colorful tone, his portrayal, his expression and his lyric melody.

With "Ariadne on Naxos," "Josefslegende" and "Woman without a Shadow" Richard Strauss detached himself from the present, its toils and problems. He created these works in a magic sphere of fancy where light and sunshine reigned while dark clouds gathered above the rest of the world. Scarcely one hundred years before, Germany's greatest poet, Goethe, had secluded himself from the French Revolution and the national upheaval of the German people and had sought majestic peace of mind among rocks and plants, statues and gems. The single epos in whose antique marble stanzas the thunder of the French Revolution is heard from a distance was the world-remote "Natuerliche Tochter," and the sole epic poem that symbolized the German uprising was a mythological drama, "Palaeophron and Neoterpe."

In the years from 1911–1915 Germany's greatest musician gave a similar answer to world questions: he offered masquerade, gala ballet and a magic opera to a world that needed not so much festive tapestries, frescoes, golden receptacles and crystal glasses as it did interpretation of its struggles.

V

As a composer of symphonies Richard Strauss had been silent since 1915. He felt that his task was done. He had joined romanticism and realism, had enriched the technique of the orchestra, augmented the media of colorful description and enhanced the lustre and beauty of the lyric melody. But with his "Alpensinfonie" he had reached the boundary where art stops and exhibition begins.

Strauss continued composing only operas. Operas of a master who lived in a world created by himself, whose every nook and cranny he knew. Knowledge and ability created these operas, not necessity. In all of them spirit, beauty, characteristics, personalities were molded with a sure theatrical technique into those patterns that are admired as the Strauss form.

Not that Richard Strauss would repeat himself—for that his mind is too keen. But he limited his fantasy to the realm that he was the first to enter. He did not search for any new territory as he did in "Salome," "Elektra," "Rosenkavalier" and "Ariadne."

Strauss, being a very clever man, did not fail to recognize the dangers which an aging artist faces. In 1916 he wrote to Hofmannsthal: "At my age it is easy to fall into routine."

From the magic world of "Woman without a Shadow" Strauss turned to one of those realistic comedies which, in his "Rosenkavalier" he brought to the music stage with the full enjoyment of realism. His "Intermezzo" (1924) depicts wife and house, maid and card parties, sleigh rides in the Bavarian Alps, argument and reconciliation with relish and, towards the finale, with warmth too. It is a dramatized "Sinfonia Domestica," and Richard Strauss himself wrote the libretto.

Strauss turned from what—in the prologue of Intermezzo—he terms "perhaps an all too bold grasp into the full life of man" to an ostentatious Greek opera "Die Aegyptische Helena" (1928) and to richly glittering Baroque containing one of those melodically enhanced love scenes that could be called Titianic, so radiant is the figure of the woman under the velvet drapes of the bed.

A comedy about old Vienna, "Arabella" (1923) is a counter-piece to "Rosenkavalier," full of realistic figures of Old Austria. In 1938 the opera "Die schweigsame Frau" (The Silent Woman) made its appearance. With a libretto by Stefan Zweig, it is a buffo opera with masquerade and mummery. Two more one-act operas followed during the second World War, "Daphne" and "Friedens-fest" (Festival of Peace). The latter brings a sublime hymnal chorus celebrating peace.

The harvest of operas that the aging Richard Strauss gathered in his barn was still a rich one. But although these works showed his intellect and his colors had the old abundance of hues, the strong spiritual trends of the time were not to be found therein. Strauss never left the field of witticism, ornamentation and play fulness into which the poet Hugo von Hofmannsthal had led him.

In a letter written in 1916 Strauss thanks his librettist for having "incised the cataract" and for having "opened up an entirely new landscape . . . the territory of the un-Wagnerian opera of play, soul and humanity." He states further that he has "definitely shed the Wagnerian music armour."

No one contributed more than Richard Strauss to the victory over Wagner romanticism that played such an important part in the musical evolution of the 20th century. Beginning with his realistic youthful opera "Feuersnoth" and continuing through the witty performances of his latest operas, there is an uninterrupted development and a departure from Wagner's romanticism. The drying heroic and romantic art of Richard Wagner, and rising modern realism approach one another in the art of Richard Strauss and in the colorful hues of Strauss music the purple and brocade tones of Wagner blend with the light of a new era that is bright and keen, the light of reality, light of materialistic mentality.

6

Gustav Mahler, The Mystic

I

WHEN GUSTAV MAHLER conducted his first symphony in Vienna, and the symphonic poems of Richard Strauss were still new, I asked Mahler about his attitude towards Richard Strauss. He replied: "Strauss and I are like two miners who dig their shafts into the same mountain from two different sides."

The mountain in question was the romantic magic mountain. Without Bruckner and Berlioz, without Wagner and Liszt the Mahler orchestra is unthinkable. All of Gustav Mahler's songs are composed to the lyrics of romantic poets. He was irresistibly attracted by the collection of "Des Knaben Wunderhorn," the masterpiece of romantic fantasy, and the poems in "Lieder eines fahrenden Gesellen" (Songs of a wandering journeyman) which he wrote himself, could easily be taken for songs from "Knaben Wunderhorn." He copies their popular tone, everything that is dark, intimate and naive in their verses.

The theme of his first cantata: "Das Klagende Lied" is a romantic folk fable. Like all romanticists Mahler longs for the simplicity and sincerity of popular melodies as they are sung by young girls promenading in village streets of a summer evening, with glow worms in their hair and love in their hearts. Music to Gustav Mahler, as to all romantic artists, is a mysterious language from Beyond. It resounds in nature, in woods and meadows, in heaven and earth. Tone represents something symbolic to him.

In comparison with Gustav Mahler Richard Strauss appears naive. The musician Richard Strauss is a narrator, a delineator who portrays reality. His perceptive faculty is unbroken, and intellectual inspiration acquired many friends for him—among them a poet like Hugo von Hofmannsthal, a stage producer like Max Reinhardt.

A friend, the composer Alexander Ritter, urged him on to compose program music. The basis of Strauss creation is the real South German appreciation of music and color. That was his environment all over Bavaria. The churches in Munich are elaborate structures in Baroque style, filled with gold altars, marble saints, trumpet music. In the Bavarian hamlets the white walls of peasant houses are adorned with frescoes, and flowerpots decorate the windows. Not far from Garmisch, where Strauss built his home, lies Oberammergau. Since the seventeenth century Bavarian peasants have presented the Passion Play here, with a wood-carver portraying Jesus.

This Bavarian pleasure in colors and bright figures is perpetuated in Richard Strauss. His enjoyment of Baroque too is Bavarian heritage. Since 1652, the year in which the Bavarian Prince Ferdinand Maria married an Italian, Adelhaid von Savoyen, the splendor of Baroque flowed across Alpine passes down to Munich. Venetian artists decorated Bavarian court festivities. Near Saint Salvador in Munich an Italian opera house was built. The printers in Munich printed Italian books. Italian architects built Jesuit churches in Munich, and in the village square the Jesuit priests presented theatrical plays with singing angels and a divine tribunal.

This, then, was the Bavarian Baroque art from which Richard Strauss was descended, and it was not entirely a joke when he told me: "I first realized in Italy that my 'Elektra' is really an Italian opera." With "Ariadne on Naxos" Strauss became altogether an Italian opera composer, even writing coloratura arias.

Gustav Mahler was not the naive and sensuous composer that Richard Strauss, in spite of all his wit, is. He was dark, Jewish looking, with the high forehead of the intellectualist and the excited nerves of his race, nerves that quivered in the memory of persecution, humiliation and death. His closest forebears were cabalistic philosophers who, sitting in dark Gothic rooms, pondered over God—the "En-Soph"—and the ten "Sephiroth," that surrounded the Divine Throne like halos.

Mahler is not a musician but a philosophical thinker who ponders over the problems of world, heaven, God, death and resurrection. The struggles of his mind turn to music. They are struggles similar to those experienced by Dostojewsky, Tolstoi and Strindberg; a painful wrestling with dark forces of the inner self, a battle that lacerates the soul, exaltation to God. Nothing is more alien to Mahler than the conception of Richard Strauss who sees in the world almost nothing but a colored superficies. All worldly phenomena are only symbols for Mahler, pointing the way to a Beyond. In a materialistic age he stands side by side with the great Russian, Scriabin, as the sole mysticist in music.

"Thinking: Fighting dark forces' spectre within oneself.
Composing: Holding judgment over one's own self"

Henrik Ibsen had written, and these lines can also be applied to Gustav Mahler. All his music: songs and symphonies, coheres in one focal point and branches out from there. Gustav Mahler never composed songs, as Richard Strauss did, because he wanted to make music, because he enjoyed singing or because he wished to portray in a melody soulful moods. His songs are the seed out of which the symphonies grow; symphonies are extended songs. Both either seek or give an answer to the same tormenting questions. The songs are sketches of symphonies, or they appear in the symphonies and give them meaning and interpretation.

At the start of every symphonic cycle by Gustav Mahler one finds a lieder cycle. Mahler's first symphony developed out of the youthful experience of "Lieder eines fahrenden Gesellen"; the second, third and fourth symphonies out of the songs of "Knaben Wunderhorn." In the fifth, sixth and seventh symphonies are expanded the melodies of "Kindertodtenlieder."

Most of the songs had orchestral timbre right from the start. Of the forty-four lieder by Gustav Mahler that have been published, the majority are provided with orchestral accompaniment, and the song cycle "Das Lied von der Erde" was termed a symphony by Mahler.

Thus the tone sphere of the songs is already symphonic. Songs and symphonies are spiritually united like big world and small world, presentiment and fulfillment, initial step and highest peak.

Gustav Mahler's symphonies themselves are again a unit. They are all associated with one another, and the fourth symphony was originally meant to be the finale of the third symphony from which it becomes disjoined as a child from its mother. All his symphonies contained the same mental conflicts and the same solutions to the problems that oppressed Mahler.

Typical symbols and ever recurring ideas reappear in all the symphonies. Anyone acquainted with the theories of Freud knows the meaning of such symbols. They are sounding forms of psychical complexes arising from the depths of unconscious emotional life.

One of these symbols is a gloomy funeral march that traverses songs and symphonies with beating drums. Another symbol is the trumpet signal which, in the form of "Reveille" or the "Great roll-call," arouses the dead. Still another is a convulsive contortion in the music that resembles a sudden cramp or swift anxiety and destroys the paradisiacal bliss in the first and fourth symphony. A fourth symbol is the Laendler dance, representing the banal pleasure in life and earthly comfort. This symbolism of Mahler's pervades all his work.

With compulsory force Mahler is drawn to the same problems of life that confront him as Oedipus standing before the interrogative sphinx. The problem of death had special significance for Mahler. The first symphony already contains thoughts about death, and the dirge sounds sneering and grotesque in the third movement, while the soul weeps.

Mahler's second symphony was devoted entirely to the question of life and death, the terrors of the Last Judgment and the eternal bliss of resurrection. It is his mystery play of the Hereafter out of which the song of the bird of death resounds. In the third movement of the fourth symphony Death plays a blaring melody on his violin. The fifth symphony starts off with dismal death thoughts, and the "Lied van der Erde" is replete with them. In the tenth symphony Mahler wrestles with death itself which had entered his working room. Beneath the third movement in the score it says: "Death! Proc! (probably: Proclamation)." At another point: "God, O God, Why didst Thou forsake me?" and several bars later, "Thy Will be done!"

Still greater emotional distress was evinced in the fourth movement. Here one reads: "The devil dances it with me. Madness seizes me, the accursed! Destroy me, that I may forget that I am! That I cease to be, that I for(get)."

The ten symphonies composed by Gustav Mahler in the years 1885 to the year of his death, 1911, contain his emotional conflicts, his development, his wrestling with the dark forces of his being, his path from Hades to Heaven and his fall from Heaven to Hell.

Gustav Mahler was always an unredeemed soul. In the finale of the third symphony the planets revolve around the sun, Divine Love pervades the universe and the fighting spirit is admitted to the eternal bliss of Heaven. Following this symphony, and the children's heaven of the fourth symphony, this Ahasueric soul plunges into the night and despair of the fifth, sixth and seventh symphonies. Having envisaged God, he again stands in solitude.

A blaring note of the trumpet, and gloomy funeral marches start the cycle of the fifth, sixth and seventh symphonies. No God, no angel sings to him. Grotesque faces grin at him. Then again follows elevation to the realm of light in the eighth symphony, with jubilant choruses and hymns of Divine Love. The "sparklet" —a term used by the mysticists to denote the human soul—rejoins the great light from which it had become detached.

In the ninth symphony, however, Mahler again conjures up dark shadows that dance, mock and threaten. There is something of the tragic in this striving for exaltation, for light and Divine Love. Gustav Mahler never found permanent peace and eternal bliss as did others who went in quest of God.

Not even in nature did Mahler find peace. He felt the beauty of nature keenly, and portrayed it accordingly. In his first symphony he gave a wonderful description of meadows in the sunlight, and the singing of the birds. His third symphony contains fascinating pictures from the world of plants and animals. In his "Lied von der Erde" he depicts beautiful young girls dancing and vigorous young men riding wild horses.

Still there was something sinister for Mahler in nature. In a conversation he described how "the blue sky suddenly becomes dreadful" and how "on the most beautiful day in the sunflooded forest one is often seized by a panicky terror." As a child Mahler could often be found sitting on a tree stump, staring into space as though terrorized. He once explained to a friend that "life sometimes becomes meaningless, and a horrible spook from which one may tear oneself with a cry of disgust."

In a similar manner the Gothic world of the middle ages sensed nature as a diabolical spectre. Out of the cathedrals of the thirteenth century animal-like demonic waterspouts erupt, and from Mahler's symphonic scenery dragons suddenly emerge.

Mahler's relation to nature is never naive. To him, nature is a stepping-stone on the path to God. It obtains significance only from a Beyond. Thus Gustav Mahler pictured, in his third symphony, the road from rigid, immobile substance to flowers, animals, angels and God.

All of Gustav Mahler's great symphonies are mystery plays in symphonic form. They are constructed like the stage of spiritual plays in the middle ages: Hell at the bottom, above that the earth, and at the top, heaven. In the finale of the third symphony, in the fourth and in the eighth symphony Mahler described Heaven: shining, gay, pervaded by light, with ringing bells, singing angels, and the sound of the trumpet. According to his communications, the heavenly choirs of the eighth symphony "should no longer be human voices, but planets and stars moving in a circle." (From a letter dated 1906.)

He was a cosmic person, like the philosopher Baruch de Spinoza to whom God represented all being, all nature and all thinking. But the way to God leads through the burning thorn bush of pain, and in the portrayal of such conflagration of the soul Mahler proves himself a modern individual with all the hysteria of a worried age. This lends Mahler's music an extraordinary emotional tension which sometimes even his purely musical genius is not able to cope with. He then becomes excessive, spasmodic, heaps media upon media: three massed choirs in his eighth symphony above a gigantic orchestra, the final scene of Goethe's "Faust" over a Latin mediaeval hymn. The orchestra assumes huge proportions, and this giant orchestra is drowned out by a massing of brass instruments pealing out chorals.

In the midst of such music, picturing a nervous Faust, there are moments of ecstatic rapture, as in the Adagio of the fifth symphony. The gigantic tableau of the third symphony is followed by the delicate miniature of the fourth symphony; the massive jubilation of the eighth symphony by the chamber music of "Lied von der Erde": a Japanese engraving after a colossal fresco.

The tragic composer, tossed about between extreme gentleness and ecstatic vision, lacks moderation and intrinsic balance. In Mahler's artistic struggling there is only exaltation and despondency, no happy medium, no lasting peace. The greatest despair becomes apparent in the sixth symphony. Here, life in a heavenly light is but a distant memory. Night devours all previous existence. Fate roars down with hammering blows that break everything asunder. The percussion instruments in this symphony are all frightening noises of the night. In the midst of this terror stands man, no, he walks, he marches, he beats the drum, nothing can keep him back, he sinks into abysses, he continues marching until, finally, at the end of the symphony he collapses: a most unusual ending for Gustav Mahler, who generally knows only triumph. Did fate completely subdue the lone, strong man?

The next symphony, the seventh, provides the answer. At the start of this work the prone man raises himself up. His collapse was merely an episode that proved how heavy were Mahler's spiritual and emotional conflicts; he escapes from them and ascends to the C-major dithyramb of the finale, in which all bells celebrate a victory which turns out to be not permanent.

Gustav Mahler belongs to the restive, tragic fighters of the nineteenth century beginning with Lord Byron and ending with August Strindberg whose proud foreheads bear the mark of the unredeemed. As an intellectual personality he is great and incomparable. Even at the age of twenty-five, when he composed his first symphony, he was entirely himself. The paradisiacal mood in the first movement of this symphony, and the Laendler dances of the second movement; the scornful parody and the harshness of the third movement, and the struggles of the final movement are Mahler. Never before had similar music been written; like the Bible it begins with Paradise and the fall of man and the expulsion from the Garden of Eden. And like the Prophets it ends with the trumpet sermon on the Glory of God.

II

Prophet, philosopher and mysticist that he was, Mahler approached music from the spiritual side. It is not the musical impulse in Mahler that creates the decisive talent for expressing himself in musical forms; rather it is the need of unburdening himself and of finding his way from the night of life to the light of heaven. A brother of Mahler's had perished by his own hand. He had lost his way in the gloominess of life. Gustav Mahler himself was able to shape the afflictions of his soul into works of art, thereby liberating himself.

An artistic personality of this kind belongs to romanticism. It was a romantic poet, Th. A. Hoffmann, who invented the figure of the conductor Kreisler, the demonic musician who is obsessed by his art and who considers reality, people and sociableness a banality.

Gustav Mahler was such a conductor Kreisler. When he was director of the Vienna opera and would cross the streets with hair flying, hat in hand; or when he stormed up the narrow winding stairs to his rehearsal room; even more so, though, when he sat at the conductor's stand in the opera, a glowing flickering flame, he gave the impression that conductor Kreisler had come to life again.

As a composer, too, he was conductor Kreisler; a mysticist like all romantic philosophers to whom world, nature, man were merely appearances of God. Again like the romantic philosophers, Mahler saw in the real world only an allegory. His scenic descriptions, unlike those in the symphonic poems of Richard Strauss which are realistic, are symbolic. In Gustav Mahler's sixth symphony there is the sound of cowbells just like at the finale of "Heldenleben" by Richard Strauss. But while they are real bells for Richard Strauss, bells that he could hear every morning on opening the windows of his study, to Mahler they are symbolic sounds: they represent the last sound heard by a wanderer making the ascent; they are similitudes of remoteness and solitude.

The cuckoo that sounds its call in Mahler's first symphony is not a realistic cuckoo which, like every other cuckoo in the world, and like the cuckoo in Beethoven's "Pastorale," calls in thirds. Mahler's cuckoo calls in fourths, a symbolic cuckoo. In Mahler's music military marches and funeral marches are all symbolic rhythms, and the sound of the hammer in the seventh symphony is a symbolic tone. The Laendler and waltzes in his scherzos are not dance music, but parables of animal love of life. All sounds and rhythms, all phenomena of the world have only spiritual meaning for Gustav Mahler. To him nature is nothing real, merely a step on the soul's path to God.

Gustav Mahler continued to develop the classical symphony form and the romantic orchestra from the spiritual side, not from the purely musical.

The classical symphony form had been a harmony. Its four movements stood at the same level. With Mahler, who fights his way upwards, the symphony becomes a gradation. The classical equilibrium of the four movements is already destroyed in Mahler's first symphony. The gay first two movements are but a prelude, the parody of the third movement an intermezzo.. They are all just a preparation for the fourth movement which is expanded mightily and gives the appearance of being the aim and meaning of the music.

The second and third symphonies are constructed in terraces, like the minarets in ancient Babylon. "My work forms a musical poem that embraces every stage of development in a step-by-step gradation. It begins with inanimate nature and increases until it reaches love." Thus Mahler himself described his third symphony in a letter.

The energy of mind with which Mahler erected these structures that aspire from earth to heaven, is extraordinary. He got the inspiration for such forms from Anton Bruckner, particularly from the latter's fifth symphony; with the fugues of the final movement this symphony works itself upwards to the glory of the choral finale: or rather, it prays itself upwards. However, what he accomplished with these inspirations is his own personal creation. Mahler's symphonies, in their ascent, became an allegory for his titanism.

For these tonal structures Mahler, like Richard Strauss and simultaneously with him, increased the instruments of the romantic orchestra to immense proportions in his work. However, this augmentation of instrumental coloring had a different significance for him than for Richard Strauss. Strauss enlarged the romantic orchestra because he needed new paint tubes for his pictures. It was materialistic pleasure in glory and splendor that augmented the orchestra of Strauss symphonies to massive proportions. The new colors were to serve festive decorations as Richard Strauss loved them; composing in his Viennese study beneath a colored wooden ceiling out of an Italian palazzo, he was surrounded by costly paintings and Greek statuettes.

Mahler's orchestra does not owe its existence to this enjoyment of color, but to the cosmic aspiration of Mahler. "I am the universe when it resounds," Mahler wrote after composing his eighth symphony. And another time: "Imagine the whole universe starting to sound and ring." Mahler's use of the chamber orchestra in his "Lied von der Erde" has similar significance. It is supposed to reproduce the gentle voices of the universe, the drifting of autumnal mists, the plaintive voices of birds, the quiet of twilight.

A number of years after Mahler's "Lied von der Erde" (composed in 1908) Richard Strauss employed a similar chamber orchestra in his "Ariadne on Naxos." But here it was an artistic mind that shaped the fine, silken tones. In Mahler's music it is always the spirit that forms the tones; in the music of Strauss it is sensuousness.

Employing tones as symbols, the way Mahler does, is romanticism. Mahler is more deeply involved in romanticism than Richard Strauss. His starting point was the poetic works of the romanticists: the songs from "Knaben Wunderhorn" and Jean Paul's novel "Flegeljahre" which had already inspired Schumann.

His eighth symphony, too, contains romance: the Latin hymn "Veni Creator Spiritus" is mediaeval poetry such as the romanticists discovered, and the ending of the Goethe-like "Faust" epic was genuine romantic poesy, inspired by the frescoes in the Gothic cemetery at Pisa. The "Lied von der Erde" took its text from Chinese poems by Li-Tai-Po, poetry of the Far East that had first been translated and imitated by the romanticists.

Romantic also are Mahler's nature scenes, the animated and spirited universe, nature as similitude, and his mysticism; his heaven, his earth and his hell. Romantic is the figure of Death bowing the shrill violin as in a picture by Boecklin, or, death potion in hand, riding a black horse like in a painting by Franz Stuck. The type of artist that Mahler represents is romantic, and differs from the type of Richard Strauss by virtue of ecstatic enthusiasm, fanaticism and conflicts with the world. Gustav Mahler is the greatest anti-realist among the artists of the twentieth century.

It is the restive spirit and the intellectuality of the modern Jew that allies Gustav Mahler with the twentieth century—the Jew who has left many generations of prophets and rabbis behind him and whose spiritual strength does not find the same peace in the study of the Bible that his ancestors did. He, too, the sensitive heir of such men, goes in quest of God as they had done.

He is visionary like the Prophet Hezekiel and the poet Kalir who, at the Sea of Tiberias, envisaged the seven heavenly halls and the choirs of angels; and like the Jewish mysticists of the thirteenth century, like Isaac Lurja in the sixteenth century and the pious Chassidim of the eighteenth century who would drive out the voices of Satan with their prayers, as Mahler did with symphonies.

Mahler carries over into the modern, scientific age this Jewish heritage of spiritual visions. He is an artist of this age, whose greatest novelist, Dostojewsky, was an epileptic as Strindberg was a paranoic, Mussorgsky a drunkard and Baudelaire indulged in erotic perversions. His nervous system was the sensitive nervous system of the era of Charcot, Liebault and Freud. Dark childhood memories oppress him, and they penetrate all his symphonies. The trumpet signals in his symphonies, the funeral marches and many other moments are such childhood memories. Sinister faces frighten him. When he was composing "Klagendes Lied" he saw his double coming through the wall of his room, and while he was writing the funeral march for his second symphony, he visualized himself laid out beneath flowers and wreaths. We find in his music hysterical cramps and convulsions. Fear suddenly cries out. The tortured nerves groan.

He was a deeply suffering man, like Blaise Pascal in the seventeenth century, and the cleft of modern time pervades Mahler's music as a similar one had passed through Pascal's thoughts. Above his symphonies he could have placed the Pascal phrase: "Car enfin qu'est ce que l'homme dans la nature? Un néant à l'égard de l'infini, un tout à l'égard du néant, un milieu entre rien et tout." (What is, of course, man in Nature? Nothing when compared with the infinite, everything when campared with the nothing; a half in between nothing and all.)

Pascal's belief that love belongs to a higher order than knowledge was also Mahler's tenet. The emotional conflicts of man, who aspires to the light were touchingly described by Pascal in his "Pensées"; in Mahler's symphonies they turn to music.

In listening to Gustav Mahler's music one realizes that the so magnificent mechanical-technical civilization of the twentieth century possessed something that was unable to satisfy a more profound nature. One of the greatest moments of Mahler's creation comes when the dark voice of an angel starts singing:

"Ich bin von Gott
Will wieder zu Gott
Der liebe Gott
Wird mir ein Lichtlein geben
Wird leuchten mir zu seel'gem, ew'gen Leben."

(I am from God; will return to God; Dear God will give me a little light; will light the way to blissful, eternal life.)

Such an artist nature would never have been satisfied with the colorful exterior of life as Richard Strauss was. "Man lies in greatest need, man lies in greatest pain" was Mahler's credo, and the third symphony proclaims with Nietzsche's words: "O Mensch, gieb acht! Die Welt ist tief und tiefer, als der Tag gedacht." (O man, have care. The world is deep and deeper than day would think.)

With the utmost spiritual energy Gustav Mahler sought the path to light, to great love, and to God in his music. Often he compared his struggles with Jacob's battle with the angel. No musical expression was sufficiently strong to picture these struggles.

The directions in his scores accumulate: "With greatest fury"; "as though lashed"; "erupting violently." "Trumpets to blow with upturned instruments." The blaring E-flat clarinet shrieks in his symphonies.

Sometimes the purely musical strength does not suffice to express that to which Mahler's titanism aspires. Then the highest enhancements become theatrical, Mayerbeer-like; a pageant with masses of comparsery, trumpet orchestras and bell-ringing in a spotlight. Or Mahler's mind, so strong and so original, begins to "talk with tongues" like the ecstatic devout of early Christendom. With the "tongues of Beethoven or Wagner," or, in the transfiguration music at the close of the third symphony, with Brahms' melody "Feldeinsamkeit."

Such monumental music as Mahler's symphonies are will always have to build with the hewn stones of triad music, just as temples will always rest upon pillars and columns. However, Mahler's counterpoint instead of uniting the various musical voices lets them go their own way side by side, and always pierces the triad structure. Mahler's counterpoint also turns the cosmos to tone; Mahler used to tell how, as a child in the forest of Iglau he would listen to the woods sounding in many voices, to the birds' songs mingling with the rustling of the leaves and the storm sounding its melody amidst the noises of the forest.

"Just so, from different sides, the themes must come." In the third symphony man marches straight through the sounds of the world, through noisy and vulgar music that goes its own way. In "Lied von der Erde" a five tone scale forms the nucleus from which all melodies grow. A "tone figure," a crystal composed of five tones, is in the centre of all tone patterns, as in the later works of Schoenberg. If Richard Strauss expanded harmonics with his naturalism, Mahler enlarges them with spiritual energy.

In a modern materialistic world, which around 1900 was great in science and research, in industry and commerce, Gustav Mahler was a herald of moral and ethical values.

The most eminent sculptor of this age, Rodin, perpetuated Mahler's features in many bronze busts: the noble head of a thinker, a fighter, a man looking up.

7

Claude Debussy, The Impressionist

In 1874 a number of young painters: Pissarro, Claude Monet, Sisley, Renoir and Cézanne, got together with several already recognized painters, like Degas and jointly exhibited their paintings in Paris, in the studio of a photographer at 35 Boulevard des Capucines. Price of admission was only one franc, but for this small sum Parisians saw something that to them appeared like a curio cabinet. People laughed, were indignant and cracked Parisian jokes.

In the pictures of these young artists the objects dissolved in a bright light that broke in hundreds of reflections. The sun burned in the landscapes. The roofs were glaring red splotches. The meadows a poisonous green. Even the shadows were tinted. Everything glittered.

In London Monet and Pissarro had seen pictures by Turner in which the fogs swam, sunsets filled the air with dancing gold, houses and bridges disappeared in the atmosphere.

Pissarro soon started placing the colors of the sun spectrum next to one another and to paint the lighting in every hour of the day and in every season; vibrations of light, and variations of the air.

Claude Monet began to paint all his pictures in the outdoors, in fields and meadows where the light could flow unhampered. He painted the same objects: Hay stacks in the field, poplars at the river bank; the portal of the cathedral at Rouen in varying lights in the morning, at noon and in the evening, in fog and mist. Claude Monet, Pissarro, Sisley, Renoir and Cézanne all reduced the light to colored atoms that moved on the canvas, swayed back and forth and dissolved.

Included in the exhibit was a painting by Claude Monet which at Renoir's suggestion was called "Impression, Sunrise" and which was to give this artist group its name. This picture showed sunlight in a blue haze, churches and houses emerging in the distance as black shadows; fishing boats upon the undulating water on which fell red light spots of the rising red run and moved up and down.

Subject of the picture was the air, the mists over the water, the flowing, fluctuating atmosphere, the light streaming into the twilight. Several visitors to this exhibit, to whom such pictures were new and embarrassing, called the painters "Impressionists," which was meant to be ridicule. Louis Leroy, the editor, adopted the word and published an abusive, scornful article about the "Impressionists" in "Charivari" on April 25th. From that date on this group of painters acquired fame.

In impressionistic painting, which retained changing and momentary colorings of air and light, it is possible to visualize a continuation and improvement of Manet's realistic painting. Like the detailed descriptions of Flaubert and Zola, it contains something scientific. The Impressionists studied light like naturalists. They wanted to reproduce reality in the lighting of the moment, and in 1874 Manet went to see Claude Monet at Argenteuil in order to study the phenomena of refracted light, as though he were a physicist.

Claude Monet analyzed light falling upon a hay stack; Sisley the light that caused the "church of Moret" to appear different every twenty minutes—each of them with the eye of a scientist and scholar.

However, there is something else and more essential in impressionism than merely a variety of realism. Impressionism does not yield objects, but moods. Not constant forms but flowing light. The forms have no meaning of their own, only the play of illumination is of significance. The picture of the world is no longer rigid, it is variable. In the glittering and glistening of the atmosphere, in its vibrating and flowing, the forms dissolve.

In 1886 the eminent physicist Ernst Mach had published his book "Analysis of Sensation" wherein he analyzed the world as a bundle of emotions. That was also the universe of the impressionist painters; no longer was it objective, but a reflection of changing subjective moods. Sun, light, haze, colors, refractions, reflexes: everything dispersed, was glittering, fleeting, vibrating effect.

During that same period similar movements had taken place in France in the poetic field. Paul Verlaine had expanded the lyrical poesy of Victor Hugo's rhetoric, and of Alfred de Vigny's declamation to a poem in which the words became music in an abundance of moods. The verses transformed themselves into music as Verlaine had demanded in his poem "Art Poetique":

"Rien plus cher que la chanson grise
Ou l'indecise au precise se joint.

Car nous voulons la nuance encore,
Pas la couleur, rien que la nuance!
Oh! la nuance seule fiance
Le rève au rève et la flute au cor.

De la musique encore et toujours!
Que ton vers soit la chose envolée
Qu'on sent qui fuit d'une âme en allée
Vers d'autres cieux a d'autres amours."

Such music sounds out of Paul Verlaine's verses, whether it be the tone of the horn that "painfully lifts its voice like an orphan in the woods" ("Le son du cor s'afflige vers les bois d'une douleur on veut croire orpheline"); or that of the violin from which "the heavy tears of Fall drop" ("Les sanglots longs des vilons de l'automne blessent mon coeur d'une langueur monotone"), or the mandolin accompanying serenades beneath a "red or gray moon" and "under a quivering breeze" ("Tourbillonent dans l'extase d'une lune rose et grise, et la mandoline jase parmi les frissons de brise").

Verlaine calls one of his poetic collections "Romance sans paroles" because the words in this poetry transform themselves into a ringing atmosphere. Hippolyte Taine must have foreseen this when he wrote: "Before 50 years have passed, poetry will have melted entirely into music."

A similar impressionism was glorified by Albert Samain when he wrote these verses:

"J'adore l'indecis, les sons, les couleurs frèles
Tout ce qui tremble, ondule et frisonne et chatoie
Les cheveux et les yeux, l'eau, les feuilles la soie
Et la spiritualité des formes grèles."

In the poems of Stéphan Mallarmé the word loses its definite meaning entirely. The world dissolves completely in symbols. Poetry becomes tone, and from out of the sounding fog glow pictures, parables, allegories, like in a mystic temple. In the visions of Arthur Rimbaud the vowels begin to change into color and the poet becomes a seer, who "arrives at his sublime and tragic visions by way of a gigantic and logical blending of all sensuous impressions."

This world of impressionism would be incomplete without a great musician: Claude Debussy. From the very moment that Debussy has attained artistic independence, his music is associated with impressionistic poetry. One of his first songs was the poem "Mandoline" by Paul Verlaine, in which Tircis and Aminte, Clitandre and Damis, garbed in silk gowns, dance in the moonlight to the accompaniment of the mandolin. (1880). In 1888 songs adapted from lyrics by Baudelaire were followed by six "Ariettes" of Verlaine, among them the wonderful "Il pleure dans mon coeur": "O Bruit doux de la pluie / Par terre et sure les toits! / Pour un coeur qui s'ennuie / O chant de la pluie!"

In 1891 he issued three songs adopted from Paul Verlaine's poems and in 1892 the first volume of his "Fètes galantes" was published, taken from texts by Verlaine. The second volume followed in 1904. Debussy, who had met Verlaine in person in Mallarmé's salon, found in his works nature dissolving in moods, the melancholia of sunsets, the sorrowful light of the moon, the weeping of the wind and the rain; a tired, elegiac world in which even the birds sing plaintively. ("Un oiseau sur l'arbre qu'on voit chante sa plainte").

Dante Gabriel Rossetti's "La Damoiselle élue" provided Debussy with the inspiration for his first important work; inspired him to pre-Raphaelite angels' choirs, to sacerdotal mystics, to a pale-blue heaven and to stars that sparkle like gems. With the adaptation of Mérrimée's "L'Après-midi d'un faune" he created his Arcadian fairy-tale that dreams in the sunshine, with transparent orchestra, freely improvising flute melodies, harps shedding silver drops from their strings, harmonies that transform themselves into tinted haze. Eleven years later Debussy dreamed three of Mallarmé's poems into his music.

A large part of Claude Debussy's compositions are impressionistic pictures that decompose the world into light and colors, motions and flowing, colored specks and mood in the same manner as Claude Monet, Sisley and Pissarro had done.

For a time young Debussy wanted to be a painter. His artistic fantasy was a color fantasy. In 1894 he reported to his friend, the violinist Ysaye, that he had written three "Nocturnes." "This is really an attempt at various mixtures that could have flowed from one color, in short, in painting it would be a study in gray." The titles of the "Estamps" and "Images" alone reveal that these piano compositions were composed as pictures. Other titles such as "Arabesque" and "Esquise" show the same picturesque fantasy.

One has only to name the titles of some of these piano pieces to realize that the pictures are impressionistic: "Jardins sous la pluie," "Reflets dans l'eau," "Le vent dans la plaine," "Ondine," "Brouillards," "Feuilles mortes," "Poissons d'or." All these names suggest dancing spots, opalescent reflections, gay color specks in motion, atmosphere that veils the objects.

Orchestral pieces, too, such as the three Nocturnes (Nuages. Fêtes. Sirenes) or "La Mer" and "Images" are conceived as impressionistic pictures. The symphonic poem "Iberia" (from "Images") portrays street noises with color blurs. The second movement does not paint anything concrete anymore; it portrays the rustling breeze in laurel shrubs and pines, flower scent and the breathing grass. The third movement represents a folk festival: noise, tumult, crowds.

Like Paul Verlaine, "Claude de la France"—the composer was called thus by D'Annunzio—loved the hours of twilight, when the shapes of objects are enveloped by mist; night, that covers things with shadows; moonlight that cloaks them with a silvery veil. He could stand for hours at the Pont des Arts, when the sun was setting and suffusing the water of the Seine with a reddish glint. He loved the ocean and its blue or gray waves, capped with white foam, that would catch the light and disperse it. He loved motion that changed objects to spots of color; goldfish flitting by in their glass bowl; fireworks that scatter in the sky. In one of his piano pieces he even painted "notes and perfumes" which "evaporate in the evening air."

He loved the "gardens during the rain" when raindrops fell from the leaves and flowers and trees disappeared behind a veil of rain. He did not like the bright light of the sun and in a poem he called it "the murderer of illusions that are the consecrated bread of suffering hearts." When Debussy did paint figures whose contours did not melt, they were like those of Paul Verlaine—men in silk dress, sword on hip, and women in crinoline who lived and danced on Watteau's "Happy Isle"; or masked dancers. He liked the genial circus clown Footit, for the circus repealed the laws of the world; it was motion, conquest of gravity, abrogation of reality.

It was this impressionistic artist's fantasy of Debussy that shaped his new music; music that causes the forms to dissolve, that veils outlines in mist and lets the colors swing and sway. The classic harmonics, out of which the classic form unfolds, begin to loosen. Augmented triads and fourth accords destroy the solid, logical construction of the harmonics. The big lines crumble and large constructions are replaced by short, repetitious motifs.

Music transforms itself into a flowing and heaving; into a dim medium, into dusk, nervous vibration. Goncourt prides himself on discovering poetry for the low brow. Debussy did something similar for music. In the articles that Claude Debussy published in "Revue Blanche" and in "Gil Blas," he fought with all the weapons of his fine intellect against "scientific construction" and against the philosophical background of classical music.

"Music is a whole consisting of variously diverted forces. . . . It has been made into a speculative song. I much prefer a few notes from the flute of an Egyptian herdsman. He is in accord with the landscape and hears harmonies of which our school books know nothing. . . . Musicians hear only music written down by skilled hands, and never that music which is legible in the landscape. It is more useful to watch a sunset than to listen to the "Pastoral Symphony." Of what good is your almost incomprehensible art? Should you not discard the parasitic compositions which, in their ingenious arrangement are reminiscent of the lock on an iron strongbox? You are saluted with high-flying titles, yet you are merely sly. A variety between the monkeys and domestics."

Those were some of the main phrases from Debussy's aesthetics. He opens up his heart when he confesses: "I believe I have been dreaming. . . . Express myself in forms? Provide compositions with an ending? . . . All questionmarks, written down by childish vanity. It is necessary that we free ourselves at any price from an idea with which we have lived long enough."

Debussy calls Beethoven plainly "a gloomy genius without taste" in whose symphonies "the tensest enhancement ends with a noisy resolution of the most pacifying banality." He calls Wagner's "Nibelungenring" simply a "bottin" (the Paris directory) and occasionally he speaks of the faisandées—"wild game taste of the masterworks of Richard Wagner." Translating this from the paradox to the reasonable, these statements express Debussy's love for music without intellectual lucidity and spiritual profundity, but with nervous mood; his inclination to music that does not construct and augment and develop, but shows a transverse section of the vibrations of the nerve plexus. In other words, Debussy's love for Debussy's music.

Music of this kind must be, above all, tone: resolved, refined, melting; just as the poetry of Paul Verlaine, Arthur Rimbaud and Stéphan Mérrimée is tone, and the pictures of the impressionist painters are color specks and light. One of Debussy's first orchestral works, "Petite Suite" (1889) already contains the Debussy tone. From out of the orchestra rise seductive tones, high, muted violins sing delicate flute passages, harp tones are blended with a sure hand. The timbre glistens like silk and satin and sparkles like light in crystal glasses.

Two years later, in "L'Après-midi d'un faune" this Debussy timbre had become all air, sun, tinted clouds and trembling light. One is inclined to dream when the flute, clarinet and oboe improvise freely, the horns call as from a distance and little bells ring. The music appears to swim in the light, a frail web of tones that turn to fragrance. A landscape where rock and wood become unreal and objects lose their gravity and just float in space as colored apparitions.

II

Claude Debussy was an unusual mind rather than a strong mind; shrewd and nervous, a man of finest taste, he instinctively hated everything that was glaring and noisy in life. Beside him Richard Strauss appears brutal, and Strauss' coloring shrill.

Debussy liked delicate, rare and frail things. Even as a child he decorated his room with rare butterflies. When he resided in Rome in the Villa Medici as recipient of the Rome Prize, he collected Japanese lacquered work and prints, kimonos and vases. His piano piece "Gold Fish" was inspired by a Japanese lacquer object, and the title page of "La Mer" was to have been adorned in the style of Hokusai.

Neither the cupola of St. Peter, nor the marble columns in the forum could make as deep an impression upon him as did a small Greek Tanagra figure that he saw in an antique shop, or a performance of Polichinell. Later Debussy collected wooden canes and dressed extravagantly, like Oscar Wilde's Dorian Gray. He surrounded himself with Tanagra figures, bibelots, artistic book bindings and perfumes.

Sometimes he appears like Des Esseintes, whom Huysmans had described in his novel "Au Rebours" as living in a room resembling a ship's cabin; his windows are an aquarium full of fish and sea-nettle, and he has the shell of a turtle painted gold because he does not like the brown color of nature.

Debussy's culinary taste, too, was over-refined. There was a time when he lived solely on "petit fours." He hated red, and wallpaper and furniture in his room had to be green. Even his walking stick was painted green.

Like all astute minds Claude Debussy was attracted by everything that was exotic and primitive, for they abducted him from banal civilization. In 1889 the World Exposition in Paris opened; exotic huts lined both sides of the Esplanade des Invalides, and from them came the sounds of Javanese and Samoan tunes, wooden rattles, gongs, kettle-drums and other drums.

Debussy and his friend Dukas were regular guests here. This music meant more to him than Beethoven's symphonies. This was not intellectualism, it was nature in its most primitive form. The music chased demons, conjured rain; out of the shrill flutes came the voices of spirits. The monotonous drumming benumbed and hypnotized the mind. The imagination was carried off to foreign seas and distant isles.

Two years before the Paris World Exposition a French painter, Paul Gauguin had gone to the isle of Martinique, and in 1891 he went to Tahiti where he painted glowing color surfaces; often in childish forms, the brown natives of the tropics under palm trees. In 1895 he settled permanently in Tahiti, and died there in 1903. Later Gauguin found successors among young German painters who, like himself, had fled modern civilization: Emil Nolde went to New Guinea; Max Pechstein to the Palau Islands.

All these inwardly agitated artists sought primitivity, for they had grown tired of technical culture. They all searched for the great silence that noisy machinery had driven out of modern cities. All of them sought simplicity, peace, ease of mind. And that was what Claude Debussy searched for among the Samoans and Javanese. Music without intellectual background, without artificial technics, a simple, direct expression of sentiment.

The flute tune that Pan plays in Debussy's "L'Après-midi" is just such a primitive melody. The little bells and the harps produce a kind of primitive music that lulls the senses like magic, as for instance the gongs in the music of the aborigines, and the monotony of the drums.

Claude Debussy continued to be attracted by the art of the Japanese. The impressionist painters had already been influenced by landscapes of Hiroshige and Utamaro. Here they found the fleeting impressions of nature reproduced with surety and delicacy. Claude Monet learned from Hokusai and Hiroshige the art of portraying the atmosphere; he studied the hundred pictures of

Fujiyama by Hokusai, the hundred pictures of the Jeddo bridge by Hiroshige with their changing light.

The Japanese painted a cherry blossom branch, and it was the whole spring; so great was their faculty of simplifying. They painted a bird, and it flew across the skies. One line, one single ornament, contained the essence of the objects. That, too, Claude Debussy learned from the Japanese. His landscapes describe the essence of a motion, or of a light and color mood. His ocean waves are what the Japanese call "Kokoro": the essential in form and color of the ocean, in condensed shape. Japanese, too, is Debussy's colouring, the timbre of his orchestra; not heavy and massive, but transparent. Manet had learned from Japanese painters the art of portraying agitated crowds. Debussy also studied—in his "Fêtes"—the reproduction of mobile masses as Hokusai painted them.

A different kind of primitivity that made an impression on Claude Debussy was Mussorgsky's music. Like Tolstoi, Mussorgsky presents the Russian people, apathetic, strong, earthborn souls. Although Debussy had been to Russia at the age of twenty, Russian music did not affect him at that time; still, there are traces of Borodin's influence in some of Debussy's compositions which could have originated then.

The strong influence of Mussorgsky's music dates from the year 1889 when Belaieff, the publisher, arranged concerts of Russian music at the Trocadero during the World Exposition. Alexander Winogradsky, director of the Kiev Music Society, conducted Mussorgsky's overture "A Night on Bald Mountain," the first composition of the famous Russian to be heard in Paris. Some time later Frau Alheim sang the "Kinderstube," seven songs in which Mussorgsky produces with forceful realism the noise of the nursery, the joy and terror of the children, the consoling words of the mother.

In 1893 a friend gave Debussy the score to "Boris Godunoff," in which Debussy recognized a kindred spirit.

To these Russian impressions is added the influence of old French music of the eighteenth century. He loved the gallant century of France as Flaubert, the two Goncourts and Paul Verlaine had loved it. He loved the tender dance music of Chambonnière that was played on small virginals painted with shepherds and shepherdesses by women with high coiffures and crinolines. He loved the suites of Couperin, the gavottes, menuets and passepieds, the bourrées and allemandes that sounded so fine and delicate. Listening to them he was reminded of festivals at the French court that took place in mirrored halls and in the gardens with the murmuring fountains.

This music, too, was not intellectual, but sensual. "Where is our French music?" Debussy exclaimed grievously in 1915. "Where are our old harpsicordists who have so much real music/ They possessed the secret of the purest charm that can also be profound; of motion that does not degenerate into spasm, and we disown them like ungrateful children. . . .!"

In 1911 he already wrote in a letter: "What I write . . . is good, old France, is it not?" He considered himself heir of the fine French composers of the seventeenth and eighteenth centuries who wrote such dainty, sensitive music with the melodic lines of rococo: music for women whose hands were kissed by gallant men in silk dress.

The music of primitive peoples, Japanese art, Russian music, music from the court of Louis XVI: all that combined to lend style and form to Debussy's music.

This refined, dreamy music, refracted in a hundred lights is very complicated. It is the last, most artful essence that has been distilled from the colorful blossoms of romanticism. The tone has turned almost entirely to fragrance. The landscape resolves in momentary mood. The world melts in color and atmosphere, in shining specks. The musician turns painter and poet, while poetry of Swinburne, Rossetti, Verlaine and Mérimée becomes music.

From the standpoint of history Claude Debussy's music is a recoil from the strong realism of Flaubert, Zola, Tolstoi and Manet that had united art with life, and an escape to a dream world, into the night and into the shadows of twilight. It presupposes realism, as this music conceives and reflects landscape and motion, atmosphere and play of lights in the unity of a momentary mood. At the same time, however, it withdraws from realism and makes reality appear merely as a dream and as a legend, as an evaporating apparition. In the music of Debussy one has again arrived at romanticism, and at a higher point of a spiral above the romantics of 1830 with the new romanticism of 1900.

In Maeterlinck's "Pélleas and Mélisande" Debussy found a libretto that corresponded completely with the special sphere of emotion that he had perfected in piano and orchestral compositions. The Maeterlinck work had been given its first performance in Paris in 1893 at the "Théâtre des Bouffes Parisiens," and the critic Francisque Sarcey, the chief critic of Paris, a mastodon of classical learning, wrote: "in witnessing this dark tragedy I feel as though I were wearing a lead cap upon my head."

The audience remained cool and Pierre Louijs advised Debussy against setting Maeterlinck's book to muisc. But Debussy knew better. This sad legend of Maeterlinck's was his romance. Mystic fogs pervaded the epic. In them, man walks, tapping in the dark, a plaything of higher powers. As in a dream dark castles stood there with secret stairways and with dungeons, with balconies high above the roaring sea, dense jungles, trickling fountains; and everywhere fate threatened with death. The people were driven by mysterious forces. They were like blind men seeking a way. Love was a light that penetrated night, and dying was night itself.

Claude Debussy had steeped the fourteen pictures of this tragic fairy legend into music in which tone and harmony, color and mood envelop the individuals like shining fog-clouds. Short motifs emerge from these clouds. The colors are refracted colors of a resolved, improved orchestra that appeared to be bedded in cotton. The accords are specks of color. Nones and changed triads cause the accords to diverge. The dramatis personae sing in the cadence of a sacred recitation, monotone, sorrowful and tired. Even the love melodies are plaintive, and love is burdened with the heavy weight of unknown fate. Much of the music sounds like prayer in a monastery cell. The final act is a funeral service at a deathbed. The nerves are soothed gently by the murmured words, the misty atmosphere of the harmonies and the artful timbre of the orchestra.

Compared to this music, every romantic symphony orchestra, be it ever so colorful, sounds brutal, and the emotional recitation of Richard Wagner sounds exaggerated. Every excess of tone is avoided; the frugality of musical lines, the art of half-tones and half spoken words, the intensity of mood is something entirely new in the history of musical expression.

April 30, 1902, the day on which "Pelléas and Mélisande" had its first performance in the Opéra Comique of Paris, is one of the decisive dates in the history of modern music.

"Pelléas and Mélisande" was a solitary work that did not establish any school and that could not be copied even by Claude Debussy. It was the most perfect expression of a mood that has vanished like fog when the sun shines; a dream, dreamed but once by a unique mind in a unique hour. The world as a dark night through which souls wander helplessly—that world is not a reality but an elegiac fairy tale that could be told only once.

Told by a master like Debussy, and surrounded by music the legendary tone of which is a ringing shadow, the visions on the stage come to life, but only for the space of two hours; after that they are forced to retreat before active, bright life. That is their immortality: to die and come to life again and again; and thus Debussy's legend emerges and disappears, like the pictures of nature that Debussy drew make their appearance and submerge in the dark and are but the fleeting apparition of a moment.

The prime of impressionistic art was short-lived. In 1904 there was an exhibition in Paris of all of Cézanne's works that proved the greatness of this painter. He had transgressed the circle of Pissarro and Monet and had proceeded from the portrayal of changing light moods to the reproduction of solid forms. His credo: "In nature everything is shaped according to globe, cone and cylinder" was in direct opposition to the impressionistic belief that everything flows.

Two years before Debussy died, while German guns were bombarding Paris, the poet Jean Cocteau inaugurated his attack against Debussy-ism (1916). But as short as was the era of Debussy, that strong was his influence. As fine, airy and frail as the music of the French master had been, as deep was its effect upon contemporary musicians, and in works by Dukas and Ravel, the English composers Cyril Scott and Frederick Delius, the Germans Franz

Schreker, Alexander von Zemlinsky, Egon Wellesz; of the Italians Respighi, Casella and Zandonai, the Spanish musicians Albeniz, Granados and De Falla, the Hungarian Bèla Bartok and the American Charles Martin Loeffler, the tone and harmony of Debussy hang suspended in air like an exotic perfume.

The soul of Debussy that vibrated with every motion of the air, every change of light and with every shadow, set all music in motion with its dreams alone. Neither the impetus and intellect of Richard Strauss, nor the sky-rocketing energy of Mahler led music so far away from the classic-romantic form as did the delicate, refined, flowing moods of Debussy. For Richard Strauss the classic-romantic symphony is still the frame of his modern house. The greatest innovations in his harmony, the most realistic descriptions, the richest colors, the most important discoveries in the realm of music are still bound in with the classical technique of thematic digest and development.

No matter how far Strauss ventures into new waters with all the colored sails rigged to the mast of his ship, the landscape of classical music remains visible in the background. This is even more true in the case of Gustav Mahler. Regardless of how strong his subjectivism is, how personal his artistic fancy and how new his expression, the classic-romantic form is just as strong. But Debussy, who retains the classic form only in his string quartette, produces a completely new pattern. In his music, the classic form with its logical development of themes melts with the harmonics that had carried it. It is not the idea that holds the musical form together, but the unity of mood. The music no longer has three dimensions, only two, like Japanese etchings. In this music, as in pictures of impressionistic painters, the objects lose their cubic shape and become a colorful vision that dissolves in light.

Imagine Debussy's music without colors, and nothing remains but a sketchy movement, not a complete, clear, plastic drawing, a reality, a solid thought structure. Debussy's music moves in new grooves. It does not ascend from the depth of emotions to the light sphere of thinking where it is expanded, developed, regulated and enhanced; as mood and transitory apparition it remains inbetween the sphere of nervous agitation and that of consciousness. It is great and masterful in the discovery and artistic formation of those rising and diffusing moods that are captured in music at the very moment in which they fade.

As great and new as Debussy's music was, in the essentials it is the last, finest light that declining romanticism cast into a mechanically-inclined world of machines, factories, and trains, of steam and electricity, of exact sciences and houses made of beton-iron. The nearest affinity to it are the poetic nocturnes of Chopin, like that of Debussy a music of dreams.

The combination of painting and music, the tone that turns to mood, the scenes in "Pelléas and Mélisande"; love of the legendary, of twilight, of everything that causes the solid form to disappear in mist; the exotic and the precious, all are a part of romanticism. Mélisande's golden hair that shines in the dark woods, the mediaeval castle with its unlit passages and dungeons, the roaring sea and the fountain are romantic requisites, and Mélisande is sister to Genovefa who was loved by romantic poets.

The small piano poem, filled with poetry, is as much romantic form as the timbre of the Debussy orchestra is romantic tone.

After Debussy no more romantic music was written. The conflicts, crises and catastrophes of the age that converged in 1914 could not find artistic expression in an art that was gentle, dreamy and precious, an art that flew over the bloody battlefields like an exotic butterfly.

8

Great Musicians from Strauss to Puccini

I

RICHARD STRAUSS, Gustav Mahler and Claude Debussy emerged
as the greatest musical personalities from an era that began after
Brahms and Bruckner and lasted until the eruption of the World
War. Gustav Mahler's feverishly agitated, aspiring mind expired
in 1911. In 1918 Debussy's fine, vibrating nerves had ceased to
oscillate under the influence of colors and forms.

Of the three leaders in modern music only Richard Strauss
remained when the first world war came to an end, when the revolution broke loose in Russia and the red flames spread to western
Europe too. But by 1918 the creative work of Strauss was essentially done. In 1915 the inventive maestro had finished up his
symphonic work, and in 1919, in "Woman without a Shadow" he
had comprised all the new forms that he had created in opera since
1902. During the war a new young generation had grown up in all
European countries who didn't want any part of romanticism, and
the work of Schoenberg and Stravinsky had started to affect the
young minds. For them music no longer meant dreaming, painting,
mood and superabundance of emotions, as it still did for Strauss,
Mahler and Debussy.

Since the first world war had destroyed the Europe of old,
music moved in new patterns towards new goals. The old ideologies
meant nothing any more to the young music generation; the young
people had become skeptical towards big words and ringing phrases,
idealistic dreams and romantic fantasia.

The young musicians were without illusions and hostile towards everything that was festive decoration in music, and splendor and magic, and towards everything that had lent color and iridescent spirit. To this disillusioned generation that was to build up a new world, the bold egotistical subjectivism of Berlioz, the grande geste of Liszt, the erotic sensuality of Wagner appeared as exaggerated play-acting.

The old world with its feudal pomp, with its grand words, with its worthless declamations and phrases had proven hollow and brittle. The ground, over which blood had spilled in streams, shook. The air was filled with the moan of the dying and with the yelling of revolutionary masses. How could one breathe peacefully, dream or indulge in fancy in that overheated atmosphere? New standards were needed to survey life.

Even science was skeptical, and the old theories with which it had analysed reality had become valueless. Towards the end of 1900 the physicist Max Planck had established the "Quantum" theory which made the theories of Newton totter, theories that were supposed to be valid for all time. In 1905 Albert Einstein published his first essay, in which he exploded the fundamental observations of the physicists on space and time. In a disillusioned world in which all old standards had lost their value, music turned from a dream and from ringing fantasies to material for the young musicians to work on. They forsook the old churches of music and, on a new foundation, began first to hew the stones with which they intended to build new houses.

Realistic art had been the first serious attempt to replace the romantic world and its sorcery, its charmed nature and its magic Beyond, with a dispassionate, real and human world. Heroic knights, the ancient kings, fairies, elves and goblins, distant landscapes, enchanted nature, heaven replete with angels and blissful souls, the world as fairy-tale, as dream or as the past,—all had become obscure. To the foreground came the world as a summary of precise observations, as a reality, as the stage of ordinary lots; the citizens' parlors in modern houses, the corners that housed misery and want, the factories and the masses.

Extending from Dickens and Turgenjeff to Ibsen, Gerhart

Hauptmann, Manet, Tolstoi, Dostojewsky, Zola and Liebermann, realism had performed strong and great things. It was a deeply human art. It embodied the spirit of the new age and its social conscience; its social compassion with the poor, the suffering, with mass poverty, with the dull existence of the proletarian, with the dark underground of life where crime grows and flourishes. In realistic art there was a hard spirit that did not dream and did not indulge in fantasy but in perception. In the deep compassion with the poor and underprivileged, with the sick and with criminals, that pervaded the novels of Dickens and Russian authors in the same manner, there was a new social conviction. In the portrayal of reality art was reunited with life from which it had become separated by romanticism.

The generation of artists to which Strauss, Mahler and Debussy belong emerges from romanticism. Young Debussy still has his big Wagner epoch. In 1888 and 1889 Debussy travels to Bayreuth where he is enraptured by "Parsifal" and "Tristan and Isolde." The English horn solo at the beginning of the third act in "Tristan," that wings into the air like a dark cloud of mourning, inspired Debussy's imagination when he was composing "Pelléas."

Debussy is influenced by Wagner to the same extent as Verlaine and Mallarmé had been Wagnerians when they dissolved lyrical poems into musical ringing; and when Mallarmé paid homage to Wagner with a sonnet ("Le silence déja funèbre d'une memoire") and Verlaine with a Parsifal poem ("Parsifal a vaincu les filles"). When Strauss, Mahler and Debussy were growing up, the whole world was satiated with Wagner music and Wagner romance. To compose meant: writing music in Wagner's style, as Strauss did in his "Guntram." Debussy did not free himself from Wagner's influence until he had read Nietzsche's "The Case of Wagner" and had let Nietzsche's hymn to "Carmen" affect him.

Neither Richard Strauss, nor Mahler nor Debussy detached themselves entirely from romanticism, but all three allowed the new trends of the time to penetrate their romantics. In the naturalism of modern art and modern life Strauss had found the new element that lent lustre and expression to his romanticism. Mahler had combined the nervous strain, and the hysteria, the emotional con-

flicts and pessimism of the new age with the romantic form. Debussy combined with it the impressionistic reproduction of nature
and atmosphere.

They were all great in that they united romantics with the
spirit of the new era, and undertook the synthesis of historical
music with modern life and modern spirit. They would have been
less great had they not possessed this power of blending old with
new, and if they had not spanned the ages with a bridge under
which the stream of life flowed into the future.

In the composers surrounding these men we find the same
blending of past and present, romanticism and modern spiritual
tendencies. One moment the romantic trend is stronger, the next
instant the modern trend. Every degree of the blend, every gradation is represented in them. One gains the impression of being in a
large experimental chamber in Europe during the decades before
the world war, where the trends of the time experiment in retorts
with all kinds of combinations of old and new.

In attempting to analyse everything associated with music life
in Europe within the period that started after the demise of Brahms
and Bruckner, and ended in 1918, it is best to begin with romantic
twilight and proceed to the bright light of realistic day.

On this road one meets one of the noblest romantic figures of
modern time, Hans Pfitzner (born in 1869). This composer, with
the appearance of a professor who has pondered too long over
manuscripts and books and has developed a hunchback from too
much night work at his desk, is the last true Wagnerian. His operas
have the heaviness, the pathos and the massiveness of Wagnerian
music. His composing contains ethics next to which the music of
Richard Strauss appears merely sensually brilliant and purely
virtuoso-like.

Hans Pfitzner composed masterful idealism. His opera "Der
Arme Heinrich" (1895) is an intensified "Tristan." His opera
"Rose vom Liebesgarten" (1901) contains Parsifal moods. Pfitzner's
"Palestrina" (1917) has as its hero a melancholy Hans Sachs and
gives the appearance of "Meistersinger of Nürnberg" on an elegiac
autumn day. Pfitzner is by no means a Wagner imitator; he creates

in the spirit of Richard Wagner. He is noble, serious and inwardly great in his music-making.

His total production is not rich—three big operas, the cantata "Von Deutscher Seele," concertos, chamber music and lieder—and he worked hard at his music, with many stops, brooding and irritable, easily intimidated and introspect; an art thinker inclined to theorize. Pfitzner stood aloof from the noise of art shops in which Richard Strauss felt at home; around him was a sphere of quiet which the voices of peddlers and dealers did not penetrate. His work is personal, masterly and great within a limited space.

This Wagnerian built his operas upon the broad foundation of Wagner's symphony orchestra and invented new colors, a new counterpoint, new harmonies that are modern. The harmonics of his early work, "Der Arme Heinrich," written at the age of 27, are Tristan harmonics, but with new intervals, realistically sharpened, forcibly enhanced.

The Gothic moyen age has new, Freudian traits in its expression: hysterical pains, emotional agony and morbid longing. Hans Pfitzner's C-major Quintet, his largest chamber-music work, has a new polyphony in which the independent voices are exerted with intensive feeling. One is reminded here of Gothic stylists such as Hans Gruenewald, with their powerful expressionism, unless one thinks of modern Gothic artists like George Minne. The latter, in his picture "Sister Beatrix" lets the fullness of the gown billow in mediaeval folds, and portrays young boys ascetically slim; he is an artist of the same generation to which Pfitzner belongs, and only three years younger than the composer.

The description in "Rose vom Liebesgarten" of the cave with drops falling from the ceiling, is reminiscent of tone coloring in "Arianne et Barbleue" by Paul Dukas. The big historical portrait of the Council of Trent in Pfitzner's "Palestrina," with the smooth Papal legates, the arguing cardinals and priests, is wholly realism of the modern age.

When the bells of Rome peal at the end of the first act in "Palestrina," a swelling chorus of high and low pitched bells that majestically fills the air, one is reminded of the ending in the first act of

Mussorgsky's "Boris Godunoff." It is the same naturalistic ringing. Everywhere in Pfitzner's romanticism there is the new coloring, new harmonics, new voice phrasing. Romanticism is to be found everywhere: in the forest scene of "Rose vom Liebesgarten" that is reminiscent of Gerhart Hauptmann's "Versunkene Glocke" (Sunken Bell), of water sprites and of Rautendelein; romantic are the angels singing the Kyrie of Missa Papae Marcelli to Palestrina; romanticism is in the danse macabre of the cantata "Von Deutscher Seele" (Der Tod als Postillion—Death as Postilion); in the Gothic style of the Palestrina music, in scenic descriptions. Still, everywhere there is also something new in color, expression and mood.

Another modern romanticist like Hans Pfitzner was Max Reger (1873–1916). No contemporary composer could compare with Reger in abundance of genuine musical powers. Music deluged him. More than 300 songs, choral works, organ music, over 70 orchestral pieces, works for chamber music, piano pieces, small and large music forms, rushed down upon the composer and crowded his imagination. When Max Reger sat at his desk, enveloped in clouds of cigar smoke, his head must have hummed like a waterfall of music. So powerful was his tone memory that he wrote down, like a letter, the most complicated polyphonous works, such as the "Hundredth Psalm" with the gigantic double fugues and the choral enhancement at the end.

Between 1898 and 1901 the twelve greatest of Max Reger's organ works were published. The organ was almost too small for the mass of music that Reger invented for it, and yet only the organ was able to absorb the roaring and storming of this music fantasy. The chromatic harmonies blew through the pipes like a hurricane, and the organ's pedals created tempests of sound.

Reger always thought and created polyphonic. In his first songs, which were influenced by Schumann and Hugo Wolf, the piano accompaniment is already polyphonous; the piano compositions, descended from Brahms, have polyphonous middle parts. In composing sonatas for a violin, viola or 'cello he himself heard in a single voice many voices. His earliest orchestral work, the "Sinfonietta" resembles a garden wherein the beds are overgrown with creepers.

Max Reger heard music as motion of harmonies. These Reger harmonies are modern chromatics. In his music the classic harmonics dissolve, as they did in the music of all composers between 1890 and 1914. The solid structure of the classic system disappears. The key-notes are veiled, harmonies become fluid.

In 1904 Max Reger published a "modulation theory" that permits every transition, every omission of intersecting harmonies, every paraphrasing of the basic chords. True, the three pillars of classic harmonics still stand: the tonic triad, the triad of the fourth step and the triad of the fifth step; but they have become insignificant and no longer support the musical structure, they vanish behind Baroque ornaments that have become essentials.

In later orchestra works Reger also turned to French impressionism.

Max Reger's music fantasy was a rich Baroque, that was often goffered, overladen and excessive. Such an imagination is not easily brought into form. Simple thoughts and large patterns cannot be built upon changeable harmonies. The liquefied base carries only short motifs which Reger likes to disperse into still smaller particles.

Debussy had recognized clearly that resolution of harmonics demanded a new form that must likewise be fluid, mobile and flexible. Max Reger took recourse to the great old forms to give his contrapuntal and harmonic fantasy solid support. One of these forms was the Bach fugue form, another the Beethovan pattern of variations. With these forms Reger had solidified his overflowing fantasy, and within them he created his greatest masterpieces: the "Telemann" variations and the "Beethoven variations," the "Bach variations," the organ passacaglia, the organ fugues, the choral preludes, and the fugues in string quartettes and in the sonorous 100th Psalm. The old classic forms provided Max Reger with a haven in which he sought protection from the storm.

There is something incongruous in Reger's music: an old form and new harmonious substance; rich harmonic and contrapuntal fancy and a form that does not grow out of this fantasy but is brought alongside it from without. All this is combined with Baroque excess, with a passionate exuberance and a genuine music mania, with true "Furor Teutonicus."

Almost all of Reger's music is absolute, the only program music being in his "Romantic Suite" which Reger wrote after poems by Eichendorf, and in the "Vier Tondichtungen nach A. Boecklin." (Four tone poems adapted from A. Boecklin).

He may have been on the way to clarify his superabundance when he died (1916).

One of his last works is a graceful "Balletsuite" which Reger announced in a letter with these words: "Next summer I want to write something infinitely graceful, something exceedingly fine in tone, dainty in music and orchestrated as fine as a cob-web."

The bear-like man who looked like a student, who drank like a whole corps of students and who enjoyed obscene jokes and clouds of cigar smoke, this man had a longing for light and fine tone figures. He had his nooks, too, where he housed an enthusiastic Catholicism. He was not strong and simple; like all modern artists, his was a multifarious nature, excessive and unharmonious; a gargantua of counterpoint, he stilled his appetite with huge portions of double fugues and canons, choral figues and variations, and for dessert he devoured quantities of small piano compositions and ballad-like songs.

Among the literary, intellectual, philosophical and picturesque musicians of his time, Max Reger is the only one in whom music was something elemental; by virtue of that fact he was the forerunner of new developments. He might have become all-important, and perhaps the Johann Sebastian Bach of our era, if he had been capable of creating new forms. He did invent new harmonies, new expression, new voice phrasing; but without the forms of Bach and Beethoven he would have drowned helplessly in the roaring tone masses of his music.

Lustre, color, ornamental splendor radiate from the music of Franz Schreker. This renowned composer was born in 1878 in Monaco, and it seems as though he had always retained the childhood memories of a brilliant landscape, a sunny sky and blue ocean, of peonies and cypresses.

Vienna, too—the Vienna in whose "Secession" in 1897 modern impressionists exhibited their pictures, Gustav Mahler became director of the opera and Olbrich and Otto Wagner built modern houses—influenced Schreker's imagination. Here, Gustav Klimt painted pictures and ceiling designs in which modern colors were blended with Byzantine gold and Japanese coloring; passion gleamed seductively from the dark eyes of beautiful women and nude bodies were coiled around one another like snakes.

Schreker's music is in affinity with the art of Gustav Klimt. It possesses the same artful colored lustre, the same decorative glamor, the same erotic heat.

Franz Schreker, who himself wrote the librettos for his operas, is a new romanticist who had traversed realism. His operas are mostly fairy tales. His opera "Die Gezeichneten" (1918) takes place in the Renaissance period, but not in the conventional Renaissance as it was presented in Schilling's opera "Mona Lisa" and in Korngold's "Violanta"—both premiered in 1915. Schreker's was an altogether fantastic Renaissance period, all myth and festive decoration.

Another of Schreker's operas, "Der Schatzgraeber" (1920) takes place in the middle ages; and again it is a wholly legendary moyen age.

In all these theatrical legends the artistic imagination shows a strong erotic tendency. The fables are carnal dreams; one act of the opera "Der Ferne Klang" (1912) plays in a "Casa di Maschere" and is filled with the orgies of a brothel. One act of "Die Gezeichneten" describes amorous intoxication in a subterranean love grotto; and in the third act of the opera "Der Schatzgraeber" a diaphanous curtain descends upon stage and bed and the orchestra intones a love symphony with motifs of embraces and themes of caresses, with tones that gleam like white limbs and sparkle like the red hair of the beautiful Els lying in bed with her boy.

Symbols glimmer in these voluptuous operatic fantasias. One of these symbols, characteristic of Schreker's fantasy, is a mysterious ringing. The hero of the opera "Der Ferne Klang," Fritz, cannot find peace until he has caught the "mysterious unworldly sound." "And I seek the master who touches the harp, and I seek the harp that bears the tone, and have I the tone, I am rich and free, an artist by the grace of God."

In the next following opera: "Spielwerk und die Prinzessin"

there is the same magic tone contained in a toy that is given voice by the flute of a young boy. In yet another operatic poem of Schreker's an artist collects the voices of nature and reproduces them in odd mechanical works. In the opera "Der Rothe Tod," adopted from Poe, a mighty old clock plays a big part. "Once it struck brightly with silver tones . . . and the work shall ring as once it did; silvery and comforting, joyfully charming." In "Schatz-graeber" it is the lute of the singer Els that resounds wherever gold is hidden in the rock.

Schreker himself, the musician, chases after mysterious, precious tones. Just as the French romanticists like Beaudelaire, Rimbaud, Théophile Gautier were attracted by everything that was unusual, artificial, exotic and colorful, so was he. Rare gems, shimmering materials and gay rugs, artistically cut crystals, sultry perfumes: that is his world too. Like Beaudelaire, he never tires of glorifying the nude body of a woman or even an agglomeration of women's torsos; bacchanals of flesh and lust.

All of this shapes his timbre which is shining, pompous and brilliant. The harmonies are differentiated; the light of the triads is decomposed and blended with colored lights. Chords are intermingled, dissonances employed as colors. Solid tonality and harmonic legality become fluid. Impressionistic nuances invade the music with gay splotches, colorful shadows, refined mixtures. The heavy, pathetic orchestral symphony of Richard Wagner has disappeared in Schreker's works. In its place steps an orchestra that shimmers like silk and satin. It is an ornamental orchestra of highest perfection and holds its own as the creation of a special tone fantasy even next to the orchestra of Strauss and Debussy.

Still, with all the dispersal of tone, harmony and motifs, Schreker does not lack firm formation. The second act of the opera "Der Ferne Klang" is constructed like a symphony. Even the orgiastic is securely formed by Schreker, and the fabulous fantastic realistically brought to life.

Franz Schreker's color and tone fantasy constitute a new romanticism that carries on art outside of life, in a dream world. Great is the visionary force of the artist who sees legendary figures. Only the hero of his first opera is a man from the present; all the other heroes are men of past ages, or from the land of legend and saga. The actions of the operas are all fantastic. The tone language, to be sure, is the modern improved declamation that lithely reproduces all psychological emotions, although Schreker is endowed with a nice lyrical talent too.

But whatever realism there is in Schreker—mostly in his first opera "Der Ferne Klang"—dissolves in his dream and fable world, in dark symbolism, in unreality. Schreker belongs to those modern artists who, like Oscar Wilde, withdraw from life with its struggles and problems and seek refuge in the ivory tower that is the precious frame of their artist fancy.

A similar frame surrounds Alexander von Zemlinsky (1872–1939), a fine, intelligent, carefully formative musician. Only his comic opera "Kleider machen Leute" contains a humorous realism. In the fairy opera "Es war einmal" (1900), in "Florentine Tragedy," in "Zwerg" (1921) and in "Kreidekreis" (Circle of Chalk) artistic refinement preponderates, and pleasure in the preciousness of tone, and the fine technical artifice that approaches the exactness of a goldsmith.

In France the opera "Ariana et Barbleu" by Paul Dukas (1865) belongs in this group. The libretto of this opera is an epic by Maeterlinck; but Dukas, a friend of Debussy's, is an artist who prefers solid form to hazy moods. The individual acts of this opera are constructed symphonically. To be sure, the symphonies are treasure houses filled with rubies and sapphires; there is gleaming and sparkling in the orchestra, and the light is refracted by fine cut crystals.

In Italy D'Annunzio's literary art fascinated opera composers. In his opera "Francesca da Rimini" (1914), Riccardo Zandonai employed a D'Annunzio text. Following his opera "L'Amore di Tre Re" in 1913 (text by San Benelli), Italo Montemezzi set to music D'Annunzio's work "La Nave" (1918) and Ildebrando Pizetti composed his "Fedra" (1915) to words by D'Annunzio.

In Russia Rimsky-Korsakoff's opera "Le Coq d'Or" (1908) may well be considered among the ranks of new-romantic operatic works. Here, too, we find select coloring, a resounding world blended from the Orient and fable; the bizarre and the fantastic formed into a play. The tonal fantasy of the great Russian composer is one of the richest known to modern music. He is a legend narrator of the first order, but his fables are not merely castles in the air; they have a landscape, and their coherence with the Russian earth makes them strong as well as gay and imaginative.

II

In Alexandre Nikolayewitsch Scriabin (1872–1915) Russia brought forth one of the greatest and most peculiar romanticists of modern time. With this mystic the romantic period in Russia came to a close shortly before the outburst of the Russian Revolution, just as it had come to a close with Strauss and Mahler in Germany, and with Debussy in France.

Scriabin died in Moscow in 1915, and with him ended the great era of Russian romantic music that had started with Glinka's opera "Life for the Czar" (1836).

The romantic trend had awakened the great art forces in Russia. In Puschkin it had produced Russia's first poet of European rank. In composers from Glinka and Dargomyschky to Borodin, Cui and Rimsky-Korsakoff and Tschaikowsky, it turned into form and tone an abundance of magnificent and colorful music that had grown out of Russian national earth.

Ever since Byron subjectivism and Byron melancholia had found kindred artist souls in all Europe, romantic poetry was stirring the emotions of artists. Everywhere it sharpened the tendency toward nationalism, the perception of an individual landscape in each country; it whetted the taste for moods of nature which are reflected in the moods of man, the taste for historical life, for sagas and legends, for the past that gives meaning to the present.

There was no Russia, and no Russian people, in music until romantic musicians gave shape to those things which previously had existed within the Russian nation only in folk songs and in the chorals of the Russian churches.

With Scriabin this important age had ended. After him there came a different Russia; not the romantic Russia with Czars, elegant aristocrats, wealthy landowners and citizens. It was a Russia of labor and national enlightenment that erected factories, dams, laboratories, schools and universities; a Russia that shaped life and economy rationally, according to plans figured out by statistics and science.

It was no longer a world for a mystic, dreamer and visionary such as Scriabin had been. He was called a "Westerner" as though Russia had never known sects which, like he, had sought mystic ecstasy; ecstasies in which spirit and flesh, thinking and passion were fused in the white heat of enthusiasm and in the drunkenness in which one visualized the arrival of the Messiah. Scriabin's mysticism had grown in Russian earth like Dostojewsky's religious mysticism and Tolstoi's primitive Christianity.

Scriabin started as a composer of romantic piano pieces, a cunning piano lyricist. Cui called these works "a trunk, full of stolen manuscripts of Chopin," but there is something new in the harmonics of this music: Arpeggios and divisions of chords, fifth and ninth chains; veiling of the tonality; crossing of several movements; melting of harmonies.

Scriabin takes the same road that Debussy took: that of impressionistic moods in which the solid forms resolve. Every music of this kind, in which clear, limited figures are transformed into flowing masses of mist can be called mystic music; for mysticism is the association of the individual with life in general, and we have mysticism in Chopin and Schumann as well as in Debussy and Scriabin.

There is a mystic instinct in every romance; love of twilight, night, the unrational, dreaminess. Scriabin's inclination to mysticism is already apparent in his piano compositions, no matter how elegant it is; mysticism in tails and white tie.

As indicated in his diaries, even as a boy Scriabin pondered over the problems of the world. The position of man in the universe, the significance of life: those were the questions that troubled him and which music was to answer. It is art that transforms pain, conflicts and tragic suffering into beauty; not one individual art, but all arts combined. United, they produce the intoxication of mystic ecstasy which alone is capable of springing the narrow limits of life and leading to the vision of God; that is what all mystics from the Pythagoreans and Plotin on rave about.

All three of Scriabin's symphonic colossi: the "Poème d'extase," the "Divin Poème" and "Prometheus" (Poème du Feu) were attempts by him to portray the flight of man into the universe. They wanted to embrace the universe, unite spirit and world. Longing of the "creative spirit" made the world; love can reunite spirit and world, which had been torn asunder. The erotic act, which consumes the individuals with its conflagration, is a means of reuniting man with the universe. It leads to self-destruction, to chaos and to a new "breath of Brahma," as the Hindus call the life of the universe, that renews itself again and again, creates and destroys life.

The symphonies wherein Scriabin attempts to portray the "breathing of Brahma" in music are of gigantic proportions. The score of "Prometheus" has forty-two lines, among them one for color piano which is supposed to accompany the music with its play of light. Like large mosaic pictures, it is composed of tiny stones. Small themes and the smallest of themes increase to the proportions of a gigantic structure. Many voices sound, and harmonies, not melodies, are the building material.

Scriabin wanted to create harmonies "with the greatest possible number of tones," and "Prometheus" in its entirety is the development of a chord that is composed of all the tones of a whole step scale. The "Poème de l'extase" also has this whole step scale as a base that becomes accords and melodies.

A boundless aspiration is contained in this music, and the words of the "Erdgeist" in Goethe's "Faust" could find no nobler musical imitation than in the three symphonies of Scriabin:

> "In Lebensfluthen, im Thatensturm
> Wall ich auf und ab
> Wehe hin und her
> Geburt und Grab,
> Ein ewiges Meer
> Ein wechselnd Weben
> Ein gluehend Leben.
> So schaff' ich am sausenden Webstuhl der Zeit
> Und wirke der Gottheit unsterbliches Kleid."

In his great works Scriabin produces a pantheistic cosmology. Not the voice of the individual shall sound, but the universe itself with which man in ecstasy blends. There is something intoxicating in this music that rustles and flows, that glows sensually and tries to describe with chords and tones longing, love, ecstasy, association with the creative mind that produces world phenomena and re-absorbs them.

The romantic idealism and high priesthood of Franz Liszt, the religious enthusiasm of the poets Lamartine and Chateaubriand created this philosophical music. Schopenhauer would have discovered in it the portrayal of "will" that pervades all creation and all being restlessly until finally it dissolves in Nirvana. The romanticism of such men lives on in Scriabin, only augmented, more excessive, more boundless. Even Gustav Mahler's philosophical titanism appears theatrical next to the obsession of the Russian whose lyrics soar into the unlimited and who would be musician, prophet and Messiah all at the same time.

Scriabin dreamed of a "mysterium" of which his three great symphonies were to be merely the prelude and the first sketches. In his estate was found the text to a "preparatory ritual" for this mysterium. Everything else remained a fancy of Scriabin's, a fancy that wanted to comprise all the arts in the planned mysterium in order to produce the grand delirium that would unite man and eternity.

Beside the great mystic of Russia stands the great realist; a composer who possesses the strength, the national power and the impressiveness of Tolstoi: Modest Petrovitsch Mussorgski (1835–1881).

If one goes by dates, of course, Mussorgski does not belong in the twentieth century, since he died in 1881 in Petersburg. However, the strong influence of his work does not begin until the start of the twentieth century, which would be unthinkable without his music. No composer affected modern musicians as deeply as this man who, at the close of the nineteenth century and at the start of the twentieth century appeared not merely as a contemporary, but more as a forerunnner who takes new paths leading to the future.

Upon no modern composer did Mussorgski have a stronger

influence than on Claude Debussy, who glorified Mussorgski in one of his most brilliant essays: "He will leave an indelible impression on the minds of those who love him or will love him in the future. No one has given utterance to the best within us in tones more gentle and profound; he is unique and will remain so, because his art is spontaneous and free from arid formulas. Never has a more refined sensibility been conveyed by such simple means; it is like the art of an inquiring savage discovering music step by step through his emotions."

Debussy was enthused about Mussorgski's songs: "songs without sunlight," the kind that this man of twilight loved. He studied the score of Mussorgski's opera "Boris Godunoff" and Charles Bordes, founder of the "Schola Cantorum" in Paris, called Mussorgski's opera the "grandfather of 'Pelleas.' "

In 1874 "Boris Godunoff" had its first performance in Petersburg; "Pelléas and Mélisande" in Paris in 1902. Today, both operas appear side by side on the opera stages all over the world. But the spirit of "Boris" is much stronger than that of "Pelléas." The opera "Boris Godunoff" is a second 'Macbeth,' and it is as remote from "Pelléas" as Shakespeare is from Maeterlinck himself.

Like the Russian composers Cui and Rimsky-Korsakoff, Mussorgski had been an officer, very elegant in the uniform of the Preobrachensky regiment; hair slicked down, manicured hands, with aristocratic manners, a friend of French conversation: thus he was described by Borodin who met the seventeen-year-old officer in a military hospital. There Mussorgski delighted the women by playing melodies from "Troubadour" or "Traviata" on the piano.

It was one of those emotional upsets and transformations that were so common among artists in old Russia that made Mussorgski a pioneer artist. It was an emotional revolution similar to that which, after a wild period of lieutenancy, after nights of gambling, carousing and love, made a great poet out of Tolstoi who donned the garb of the muzhik.

As it did for Tolstoi, so did the Russian landscape and the Russian people reveal itself to Mussorgski. His brother, Filaretes, writes that Mussorgski "considers the Russian muzhik to be the real human," just as Tolstoi had. Russian humility and Russian compassion strike him as Dostojewsky had been touched; he displays devotion to the wretched, to the poor and the criminal, all of them creatures of God.

"The other day," Mussorgski writes to Cui, "I found a small poem by Goethe, and enthused, I set it to music. The subject is 'The Beggar' (from Wilhelm Meister). I think the beggar can sing my music without hesitation."

One composition by Mussorgski: "The cradle song of the laborer" was inspired by the Russian peasant. The scene that stimulated Mussorgski to write this music is worthy of a Dostojewsky. One day Mussorgski happened to overhear a poor idiot in front of his window begging for the love of a pretty peasant girl, despite his knowledge that he is weak and ugly and that pleasure and love do not exist for him. Mussorgski was deeply moved. The scene just witnessed, the humanity of it, clung to his mind. He attempted to reproduce musically the monotone rhythm of the idiot's words, the breathless pleas, the persuasiveness.

Other works by Mussorgski are also inspired by true experiences in Russian peasant huts or in field and forest. So, for instance, in "Intermezzo" is perpetuated the memory of a winter's day on which Mussorgski watched some peasants trudging through the snow, while laughing, singing young girls came towards them, all of them radiant in the clear winter sun.

Passionately adoring life and enraptured by reality, be it ever so lowly, Mussorgski strove for direct art effect. Like Tolstoi he hated everything that was "Art pour art," and he knew that the folk song that originated from simple souls, could be deeply stirring. Every simple conversation could be a revelation of the soul if it expressed emotions that were true, though artless.

He was influenced by Dargomyiski who had stated: "I want the tone to express directly the word. It is not my intention to trace music to a play for the benefit of dilettantes. I want the truth." Mussorgski considered everything that was technical as hampering direct expression.

In a letter to Stassow he wrote: "Tell me why, when I talk with young painters or sculptors, I can follow their thoughts, understand their opinions and intentions, and rarely hear them speak of technics except in cases of absolute necessity. Yet when I am among musicians I seldom hear a live thought spoken. One would think they are sitting on a school bench. All they know are technics and the vocabulary of the trade. Is music such a young art that it need be studied in such a childish manner?"

Similar thoughts were expressed even more beautifully by Mussorgski in a second letter: "When will the young folks, instead of manufacturing their fugues and their three obligatory acts, open the Holy Scriptures and converse in these books of the wise? Will modern man not find here the best way to art, and justification for the task of an artist? Life, wherever it manifests itself; reality, and be it ever so bitter; boldness, a frank word . . . that is my leaven. That is what I want, and I don't wish to weaken here. I have pushed forward to here, and will remain thus."

In the fanatical hate that Mussorgski feels against intellectualism in art, against everything formal, everything technical, there is something of the great hate that filled Tolstoi, hate against all forms of civilization that barred the way to God. Mussorgski is a primitive man who wants to reproduce in piano compositions, songs and operas reality without any styling and without any enhancement, led merely by his Russian genius.

The two scenes of the prelude, and the four acts of his opera "Boris Godunoff" are replete with this national primitivity. Puschkin's historical drama that provided the text which Mussorgski himself wrote in prose changed under his pen from a romantic story to a piece of the present. The chief figure is the Russian people itself, the great crowd surging in front of the monastery in which Boris is concealed in the prelude, and which in the final scene revoltingly pays homage to the false Demetrius. "The masses," Mussorgski states in a letter, "always have subtle traits that are difficult to penetrate and are not yet fully understood. To notice these fine features, to read them, to get acquainted with them either through observation or hypothesis, to study them thoroughly, to reinforce humanity with their reproduction—that is my duty and my greatest pleasure."

The Macbeth drama of "Boris" is accompanied by the chorus

of massed people that swells to the proportion of a revolution in the end. "Weep, weep, weep, Russian people, hungry people": with this monotone lament of the poor idiot the opera closes. The wide snowy plains and the Russian fir forest are filled with this lament—a magnificent finale for an opera, but one that Rimsky-Korsakoff's arrangement made conventional. Mussorgski gave the last word not to the Czar, but to the poor, simple muzhik.

If "Boris Godunoff" presents a realistic national drama in its mass scenes, the figure of the murderer and usurper Boris is a grand, gripping psychological picture. The mental torment of the Czar, the terror of bloody ghosts that frighten him, the gentle love for his son, the taciturnity, the dismal dignity of the Czar who ends up a penitent—all this is reproduced by Mussorgski with a forceful simplicity that has its equal only in Shakespeare's tragedies.

There is nothing of the old opera here, one can feel the very breath of life in every tone. Fourteen years after the first performance of "Boris" Verdi invented a kindred style of soul narrative in his opera "Othello," and introduced into Italian opera the realism of modern times. But Mussorgski's style is far greater, simpler, stronger. He is genius personified.

Mussorgski started working on "Boris" in 1868 and by 1869 the composition was completed. In 1870 he finished the orchestration. But every theatre turned the new opera down for containing too many choruses. Just that which was so great in this work: the Russian nation as hero, was not recognized and Mussorgski had to agree to a re-arrangement of the opera in which he was assisted fraternally by Rimsky-Korsakoff.

Three excerpts of this new form were presented in 1873 at the Marientheater in Petersburg and, inasmuch as it was a successful performance, the whole opera was given in 1874. The reviews called Mussorgski a dilettant and an ignoramus, but the young people in Petersburg sang the choruses from "Boris" when they marched across the Newa bridges.

Thirty-three years were yet to pass before the fame of "Boris" began to spread across the world. In 1907 Diaghileff, who later founded the Russian Ballet, arranged two concerts in the grand opera house in Paris. Included in the repertoire were compositions of Russian masters, among them excerpts of operas. Nikisch, Glazunov, Rachmaninoff, Rimsky-Korsakoff conducted; Joseph Hoffmann played a piano concerto by Scriabin; the orchestra and chorus of the Petersburg opera took part.

A singer who until then was unknown in Paris gained fame overnight when in excerpts from "Boris" he sang the Czar with powerful basso and unheard of dramatic force: it was Chaliapin.

So great was the success that the enterprising Diaghileff could afford the risk of producing a Russian performance of "Boris Godunoff" in the Paris Opera in 1908. Bilibin and Yon had painted the decorations which portrayed realistically the Russia of old, the mighty Kremlin walls, the gold mosaics, the birch woods. Golovin had designed the costumes with the gold and lace collars of the Bojares; gay, gaudy, Oriental splendor. Diaghileff and Benois mustered the crowds as Paris had never seen the likes; no longer were they drilled extras, but a gesticulating, yelling, revolutionary mass.

Chaliapin was impressive when, gloomily brooding, staff in hand, he strode down the stairs of the convent; when he caressed his son, when the ghost of the murdered Dimitri appeared before his eyes, when he died.

From that performance on Mussorgski's spread over all the opera stages in the world, and the great influence of the mighty realist began to affect composers everywhere.

Even during a period in which Wagner romance was spreading in music in Russia, too, this great realist reached into life with full force. No composer is more akin to him than the Czech Leos Janacek (born 1854). Janacek made two study trips to Russia, and it is possible that he heard Mussorgski's music there.

Even stronger is the effect that Tolstoi's poetry had upon him, and the string quartette and a piano trio by Janacek are influenced by Tolstoi's "Kreutzersonate."

But the little man with the upturned white mustache and baby blue eyes, son of a teacher and himself an instructor of the organ in Bruenn, was of an entirely self-reliant nature with a special kind of fantasy. His masterpiece, the opera "Jenufa," although reminiscent of Mussorgski's, displays a different kind of realistic style than Mussorgski's was.

Both composers are akin in their bold endeavor to grasp full reality and life without embellishment; both view human fate in an inexorable, strong light. But Janacek does not possess the greatness that enabled Mussorgski to portray nation and people upon a large historical background.

"Jenufa" takes place in a Czech village, in low huts with little gardens and gayly painted doors. Its chief characters are peasant boys and peasant women.

A village is also the scene of the opera "Katja Kabanova" (1921) adapted from the drama "The Storm" by Ostrovski. A small Prague house owner who likes to eat and drink and prattles about politics at his reserved table in the tavern is the hero of Janacek's operatic satire "The excursions of Mr. Broucek" (1919). The opera "The Makropoulos Case" (1924) transplants a three hundred year old demonic woman into a contemporary sitting-room. And Janacek's fine, witty opera "The Sly Little Fox" (1923) has its action among the animals of the forest, under singing trees and flowers.

Janacek's artistic world is his Moravian homeland. It is not boundless like the steppes of Russia, nor can it boast of a grand history with Czars and usurpers and troops of horsemen galloping across the wide plains; it is composed of small landscapes in which the forest is visible behind the yellow corn fields, and small towns behind the villages.

The music that Janacek discovered for this artistic world is not as generally appreciated as it deserves. The composer learned it from nature rather than out of books. "I listen to the gnat and the fly, the sad melody of the owl etc. My notes on human speech melody are increasing. I gaze with astonishment at the many thousand phenomena of rhythm in the world of light, color and matter, and my tone is rejuvenated by the eternal rhythmic youth of eternally young nature." Thus Janacek described his working method.

When he went for a walk he noted tirelessly, like a naturalist, the voices of the birds, and like a philologist all inflections of speech. "The theory of composition," he stated, "will have to be enriched by a new chapter. Just as today one practices and studies counterpoint, harmony and forms, the young opera composer will, to some extent, have to learn to draw from nature. The sketching of true speech melodies is as much as nude drawing of music. Of course I would not think of confusing a good sketcher of nude figures with a creative artist. Nude drawing is and remains an elementary course, a trade. However, it seems to me it is a necessary trade, necessary preparation."

Janacek's opera "Jenufa," a gripping village tragedy, is crowded with speech melodies with realistic intonation that have been learned from reality. These declamatory melodies overflow from the stage to the orchestra, melodies of primitive souls that give Janacek's tonal language something impelling.

Janacek's work has no room for musical rhetorics. There is something sparse and restrained in his expression. Only in two climactic points of the opera—in Jenufa's prayer and in the finale—does the melody broaden: it is song of the soul, not language of the soul. The choruses too, full of life as they are—the chorus of the recruits and the wedding chorus—are terse. Short melodies repeat themselves, like in Slav folk dances, they turn and twist. But they contain full reality and the gay colors of pictures by Uprka who painted the peasant girls and boys of Janacek's Moravian villages: the girls with colorful, wide skirts and flowered head shawls, the boys with caps adorned with shining field flowers.

Thirty years before Janacek began the composition of "Jenufa" (1896–1903), Smetana first brought the Czech village to the opera stage in his "Bartered Bride" (1866). This was in the days of the first romanticism, and all his melodies have the freshness and melodic beauty of folk songs. The opera is like a day in spring, glowing and warm, a blooming garden. Janacek's Slav village is entirely without romance. One is not in a blooming garden, but on a muddy village road. The air in the peasants' huts is heavy. Wet earth and dust cling to the people's boots. Reality is severe, inexorable, tragic. But true Slavic compassion bursts from the dull souls

of these people in the finale of the opera, and in "Jenufa" (as well
as in "Katja Kabanova") the sinners confess: Christian souls who
believe in the forgiveness of their God. The light of kindness that
strikes the poor peasant hut in "Jenufa" and covers everything with
a gold sheen is one of the biggest moments in modern opera.

Janacek's orchestra has no colorful varnish. It is unadorned,
hard and frugal. The colors are applied without mixing and are
placed next to one another haphazardly. Listening to this orchestra
one is reminded of the gay colors with which the wooden plates
are decorated in Janacek's homeland: primitive, clear colors that
reproduce simple ornaments.

Even this totally unromantic orchestra coloring contributes to
the impression of faithful reality. It does not embellish anything.
It allows the light of an ordinary day to flow through the voices
without refracting this light and without those mixtures that the
impressionistic orchestra likes. It does not possess the rich timbre of
the Smetana orchestra, the timbre that is Schubert-like with lights
from the shining tone world of Wagner and Liszt. Janacek's
orchestra has the colors of peasant soil, the colors of the highways
leading to the hamlets of his homeland, past ponds with swimming
ducks; the colors of unadorned rooms with their tables and benches
of unpolished wood. The orchestra itself is like carved from wood.
It was not until many years later that Stravinsky wrote such unromantic orchestra scores.

The reproach of naturalism was hurled against Janacek at an
early date. The foremost music scholar of Czechslovakia, Professor
Nejedly, custodian of the Smetana legacy, criticized Janacek's use
of word melodies and fought against his naturalism. The Czech
National Theatre in Prague turned down Janacek's opera, which
was first performed in Bruenn in 1904. Janacek had to reach the
age of sixty-two before "Jenufa" was performed in Prague; but it
was the success of the powerful work in the Vienna opera house in
1918 that first opened his path to the stages of foreign countries,
to Cologne, Frankfurt, Berlin and New York.

III

In Italy the aging Verdi had completed a turn to realism with his "Othello" in 1887. "We are intent on clarity, and to a great degree, we are skeptics," wrote the great old man of Roncole at that time—he who since 1839 had portrayed great romantic passions in gripping opera melodies—the first being the opera "Oberto, conte di San Bonifazio." The blood boiled in his arias and strettas. Love, hate, jealousy, revenge gushed across the stage with elemental force. One has only to read the critiques of Eduard Hanslick about Verdi's first operas to realize how violent and brutal these Verdi arias appeared when they broke into the melody realm of Bellini and Donizetti. They attacked the audience like a horde of brigands with knives and daggers.

Verdi's opera librettos were romantic texts, among them Victor Hugo's "Ernani" that had given the signal for the romantic revolution in France. Only two of Verdi's operas are in modern costume: "Luisa Miller" and "La Traviata," but even here the emotional sphere in the Verdi melodies was romantic. Schiller's realistic small-town drama "Love and Intrigue" and Alexander Dumas' Paris salon of "Demimondaine" are merely the scenes of passion and love that sing melodies similar to those of the chivalrous brigand chief Ernani and the Troubadour.

"Othello" is something else again. The opera was originally to have been called "Jago," and Verdi wanted to set to music character description and portrayal of psychological evolutions: music that would reproduce the dark thoughts that stir, grow and expand in the soul. It is not passion as elemental outburst and the blazing flame of emotions that sings in this music, as was the case in "Aida"; rather it is the inception and growing of passion.

As much as Verdi's "Othello" is Italian melody opera, with the tender love duet and the larger ensemble, it is equally novel as realistic soul analysis.

A wholly realistic comedy was "Falstaff" (1893) that came to be be considered the miracle work of the octogenarian Verdi. From the height of his old-age wisdom he smiles down upon love and jealousy and is amused by everything passionate that he portrayed in his operas: "Tutto nel mond' e burla. L'huom' e nato buffone." (Everything in the world is fun. Man is born as joker.)

In this opera the people chat as in real life; they joke and laugh, prattle and gesticulate. Ironic lights fall on love and grand emotions. The ensembles are continuous babbling. The love duets a fleeting play that comes and goes, and ends with a quick kiss. Everything is merry motion, and the orchestra gives sketchy glossaries to the happenings on the stage. This is an altogether new style of realism, compared to which the comedy of "Meistersinger of Nuernberg" appears heavy and pathetic.

Life is presented with very light strokes of the pen, such as great artists like Daumier or Forain employed for their sketches. Everything is "pris sur le vif"; reality in flight caught in a net. The influence of this new comedy style makes itself felt as far as Puccini's buffo comedy "Gianni Schicchi" and Ravel's "L'Heure Espagnole." And then it did not exercise all the influence of which it was capable.

Italy had tired of the heroic and historical tones that romanticism loved. Three years after Verdi's "Othello" Pietro Mascagni had composed his "Cavalleria Rusticana" (1890) and the new Italian "Verismo" was a world success. The realism of Bizet's "Carmen" and Verdi's "Othello" was joined in Mascagni's opera by popular Italian theatre melodies.

Italian peasants from a Sicilian village—portrayed true to nature by Verga in his "Novelle Rusticana"—sang love and hate to a brutal orchestra.

Two years later came "Pagliacci" by Leoncavallo who set to music Catulle Mendes' "Tabarin" with similar cheap naturalism and with equal effectiveness. Each year brought a new Italian opera in which peasant or small-town burghers sang arias and in which blood ran in streams across the stage. There was no opera without knives, and the drawn swords of the Verdi operas had become historical memory.

The theatrical naturalism became a universal style. In France Massenet wrote his "Navarraise" (1894) in bloody Mascagni style, which also includes an Intermezzo. In Germany Eugen D'Albert wrote his brutal "Tiefland" (1903) and Wilhelm Kienzl his folk opera "Der Evangelimann" (1895) with lively Lower Austrian folk scenes, a blend of cheap naturalism and cheap Wagner imitation.

The realistic folk opera found in Julius Bittner ("Die rothe Gred"—1906; "Der Musikant"—1907/8) a gracious representative who resumed the traditions of the Austrian popular stage.

Beside Mascagni and Leoncavallo two successful theatre composers rose to fame from the Italian Verismo: Umberto Giordano ("Andre Chenier"—1896) and Giacomo Puccini ("Le Villi"—1884).

Puccini's love melody has become a universal melody. Next to the soignée, well-bred love melody of Gounod and the tender love melodies of Massenet, it retains its own timbre. It is more strained, more intensive; and when the violins sing and the harps ripple, while the tenor voice rises to high C, the air is filled with a fine perfume like the parlor dandies use.

The sweet love melodies of Puccini do not have the timbre of great passion, nor the impassionate tone of the "Traviata" melody nor the overpowering force of Desdemona melodies. Puccini's melody is the song of a cultured cosmopolite who gently presses the hand of young girls and embraces them with a somewhat melancholy glance. The little salesgirl dreams of being loved by such an homme du monde and Puccini was successful in that his melodies were understood by these little salesgirls who occupy the gallery in the opera houses.

Puccini was well aware that the success of his operas depended on the lowly people. "We must amuse the organ grinder," he wrote to one of his librettists. "If not, we fail utterly and that must not happen."

Puccini loved the theatre, and he wrote only theatre music. "Music?" one reads in a letter. "Useless if I have no libretto. I have the great weakness of being able to write only when my puppet executioners are moving on the scene. . . . Almighty God touched me with his little finger and said: 'Write for the theatre—mind, only for the theatre.' And I have obeyed the supreme command."

Presumably Almighty God too enjoyed Puccini's tunes—albeit only during the hours in which He wanted to rest, when he wanted to listen to music that was charming, human and not too heavy.

Unlike Verdi, Puccini was not a composer who represented a whole nation. He was not of the material from which the people had been made. He was cultured and sensitive, and he wrote operas for the theatre in the same manner as Sardou or Dumas wrote plays for the theatre; a connoisseur of theatre technique, he was an artist who could calculate exactly what is effective and what is not effective, how to provoke applause and how to write effective parts.

The theatre as Puccini loved it is not chiefly a theatre of artistic fantasy, but a place for entertainment, suspense, excitement.

One day Puccini called upon Maeterlinck and requested his permission to compose "Pelleas and Melisande." Maeterlinck refused, having already given Debussy this permission. What would have become of Maeterlinck's gentle legend under Puccini's pen? One can readily imagine: a kind of Madame Butterfly who sings beautiful love songs and, on her deathbed, a second Mimi. Pelleas would have had his aria with a high "B." Puccini would never have made a new musical art production out of the Pelleas poetry, a work of art that has a language and an atmosphere all its own, that is enveloped in a cloud of grief, mystical quiet and dream.

The fantasy theatre did not exist for Puccini. He was a man of the realistic theatre and the "piece bien faite" as it was written in Paris by successful theatrical authors and as he saw it in Belasco's theatre in New York. This was where he found his "Madame Butterfly" and his "Girl of the Golden West."

Puccini himself always suggested his opera texts to his librettists. Many parts of his operas were his own invention, as for instance the waltz of Musette in "Boheme." The third act of his "Girl of the Golden West" was completed according to his directions. He wanted effect, and again, effect. How painful it must have been for a man like Puccini when his "Butterfly" failed in Milan in 1904. "Poor, crushed Butterfly! With what feline rage did they hurl themselves upon her," he wrote to his publisher, Ricordi.

But his faith was unbroken. "Butterfly is alive and real and will soon rise again. I say and believe it with an unalterable faith—you will see—and it will be in a couple of months." Puccini knew his theatre well.

The man who saw in the theatre a reality, not an artistic dream, is himself a realist, and his romanticism had to pass through realism. The first act of Boheme is all reality, life and motion. The second act with its Christmas frolic, its crowds, its cafe bustle could not have been written prior to 1896. It presupposes the complete evolution of the naturalistic theatre. "Tosca," written in 1900, is a crassly naturalistic opera wherein the violet fragrance of Puccini melodies mingles with the odor of blood.

"The Cloak" is a naturalistic sketch. "The Girl of the Golden West" a Belasco play of the wild west. For Belasco's "Madame Butterfly" Puccini studied Japanese melodies to give the opera the right local color. "Turandot" also has its Chinese atmosphere. Only Puccini's first two operas—"Villi" and "Edgar"—are completely steeped in romance. Everything else is realistic art in the approved French theatre form, with Italian melody.

In every one of Puccini's operas one finds that pleasure in portraying details that characterizes all realistic art and that put life into the first act of "Boheme." In all of the operas there is a natural conversational tone that gives way only to the Puccini love tune. In all of them the figures are alive and even in exotic costume they are reality and the present.

One has only to look at the woman figures that Puccini created: Mimi and Musette, Floria Tosca, Butterfly, Minnie, Turandot— to realize that there was something of a modern realistic poet in this theatre connoisseur Puccini; for to him the theatre meant as much as it did to film authors or to producers of Broadway hits: a chance for impressing the masses.

He loved life, frail or proud-spirited women who love and suffer; young girls, elegant women, exotic females who loved just exactly as the little milliner did. He had in him something of the modern stage authors like Arthur Schnitzler who invented Viennese women with similar love, or like Maurice Donnay who brought elegant Parisiennes to the stage.

In the history of modern realistic art Puccini must not be missing, for he enriched the opera not only with lovely Italian melodies but with warm human emotion as well, and with beautiful appreciation of life. One gets acquainted with Puccini, the modern poet, from words spoken to his friend (Arnaldo Fraccaroli) after the fiasco of his "Butterfly": "It was a human thing that I felt deeply: love, pain, a tender emotion. I am not made for heroic gestures. I love the souls that feel as we do, that consist of hope and illusion, that sense gleaming joy and tearful melancholy."

Puccini's greatness consists not merely of his warm humaneness, his brilliant theatre talent, his sure technique and his beautiful melody, but rather in the harmonic combination and dosage of these talents. He blends all these faculties in such quantities that even the little man understands the opera. Puccini considers the theatre audience a crowd of people who cannot stand too much genius. It is not an intellectual crowd, but a throng with primitive instincts. They want to see on the stage the simple human passions that regulate their lives.

They resist profundity of intellect, artitsic peculiarity, the power of creative personality. What Puccini gives them is genius in such a proportion of all component parts that his genius is not oppressive but finds a niche in the small homes of the average man. He is everyone's friend.

IV

Around 1900 the artists living in the Montmartre in Paris designated that district as the "brain" of the world. Modern poets, painters and musicians lived here in the houses that were built at the slope of the hill, upon which rose the white mass of "Sacre Coeur" dome. They populated all the cafes on the Boulevard Clichy and Boulevard Rochechouart. In the cafe "Nouvelles Athens" opposite the red glowing mill wheels of the "Moulin Rouge" sat the most modern painters. In the bar of the "Chat Noir," the poets.

On Montmartre Wilette sketched and painted his melancholy pierrots and pierrettes with the wondering children's eyes. The hunchback Toulouse Lautrec painted over-rouged prostitutes in the cafes. In the Cafe Nouvelles Athènes sat Debussy. In a neighborhood cabaret Aristide Bruant, in red shirt and velvet trousers, sang his poems about pimps and prostitutes, and men in tails and women in evening toilette came to hear him. In the "Chat Noir" Maurice Donnay wrote and Paul Delmet sang his latest songs.

In the Rue Clichy that led to the top of Montmartre there were no new houses. Here the artists lived behind garden walls in little cottages. After nightfall, one could see from here the lights of Paris, and the noises of the big city's traffic penetrated to the summit like a dull roaring.

In one of these cottages lived the composer Gustave Charpentier. For him, too, Montmartre was the center of the world. In the company of one of those young girls he loved, he would look down upon Paris, the big, shining city, and imagine he heard hundreds of voices calling, tempting, luring.

This city was a mighty monster that devoured human lives and supported itself with the flesh of women. This insatiable city reached out for the girls of Montmartre who sat in the cafes with the young artists, their absinthe glass in front of them; or who went up to the "butte," across the little "Place du Tertre" where burghers sat under chestnut trees and drank their wine at small inn tables; and to the dome from where one could look down on Paris.

Charpentier loved the Montmartre where the old windmills of the "Moulin de la Galette" stand beside the "Sacre Coeur" dome; and it was to Montmartre that he dedicated his opera "Louise" (1900) in which his heart beats.

This opera contains everything that endeared the Montmartre to the artists. The little houses and the little gardens, the quiet squares, the chatting girls in the dressmaking establishments, the artist fêtes, the street peddlers, the lights of Paris below, and above all, the memory of vanished love that, like every young love, was a dream.

There is gracious realism in this work. Even the voices that lure Louise from her domestic home to Paris are not really romantic voices; Charpentier actually heard them when he embraced his girl, and was afraid of losing her to the big city whose thousand lights shone up to Montmartre. These voices were as real to him as the calls of the street peddlers. In one of the most beautiful of his opera scenes, they sound from the distance across the little square lying in the broiling sun. They are as real as the clattering of the sewing machines in another of his scenes, and the monotony, the oppressive mood, the poverty of the proletarian home which he described so true to life in the last act of his opera.

It was not great art but the realism contained in this opera that made Charpentier's work an important one. The opera is more alive than the Wagnerizing "Sigurd" which August Reyer had composed in 1884, or the serious and heavy "Fervaal" by Vincent D'Indy, or the three massive Zola operas (La Rêve—1891; L'Attaque du Moulin—1893; Messidor—1897), written by Alfred Brumeau. In "Louise" we have less art, but more life. Massenet's "Manon" and "Werther" are clever art craft compared to the true experience and fresh memory in "Louise."

When the first world war broke out the artists moved from Montmartre to the cafes of Montparnasse and in "La Coupole," "Closerie des Lilas" and "Dome" one could see Stravinsky, Cocteau and Picasso at their tables. From an artist mountain Montmartre became a caravansary for foreigners who danced to the music of Negro bands in dance halls and drank champagne. But in Charpentier's "Louise" the Montmartre of the artists is perpetuated as the Quartier Latin of the Fifties is perpetuated in Murger's "Boheme."

9

The Fight Against Wagner

REALISM WAS A success on the operatic stages all over the world between 1890 and 1910. It not only penetrated the romantic art world with two great art productions, "Salome" and "Elektra"; since the year of "Cavalleria" (1890) it produced effective theatrical operas, in fact a new effect opera practically every year. These naturalistic operas were crass, often vulgar, and rarely were they creations of a refined artistic mind.

However, they were the first operas in modern times to eliminate the great romantic orchestra, to omit the symphonic juncture and enhancement of the leitmotifs. They were the first to mold the theatre melody into a set form, and to fill the theatre—the ordinary theatre—with everyday life.

Mascagni, Leoncavallo, Giordano, Puccini, D'Albert, Kienzl—all of them successful exponents of the banal operatic theatre—deprived the operatic stage of all its romantic decorations, of the historic or mythological costumes, of its ideological value and of the intellectual background. Their opera theatre had only three dimensions; it lacked a fourth dimension that could be called poetic, or philosophical, or even religious. It was reality in the nude, or at least something that resembled naked realism. One has to force oneself to remember that Mascagni's "Cavalleria" had been composed a mere eight years after Wagner's "Parsifal."

The attitude of the present age towards Richard Wagner had slowly undergone a change after Wagnerian art had become victorious the world over. To the men surrounding Wagner, he was an heroic figure, like Bismarck, and his art production strong and mighty, heroic and full of grandeur. When Hans Richter led the

orchestra in one of Wagner's music dramas, with a broad swing of
the baton, he conducted it as he would a Beethoven symphony.

The orchestra was like a wide stream. There was something
solemn in the gesture of the conductor with which he caused this
stream to gush. The great Wagnerian singers: Winkelmann
Materna, Lilli Lehmann, Theodore Reichmann, all possessed a
strong, heroic simplicity and broad pathos. When young modern
conductors directed the same works around 1890, they transferred
Wagner's language into a modern idiom. Gustav Mahler lent
nervous intensity to the music, Richard Strauss sensual rhythm.
The "Meistersinger of Nürenberg" was transformed into a spirited
modern comedy by Mahler, "Tristan and Isolde" into a high-strung
epos of passion.

Eight years after Richard Wagner's death the changed emotions
of a new era began to regard him in a different light than the old
Wagner generation did that had fought the first battles for these
works.

Of Wagner's works "Tristan and Isolde" was considered the
opera closest to modern sentiment. One has only to read the description of the "Tristan" music in D'Annunzio's novel "Il Trionfo de
la Morte" in order to realize that in 1895 this music was no longer
felt to be a Beethoven symphony. Rather it was nerve music, with
hundreds of different fine gradations such as are found in the works
of Flaubert or Dostojewsky.

The Wagner whom Mallarmé described in his Wagner sonnets
and whom Baudelaire glorified in his "Tannhaeuser" essay—that
Wagner was a French romanticist who happened to be born in
Leipzig but who nevertheless was akin to Victor Hugo and Delacroix. D'Annunzio's Wagner is a refined "symbolist."

Such a change in the attitude towards Wagner was possible
because, like every art creator, Wagner himself had many different
aspects and his great light is refracted in many colors. There is
much in Wagner that points to future times and prepares for them.
In Senta's hysteria in "The Flying Dutchman," one finds a great
deal that could be considered a preview of Henrik Ibsen's "Lady
of the Sea."

Alberich's recitation, the furious shrieking and hateful yelling are of a crass naturalistic keenness. The picturization of an emotional underground in "Tristan and Isolde" is already a portrayal of Freudian "subconscious." The Meistersinger of Nuernberg are fully realistic in the description of old Nuremberg with its crooked lanes, its Gothic windows, its churches and its architecture.

Even the tone of conversation between Hans Sachs, Walter Stolzing and Eva is realistic. "A great man is many men in one," Emerson had stated. Thus in Wagner there are realistic and psychological artists in one, and it was especially this modern trait in Wagner that was felt keenly and portrayed by young musicians at the close of the nineteenth century.

Mahler had staged "Tristan and Isolde" with decorations by Roller which reflected the moods of the three acts in an impressionistic manner. Whistler would have called Roller's first act an "impression in yellow"; the second a "nocturne in blue," the third a "symphony in gray." Only the theatre in Bayreuth retained the old Wagner style which gradually appeared to be getting more and more hollow and antiquated. Claude Debussy found it to be a "mausoleum" when he came to Bayreuth.

Even the acting style of Wagnerian singers had undergone a change since great naturalistic actors appeared on European stages. In Naples in 1884 Eleanora Duse had played Santuzza for the first time at the initial performance of Verga's "Cavalleria Rusticana." Garbed in the simple dress of the Sicilian peasant woman, a black woolen shawl framing her pale Mater Dolorosa face, she played with tired steps and simple, touching emotional tone.

She had achieved her first great success in Italy when she appeared in Zola's "Therese Raquin," and since 1884 had stirred audiences in European capitals with her performances as Nora, as the Lady of the Sea, and as Hedda Gabler. She played woman's sorrow quite naturally, even in theatrical parts such as Dumas' "Camille" and Sardou's Feodora.

Her acting as well as that of the new naturalistic actors in Germany: Kainz, Mitterwuzer, Bassermann, was bound to change the old, pathetic Wagner style with its grand gestures and solemn motions—Wagner in cuirassier's boot! The Wagnerian heroes lost the flowing beards of the Wagner era—Niemann as Tristan and

Winkelmann as Tannhaeuser had worn them—and appeared on stage looking like striplings without the hirsute adornment which in the Germany of Bismarck signified masculine dignity. (The first singer who dared to play Tannhaeuser without heroic beard was Alvary in Düsseldorf.)

The voices grew less heroic and more human, more lyrical. Michael Bohnen even sang Hans Sachs in an everyday tone of voice as though he were a figure out of a Gerhart Hauptmann drama.

However, all this new interpretation of Wagner into the realistic or the psychological, into the unemotional and the nervous, did not alter the fact that Richard Wagner's art production had been a comprisal of all European romanticism, and the trends of the time were leading away from romanticism.

The greater Wagner's genius had been, and the mightier he controlled spiritual life in all Europe and throughout the world, the more violent waxed the struggle—not so much against Wagner himself as against Wagnerism, against his artistic system and his art theories.

Wagner had been a tyrant who used his energy to shape music after his own personality and to pattern his theories according to the laws of this unique personality. He considered his art production the generally valid "art production of the future"; his romantic art pattern, which tried to join all arts to a unit was for him the universal law of art.

Broad and mighty like a boulder, this Wagnerian art creation blocked the way that led to the new world—a world that thought not in romantic terms, but rationally, materialistically, exact; a world for which historic costumes, legendary and mythical figures lost their significance.

The first great opposition to Wagner's romanticism came from the philosopher Friedrich Nietzsche. As a young professor of the university in Basle, Nietzsche had been among Wagner's intimate friends. In his writings "The Birth of Tragedy from the Spirit of Music" (1870/71) and "Richard Wagner in Bayreuth" (1873–1876) he had glorified Wagner's art with profundity and enthusiasm.

Promenading along the banks of Lake Lucerne with Richard

and Cosima Wagner and their big Newfoundland dog, discussing art with them, he was lifted from the banality of the present to an elevated world of magic in which great works of art and great philosophical ideas lent dignity to human existence. The composer and poet, covering his large head with a velvet beret and garbed in velvets and silks, appeared to Nietzsche as a great tragedian who, in a bourgeois world, looked deep into the abysses of life.

When Nietzsche's legacy was published it became apparent that even at the time of writing his two admiring Wagner essays, critical thoughts were not missing in the background of his reflections.

In the preliminary studies to "Birth of Tragedy" he already calls Wagner's interpretation of Beethoven's Ninth Symphony a "monstrous aesthetic superstition." Tannhaeuser has a "dramatic-pathological condition." "He is never naive." "Wagner is to grand opera as Schiller was to the French tragedy; the fundamental error remains." The main thought of Nietzsche's future Wagner critique is already contained in "Birth of Tragedy": "Wagner's relation to music is that of an actor . . . it is a theatrical language that speaks Wagner's art."

At that time Nietzsche did not fully appreciate the conflict that was already separating him from Wagner, and he wrote puzzled: "Only God alone knows how often I offend the Maestro; I am astonished anew each time, and yet I cannot ascertain the cause of it." Wagner himself tried to hold on to the escaping friend. "O friend! Why do you not come to us! I will find a way out for everything. . . . Still—or rather: Nevertheless! Or even: So what!" And Nietzsche came.

In the year of the first Bayreuth Festspiel the inner conflict between Nietzsche and Wagner becomes evident, although powerful spiritual ties between the two attempt to prevent it. During the Festspiel Nietzsche departs from Bayreuth; enroute, terrified by his loneliness, he turns back and then, certain of his facts, leaves again.

The romantic spirit world of his youth had lost its value for him and lay far behind him. A new landscape, remote from Schopenhauer's philosophy and Wagner's art, offered itself to his eye: a landscape that was no longer romantic, pessimistic, hostile to the whole world, but light, optimistic and positive. French positivism, the scientific theories of the new era, the lucid wisdom of Greek philosophers before Socrates, Voltaire's brilliant mind had re-formed his thinking.

In 1878 appeared the first book of this new Nietzsche, to whom Schopenhauer's romantic philosophy had become a symbol of decay, and Wagnerian art a dissolution of style, the opposite of classicism, painting and literature in a polluted mixture with sensual music.

In 1888 Nietzsche's writing "The Wagner Case" was published wherein Bizet's opera "Carmen" is played against Wagner's romanticism. Bizet's naturalism, the elemental passion of the opera, the bright light of Mediterranean sunshine were objects of Nietzsche's admiration ever since he had first heard this opera in the Politeama Theatre in Genoa on November 27, 1881. "The day before yesterday I heard an opera, 'Carmen' "—Nietzsche wrote his sister—"and I was deeply moved. So strong, so passionate, so graceful and so southern." He calls "Carmen" "the best opera extant." Every time he heard "Carmen" he "seemed more of a philosopher and a better one than I otherwise seem to be. In my estimation this music is perfect. It approaches lightly, supple with courtesy. It is gracious, it does not perspire. . . . It is light, it is precise. It constructs, organizes, is complete. That is what makes it different from the polyps in music, from the 'infinite melody.' "

What Friedrich Nietzsche seemed to hear in "Carmen" was the music of his own new world of thoughts, in which there was no more room for romantic tricks of magic. In "Ecce Homo" Nietzsche formulated his conception of music: "It should be gay and profound as an afternoon in October. It should be specific, merry, affectionate, a little woman of nastiness and grace." To the romanticists music had not been gay; it was a serious revelation; not a little woman but the great love itself. Or, as Wagner put it: "I cannot grasp the soul of music except in love."

Among Friedrich Nietzsche's 1052 aphorisms which are splinters of his projected great work "The Will to Power," we find many that analyze Wagner's art production in association with romanticism. According to Nietzsche, Wagner belongs to French romanticism, to Delacroix and to Victor Hugo, who are "great discoverers in the sphere of the sublime as well as in the sphere of the odious and the monstrous; greater discoverers yet in effect, in exhibition, in the art of display." Their art, Nietzsche continues, is overwhelming by its bulk, rather than by virtue of lucid patterns. They are incompetent in the use of a "strict style" that "arranges, fixes, limits and concentrates."

"What good is the expansion of expressive means when their employer, art, has lost its own rules! The pictorial splendor and power of tone, the symbolism of timbre, rhythm, color hues of harmony and discord, the suggestive significance of the music, all the sensuality of music that gained control with Wagner—all these qualities in music were recognized by Wagner, extracted and developed.

"Victor Hugo performed a similar task for the language; but even now in France one already ponders the question, in the case of Victor Hugo, whether it was not for the corruption of the language. 'Dramatic music. Nonsense! That is simply poorer music . . .' Passion is easier than 'high spirituality and ensuing happiness'—it presupposes much poorer artists. Stunting the melody is the same as stunting the idea, or dialectics, or freedom of intellectual motion—it is a bluntness and stuffiness that develops into new enterprises, even into principles. Descriptive music is: 'lighter, more imitable, within reach of those less talented; it is an appeal to the instincts; suggestive art.' "

Nietzsche characterizes modern art as an art of tyrannizing. "A coarse exaggerated logic of lineament; the motif simplified to a formula; the formula tyrannizes. Within the lines a wild variety, an overwhelming mass that confuses the senses; brutality of colors, substance, and desires. Examples: Zola, Wagner."

In these and similar phrases by Nietzsche one re-discovers the entire aesthetics of modern music. A Satie, a Schoenberg, a Debussy, a Stravinsky could underwrite every single one of these sentences. The following sentence: "One is an artist for the price of perceiving as purport, as the substance itself that which all non-artists call 'form' "—can be accepted as the truth as much by Arnold Schoenberg as by Picasso.

Friedrich Nietzsche belonged to the foremost forces that prepared both the alienation from Wagner's romanticism and the formation of a new, unromantically objective music style. The spiritual effect of his philosophy was felt all over Europe at the turn of the century, particularly by young artists. He made a deep impression on them with his ideas and the artistic form of his books which, in "Thus Spake Zarathustra," was enhanced to the language of a new bible. Musicians like Richard Strauss and Claude Debussy were equally fascinated by Nietzsche's thoughts as was D'Annunzio. The English impressionist Frederick Delius composed his "Life Mass" to words from Nietzsche's "Zarathustra."

Overcoming the Wagner romance, and detachment of music from literary or pictorial substances had become an essential artistic problem in France before the first World War. In 1903 "Mercure de France" arranged an inquiry: "Sur l'influence de la musique Allemande en France." The responses by all the musicians and critics disavowed the influence of Richard Wagner's art as being no longer suitable to the changed epoch.

A year later Paul Landormy, in the "Revue Blanche"—the review of the progressive artists in Paris—conducted a similar inquiry: "L'état actuel de la musique française," which resulted in similar replies.

For a number of years Claude Debussy had led the fight against Wagnerian art in "Revue Blanche" and in "Gil Blas." Pierre Lalo did likewise in "Le Temps," Louis Laloy in the "Revue Musicale," Marnold in "Mercure de France."

Even as fine and poetic a genius as Romain Rolland wrote that Wagnerian art "is in no way adequate to the French mind, neither to the artistic taste of France nor to her conception of the theatre, nor to her musical temperament. Wagner's art was able to thrive in France thanks to the might of the conqueror, it could—and still can—dominate the French spirit by right of a victorious genius; however, that does not alter the fact that it is, and will remain, alien to us, for the Wagnerian ideal is above all an ideal of brutal force." (In "Musiciens d'aujourd'hui.")

In a land of intellect such as France was, as well as in the rest of the world, Richard Wagner's art production had evoked battles in which especially the artists took part with vehemence. The poets

Baudelaire and Théophile Gautier, later Paul Verlaine and Stéphan Mallarmé, had been among the most enthusiastic of Wagner's apostles, and in the "Revue Wagnerienne" that made its initial appearance in Paris in 1885, there are represented such poets as Huysmans, Villiers de l'Isle Adam, Richepin, Catulle Mendes and Verlaine, and painters such as Fantin Latour, Jacques Blanche, Odilon Redon.

The intellectual youth of Paris, and the great masses had been won over to Wagner music by the Wagner concerts of Charles Lamoureux, and joined the "Lohengrin" battles in the Eden Theatre. According to Romain Rolland the influence of Wagner and Wagnerian art production "dominated the entire artistic manner of thinking in Paris from 1885 on."

Starting in 1890 in France—first quietly and slowly, then louder and faster—there grew a reactionary movement against Wagner enthusiasm and against the exclusive rule of Wagner's art ideas. The moral influence that emanated from Cèsar Franck had led his pupils Vincent d'Indy, Ernest Chausson, Guy Ropartz, Guillaume Lekeu, and his admirers such as Gabriel Faurè, Paul Dukas, Emmanuel Chabrier, to classical music, to pure music. The music written by the organist of St Clotilde was music of noble form, clear construction; music that was supported by its own powers and neither described, nor painted, nor philosophized.

Only in his youth had Cèsar Franck composed descriptive music in the romantic style of Hector Berlioz. That was in his "Chausseur maudit." All his other music has classic poise and is the expression of his peaceful, ardent, mystic love emotions in beautiful forms that were suited to French taste. Sometimes, as for instance in his two choral works, "La Rédemption" and "Les Béatitudes," Franck rises to the region of a gentle Christian mysticism, and his music has the lustre of a saint.

But here too the music is not formless; it has the greatest clarity of design and gentle lines such as are found in the frescoes of Puvis de Chavannes.

When Cèsar Franck died in 1890 he left a school of French musicians who carried on his traditions and his doctrine. Four years after his death, his pupils Alexandre Guilmant, Charles Bordes and Vincent d'Indy established the "Schola Cantorum" (1894) which performed the Gregorian Chorals and Palestrina's Masses in the church of Saint Gervais.

Bordes conducted Bach's cantatas in the "Salle d'Harcourt" and in Paris as well as in provincial towns there were regular concerts in which the old masters of past eras in France were performed, from Couperin and Rameau on.

In 1903 Charles Bordes published a program oration in the "Tribune de Saint Gervais," the "Credo" of young French composers: "We want free speech in free music, the eternal melody, the infinite variation as well as the freedom of the musical phrase. We want the triumph of music that is natural and free, gripping as speech and plastic and rhythmic as a Greek dance." It was the ideological influence of the "Schola" that led Claude Debussy to his adoration of old French music.

Rarely did the moral authority of a pure musician as Cèsar Franck change the spiritual climate in a country to the extent that the simple man did who on weekdays in the organ class of the Paris Conservatorium taught the young musicians the gospel of the ideal musical form, and on Sundays played his organ chorales in the church of Saint Clotilde.

His pupils comprised a group of symphonic and chamber-music composers, the likes of which had never before existed in France. In the works of Vincent d'Indy and Dukas one finds again the logical construction of Cèsar Franck; in the music of Chausson and Faurè his gentle mystic emotion; in Debussy his French sense of forming.

His pure personality gave all French musicians the assurance that French music need not imitate foreign ideals and that it was strong enough to create in a style of its own. This style was to continue the French tradition of lucid forms and provide it with new expression. It was to be a pure music style in symphonies, chamber music and songs, music within its own legality; tone, melody and harmony to move from within and spend themselves in forms that were purely musical patterns.

The gentle doctrine of Cèsar Franck, a moral force like the tenets of Anton Bruckner, changed the spiritual outlook in France.

True, it did not preach with loud voice a revolt against romanticism and against Richard Wagner's art production which was the greatest romantic authority and which, in France as everywhere else had assumed power. But it did change the hearts, and the contrast between the perception of the musicians and romantic music waxed larger. That which had been the greatness of romantic music: its poetic and descriptive power, its fantasy in the tonal sphere, its new colors, its association with other arts, its strong subjectivism, its overflowing erotic brightness—now appeared as impurity of style.

Wagner's art uniformity appeared just as unilateral as Victor Hugo's claim that he "had made all verses." Wagner's greatness was acknowledged, but Wagner romance turned down.

Wagner's art production had filled the whole breadth of the world. However, in France new ways had been found that led around the block.

The turn against romanticism was so radical that it did not even spare impressionism, which had dissolved the world portrait and transformed it into light vibrations; nor did it exempt Debussy's art that set to music this flickering world that melted in colors.

Paul Cezanne, a friend of Claude Monet and of Pisarro, and a comrade of Zola, painted as architectural unity the landscape of his Provençal home: the red soil, the stony hills and the houses that are piled like stone heaps. The landscape appeared to him as bulk, and the people, the players in the tavern, and the bathing women, as statues.

Matisse led the landscapes back to the essentials of their structure. Gauguin revolted against impressionism with emphasis of abstract forms and colors and with the return to decorative forms as he found them among Polynesians weaving straw mats.

Braque took the bold step of visualizing world objects in geometrical shapes. Reaction against impressionism, which had started as monumentalization of world phenomena, finally developed into pure form abstraction. Impressionism had been entirely subjective mood. The movement against impressionism ended as geometrization of world phases.

Impressionism had begun to take firmer shape with Maurice Ravel. Ravel is the most important musician to come out of Debussy's school. His art of describing fountains so that one sees the water ripple and spray; or his art of bringing forth from the music the ghost-like apparition of a gallows in the dark of night as out of a fog—this art is just as great as the descriptive art of Debussy had been. Debussy's "Iberia" and Ravel's "Rhapsodie Espagnole," which were composed almost at the same time (1908), both employed the same glimmer and light technique. Like Debussy Ravel paints Spanish street scenes and the bustle of fandango melodies.

In spite of all its refinement, though, Ravel's orchestra is much less scent and cloud than Debussy's. It has a keener line, and is less poetic and dreamy than intelligent. It has a peculiar bright silver lustre as it prefers woodwinds and strings, lets harp and celesta tones drip in and blends silk colors.

Debussy never employed an orchestra that was a mythological fairy tale and an ornamental glamour painting, such as Ravel's in the ballet "Daphnis and Chloe" (performed by the Russian Ballet in 1912).

Debussy's tonal fantasy was sensitive, personal, picturesque, but the deluge of sensual tones and the gay fresco style of Ravel were alien to him. What Ravel paints is a large fresco with figures from the Greek saga. Debussy paints intimate landscapes. Ravel covers the canvas with a profusion of shining colors and the gleam of nude bodies. Debussy paints water, air, branches, mists with vibrating colorful specks.

Ravel's fantasy is the classical French fantasy. It is clear, bright, intelligent and witty. Ravel's sense of form is the surest there is. Even the smallest piano composition of Ravel's is masterful in the form and complete in itself.

Impressionism alone could not suffice Ravel, since in its essentials it is an art of sketch. Even an impressionistic piano piece like "Ondine," which is merely play of the waves and rustling and performance of lights upon the rippling water, is covered by a line that rises and sinks. Ravel's "Bolero" is a solid construction, not just Spanish color display.

Like all French artists of the generation that was born around 1870, Ravel loved the artificial, the artful and the mysterious. In his texts Ravel gave preference to the poems of Mallarmè, to the costly symbolism, the pictures arising out of precious words, and to the resounding words which are shown like the Host to the consecrated.

A poem by Tristan Klingsor glorifying the virginal eyes and the lithe hips of a young boy, which was set to music by Ravel, shows this peculiar, super-refined taste. The Three Poems by Mallarmè for voice and small orchestra—string quartette, two flutes, two clarinets and piano—are as much art of hyper-refined emotions as the four orchestra songs which Schoenberg composed to verses of Georges and Rilke at almost the same time.

Still, the same composer who possesses the nervous delicacy for verses that are cool and shining like marble, can also be acidly ironic in "Histoires Naturelles." He has the wit and brilliant serenity of the Frenchman. His one-act play: "Heure Espagnole" is one of those merry sex stories that were told as early as the French moyen age in castles and in roadway inns. It is a story for gay women and courageous young men just before bedtime, and is told by Ravel with French clarity, French wit and sense of form.

Ravel was one of the first musicians to introduce jazz into serious music. But side by side with modern dance rhythms he always retained his love for the waltz which he first glorified in his "Valses nobles et sentimentales." In 1922 he composed "La Valse" for the Russian Ballet with a preface that read: "Whirling clouds, struck by bright light darts, show dancing waltz couples. The clouds gradually lift. One sees a huge hall crowded with rotating people. The scenes get brighter and brighter."

In this musical picture, Ravel portrays the waltz as motion, as, rhythm; he paints the atmosphere of the ballroom, the illumination, the whirling crowds; luxury, girandoles, uniforms, diamonds, naked shoulders, the Tuileries around 1855.

Ravel was a great admirer of Degas and of the pictures in which Degas painted the ballet dancers of grand opera at rehearsals and before the footlights, in tinsel dress, bending forwards and tying their shoelaces, pirouetting on tiptoe and balancing. That is what he wanted to reproduce in his "Valse"; the glitter of white satin ball gowns, lights and spots that sparkle in the big mirrors, the glossiness of the brown inlaid floors, the hot air, the hot wave of sensuality, motion in three-quarter time.

The technique is again impressionistic, but the many ingeniously employed percussion instruments—three kettle-drums, triangle, tambourine, cymbal, drum, bass drum, castanets, tamtam, woods, crotales (Greek castagnetes)—belong already to the Stravinsky era.

Eight years after this last great impressionistic work Ravel composed a piano concerto (1930/31) in baroque style as introduced by Stravinsky. However, he used the clear shining French taste and the polished piano tone that always was a part of French piano music.

One learns the meaning of French art taste just as well from Ravel as in the art of Chambonnières, Watteau, Auber or Anatole France. His is a rich personality of the greatest brightness of mind and finest treatment of material. The impressionistic colors are but a part of Ravel's artistic means; in his ingenious music is reflected the entire evolution of the European art spirit from Debussy and the symbolism of Mallarmé's age to the construction of the post-war era.

Ravel is among the best representatives of French intellect; lucid, gay, witty, ironic, he is the last musician to represent an old tradition of French intellect that has a grand history. From the Middle Ages to the time of Anatole France, this tradition has produced without interruption works that possessed the lustre and clear outline of crystals.

An absolute contrast to impressionism is personified in France around 1890 in Eric Satie in most original manner. Satie was one of those paradox, brilliant personalities, half childish, half whimsical, such as one finds so often in the artist cafes of Paris.

Paul Verlaine had been such a personality that concealed its delicate soul behind a Boheme existence, and Satie was a modern Socrates who hid his child-like disposition, his kindness and wisdom behind clownish wit. In derision of impressionism, he gave his piano pieces grotesque titles: "Embryons dessèchés"—"Avant-Dernières

Pensees"—"Air à faire fuir"—"Morceaux en forme d'une poire"—
"Morning twilight at noon."

The precious titles of Debussy, like: "Et la lune descends sur
le temple qui fut" evoked his ridicule; as early as 1890 he wrote his
"Trois valses du precieux dègouté." His instructions on execution
too are those of a mocker who laughs about romantic sentimentality: "Don't get too excited," or: "In the most profound silence."

From behind all romance Satie appears as the jester who makes
his jokes. In his "Papillons" Robert Schumann had made a notation
in the last piece: "The noise of the carnival night has stopped. The
clock on the tower strikes six." With that the piano sounds the six
strokes of the clock. Satie writes similarly, but he uses parodies. To
the words "The shadow of millennial trees marks 9/17 o'clock" he
writes an accompaniment in which a deep bass sounds the hour of
9, and the 17 minutes are heard in a high soprano.

That Satie hid a pure soul behind the white costume and the
white-painted face of a clown is most apparent in his "Socrates"
wherein Plato's narration of the death of Socrates is composed in
a sort of Gregorian recitativ as psalmody. In this music there is a
transfigured, holy mood that shows the true Satie.

Satie's piano pieces, simple in their harmony and in the musical
line, triad music with an occasional hue of fourths and chord blending, are a kind of unromantic "Davidsbuendlertaenze." There is no
emotional exuberance, no poetic admixtures, nothing fantastic. It is
all pure music, hovering in clear air, all lyric has an ornamental line.
It seems as though after the period of romantic piano virtuosity and
color splendor Satie had re-discovered the paradisiacal landscape
which music had deserted for adventures in the land of fantasy.

Satie opposes everything that is intellectual in music, all elaboration of themes, all counterpoint. He called such music "Musique
d'Ameublément" as in it "one musical pattern repeats like wall
paper pattern." He hated all realism. His ballet "Parade" (composed to Cocteau's text) was first performed by the Russian Ballet
in 1917 with decorations by Picasso; and while Cocteau called it a
"realistic ballet," it is anything but realistic in the ordinary sense
of the word.

The circus parade and the circus performance are presented

simultaneously, the outside and the inside of the fair booth, parade and show.

Satie's sketch "La boeuf sur le toit" that plays in a speakeasy is entirely fantastic; to the accompaniment of ragtime rhythms, actors in painted masks appear on the stage with very slow motions. Another of these Satie joke-plays is "Le Mariés de la tour d'Eiffel" for which all "Six" wrote the music. This sketch exaggerates banal conversations and platitudes a hundredfold until they become sur-reality.

Eric Satie's idea of the highest form in music was music without rhetorics, without literature, without trimmings of colors and without bombast. Music that flows out of simplicity as out of a clear spring.

That was the doctrine that he taught to the young musicians who congregated about him as around a new saint, the group of "Six": Arthur Honegger, Georges Auric, Francis Poulenc, Germaine Tailleferre, Durey and, since 1910, Darius Milhaud. A young critic and author, Jean Cocteau, belongs to this group intellectually. For him, too, the meeting with Satie was an event, and he wrote later: "In 1916 Satie was our schoolmaster."

He gave Satie's aesthetic tenets literary formulation. He preached with dazzling spirit on "disenchanting French music"—the liberation of French music from romantic spell, particularly from Wagner's arts. He opposed all emotional music, which he called "music of the bowels," and all narrative music: "Music that can be heard with the hands." Music should be "plastic apparition, to be heard objectively in a magic distance."

He calls Stravinsky's "Sacre du printemps" the most "revolutionary contemporary work of art" and lauds Stravinsky for deflecting his perceptions "into an apparatus."

Milhaud, Satie and Honegger composed to the texts of Cocteau.

In 1916 Cocteau attacked Debussy's impressionism. He spoke on behalf of the young musicians. He himself was very young at that time, just twenty-four years old. Milhaud and Honegger were also twenty-four then, Poulenc and Auric but seventeen. This was the new generation that had alienated itself from impressionism, a young generation without romance.

Debussy was deeply hurt by this attack, and later, in 1926, Cocteau attempted to justify it: "To act and to revere are two different things. To my lively regret, I was forced in 1916 to pretend to attack Debussy. In reality I was attacking Debussy-ism."

Cocteau criticized in Debussyism romantic art which had lost its significance in the serious crisis of the era. One could no longer live in dreams when reality predominated. One could not live by emotions when the dire necessities of a threatened existence forced all tender sentiments into the innermost depths of the soul. Neither could one continue to revel in the subjectivity of mood when the needs and insecurity of the age demanded activity. Pomp, splendor, sensual gleam, pathos, as they were embodied in the art of Richard Wagner in their grandest style, gave the impression of being magic means of overpowering the soul with the combined forces of all arts. Cocteau fought against the "hypnotism of Bayreuth"— Nietzsche having already pictured Wagner as an old sorcerer in "Zarathustra."

The anti-romantic trend was not limited just to France, though. It had become a European trend. Since 1890 Feruccio Busoni had transformed ideas similar to those of Cocteau and Satie into the doctrine of a "new classicality," and had passed them on to his pupils.

The brilliant piano virtuoso, half German, half Italian, was an intellectual personality of the first degree. He was extremely cultured, one of the last artistic figures whose mind was imbued with some of the Goethe-like universality and lucidity. His musical education was extensive; the circle of his literary interests wide. Busoni personifies what Nietzsche had termed a "good European" in a vivid, intelligent, distinct personality that looks across ages and countries from a high watchtower.

Busoni's musical mind was not creative, he did not invent new forms, as Liszt did, that had historical after-effects. But he had a sense of beauty, originality, fine culture and a Faust-like ambition to progress further and into ever new intellectual territory.

In 1907 Busoni put down his ideas in the "Sketch of a new tone art" (English translation 1911; Russian translation 1912), and within just a few pages he propounded an abundance of ideas on the essence of music. These ideas were the thoughts of a new era that wanted to return music to pure forms and to a new formation of its most specific materials.

Like Debussy, Busoni is a foe of all historic form, all the symmetries that are found in classic music. "The creative man should not accept traditional law bona fide and consider his work an exception thereto eo ipso. He should look for a law of his own to fit his particular case and destroy it after the first perfect application, so that in his next creation he may not become repetitious." "The man born to create will first have the negative, very responsible task of freeing himself from everything that he has learned and heard, everything that is apparently musical, so that, removal completed, he may conjure within himself a fervent, aesthetic concentration that will enable him to hear the inner tone and to make further progress by passing it on to the people."

"Let us free ourselves from architectural, acoustical and aesthetic dogmas, let music be pure invention and sensation, in harmonies, in forms and tone colors. . . . Let it follow the line of the rainbow and compete with the clouds in refracting the sun's rays, it is nothing but nature mirrored in the human soul and reflected." Conventionalities and formulas are like a worn dress, according to Busoni. The qualities one should strive for are: the abstract tone, unhampered technique, tonal boundlessness.

Taken from this viewpoint, descriptive program music is "a primitive, limited art." It is just as unilateral and bounded as "the tonal tapestry designs glorified by Hanslick which were proclaimed absolute music. (In his book "Vom Musikalisch Schoenen" Hanslick characterized music as play of "sounding moving forms." Eric Satie also designated the repetitions and symmetries of the classic form "tapestry design.") Instead of architectural and symmetrical formulas, instead of tonica and dominant relations program music has strapped on like a splint the binding, poetic, sometimes even philosophical program. "What can . . . portrayal of a small event on earth have in common . . . with the music that pervades the universe?"

Wagnerian art production has personal greatness, as far as Busoni is concerned, but it is not a generally valid greatness.

"Wagner, a Teutonic giant, grazed the terrestrial horizon in the timbre of his orchestra. While he enhanced the expressive pattern, he also systematized it (music drama, declamation, leitmotif) and is incapable of further augmentation due to these self-imposed limitations. His category begins and ends with himself; in the first place because he brought it to its highest perfection, to a finish, and secondly because the self-imposed task was such that it could be accomplished by a single person alone.

On the other hand the paths that Beethoven opens up to us can be traveled only by generations. Like everything else in the system of the universe, they may just form a circle; but this circle is of such huge dimensions that the part which we see before us appears as a straight line. Wagner's circle can be surveyed in its entirety,—a circle within a large circle."

Busoni's idea on opera had a strong influence on opera production in his time. "The largest part of newer theatre music suffers under the fallacy of wanting to repeat the events taking place on the stage." Busoni considers verisimilitude untenable for the music stage, likewise realistic portrayal of human experiences. The audience that wants to be gripped by realistic passions on the stage is "absolutely criminally inclined as far as the theatre is concerned, and it can be assumed that most people demand an intense human experience from the stage for the reason that it is lacking in their average existence and perhaps also for the reason that they lack the courage for the kind of conflicts they desire. And the stage offers them these conflicts without the accompanying dangers and evil consequences, uncompromising and above all, without exertion."

Right from the start opera must be geared to the incredible, the untrue and the improbable, "an imaginary world that reflects life either in a magic mirror or in a mocking mirror; the magic mirror for the serious opera, the mocking mirror for the gay opera. And let dance and mummery and spook be entwined so that the spectator be aware of the graceful lie at every step and not imagine it to be a true experience."

In his opera "Turandot" (and in the brilliant play: "Arlecchino" —1918) Busoni brought to the stage the Italian commedia del arte and its masked actors. Richard Strauss had already amused the spectators of the opera stage in 1912 with "danse and mummery" in the manner which Busoni demanded of the comic opera stage. The Goldoni operas of Ermanno Wolf Ferrari, "The Curious Women" (1903) and "Quattro Rusteghi," conform as much to Busoni's ideas as Puccini's "Gianni Schicchi" (1919).

Busoni held that the old opera was justified in its custom of comprising in a separate piece the mood derived from a dramatically moving scene and letting it fade out (aria), but the romanticism of Richard Wagner had become past history for him.

The new century no longer belonged to Wagner alone, but to new ideas, new artists. Although not a single one of them could compare with Wagner as far as ingenious creative power was concerned, all together they formed a new generation whose combined artistic strength set music in motion.

After 1919, the year in which Richard Strauss had composed his "Woman without a Shadow," no important opera was written in the style of Richard the Great. The opera with symphonic music and leitmotif had become a thing of the past, just as the Berlioz-Liszt program symphony had, and the romantic color orchestra.

In the Strauss "Alpensinfonie" (1915), in Schoenberg's "Pelléas and Mélisande" and in the Gurrelieder" (1911), in the music of Ravel's "Daphnis et Chloe" (1912) and in Stravinsky's "Fire Bird" (1910) this color orchestra had spread out for the last time its wealth of hues in their greatest enhancement.

10

The Path of Arnold Schoenberg

I

THE EVOLUTION OF music from the time of Brahms' death to the outbreak of World War I had no more forceful representative than Arnold Schoenberg. In his artistic personality were united all the spiritual trends that had pierced old dams in Europe during an age of crisis. His emotional world was set in vibration by all the movements of the spiritual atmosphere in Europe. His keen intellect studied all the problems of the era. His artistic development contained the most severe logic. Every composition he ever wrote is a step forward.

Compared with the dire necessity that governed Schoenberg's development, the evolution of Richard Strauss appears versatile and motivated by varying impulses. Strauss stands between romanticism and realism and is in one instant closer to romance, the next instant closer to reality. They are blended in various proportions in his works.

Arnold Schoenberg moves out of romanticism straight ahead into territory never before touched by man—considered a desert by his contemporaries—where he seems to know every spot of soil. He examines the ground carefully before taking each new step, proving himself a keen thinker and clear-sighted dialectician, not just a man possessed of artistic divination.

After composing his songs to lyrics by George (1907), Arnold Schoenberg wrote: "With the George songs I have succeeded for the first time in approaching an ideal of expression and form that I have had in mind for years. So far I have lacked the strength and assurance necessary for its realization. Now I am aware of having broken through all the barricades of past aesthetics; and even in striving for a goal that seems sure to me, I still can feel in advance the resistance that I will have to overcome. I can feel the boiling point of the opposition which even the pettiest temperaments will reach, and suspect that even those people who believed in me thus far will not want to admit the necessity of this development."

It took great moral courage to foresee so distinctly the "resistance of the apathetic world" and nevertheless continue on his way with the sure feeling of entering the "seventh solitude"—just as Friedrich Nietzsche envisaged it while writing "Zarathustra." Everything is over," Nietzsche wrote to his friend Rohde at the time, "everything is past, and consideration; one meets again, one talks in order not to be silent—one corresponds so as not to be silent. But the look speaks the truth; and it tells me (I hear it well enough!) 'Friend Nietzsche, you are now all alone.' "

It was Schoenberg's conviction that his music conformed to the laws of his nature that gave him the moral courage to withdraw into solitude. "Beauty exists only from the moment in which the unproductive begin to miss it," he write in "Harmonielehre" (published 1911/12). "It does not exist earlier, for the artist does not require it. He is content with the truth. It is sufficient for him to have expressed himself; to say that which had to be said according to the laws of his nature. However, the laws of nature of an ingenious man are the laws of future humanity."

Every great artist, every great musician occupies a place in his era as a man whose fantasy reacts to the intellectual trends of his time like a sensitive apparatus. We have already seen some of these movements that pervaded Europe at the start of the twentieth century: passing romanticism, naturalism, the impressionistic wave, the "l'art pour l'art," music as the art of pure tone. They can all be found again in Arnold Schoenberg, in addition to other, newer ones: constructivism and expressionism.

No other important composer of the twentieth century, not even Stravinsky, can compare with Schoenberg's strength to utilize independently and sovereign everything that his time brought him in forms of intellect and emotion, in artistic impressions and in ideas of a new evolution, and to join it to his individual personality. The most important component part of the Schoenberg fantasy remains always "Schoenbergism," the forming artistic energy of the peculiar artist personality.

In a torn and dissonant era writing in the travail of a new future, this personality of Arnold Schoenberg's with its mixture of imagination and logic, boldness of artistic vision and energy of thinking, sensitivity and moral courage retains its intrinsic soundness.

Gustav Mahler's was a bold mind, unequalled energy, a prophetic nature. But his personality is tragic and torn, tied to his era by nervous agitation. Richard Strauss was bold and novel, but he fled from the conflicts of his time to a pompous palace of colorful fantasia. Stravinsky is bold and, as creator of "Histoire d'un soldat," of "Les Noces" and "Sacre du printemps" he is a grand representative of Russian power, who turns into a brilliant artist. Inspired by Cocteau, Picasso and the Russian Ballet he allies himself with modern Parisian art.

Arnold Schoenberg courageously walks straight through his time. He does not stop in the middle, like Gustav Mahler, nor does he escape it as Richard Strauss finally did. Neither is he continually inspired by modern literary or pictorial programs as were Debussy and, in later years, Stravinsky. He absorbs it all, utilizes it and continues on his way; neither the hissing of the crowds nor the ridicule of the art custodians frighten him, neither the storms and tempests of his era, nor the changing fashions in which the feverish agitation of the time gives vent.

Unlike D'Annunzio, the English Pre-raphaelites and Stephen George, he does not live in an ivory tower. He is a fighter, and even the last work of the septuagenarian, the "Ode to Napoleon," contains a passionate inner excitement that makes the severe musical construction glow. He always hears the words of the archangel Gabriel which he wrote in "Jacob's Ladder": "Whether right or left, forward or backward, uphill or downhill—one has to go on without questioning what lies ahead or behind one."

At the start of the twentieth century there were many versatile, impressible composers in every country of the globe who appreciated modernism and who utilized new forms and new ideas rapidly. In Germany the greatest talent among those intellects that followed all trends of the new age was Paul Hindemith. Arnold Schoenberg was a composer of a different sort. He was a creative spirit with an intellectual form of his own, and he listened to the voices of his age because he wanted to discover his own beauty or his own truth. In the history of modern music only Mussorgski, Janacek, Bela Bartok and Stravinsky could equal him in independence as a musician. What he inherited and experienced in music was merely like a drink that a wanderer takes on the road, in order to renew his strength and continue his journey.

In his very beautiful book that describes the spiritual figure of Goethe, Friedrich Gundolf explained that there are two different kinds of experience within a creative artist: the "elemental experience" and the "educational experience." "Elemental experience" is that which exists in the depths of his personality as mysteriously forming force. "Educational experience" is everything that life and experience, travel and reading offer the artist.

In Arnold Schoenberg the "Elemental experience" was so powerful that it completely overshadowed the "educational experience." In contrast to Richard Strauss, his educational experiences did not accompany him all through his life. He left far behind him everything that was inherited and everything that was traditional, as well as everything that crimped the surface of contemporary life so that he might be able to listen to the unusual voices that sounded from the deep recesses of his own personality and which were comprehensible only to him.

Without pathos and without loud sounding words, going his own way forcefully and consciously, Schoenberg was one of the great Jewish revolutionaries that modern times saw and who was motivated by the new times; a revolutionary like Karl Marx, Einstein and Freud.

After Schoenberg's time music was something entirely different than it was before him. Traditional patterns, traditional harmonics, the traditional timbre, the traditional orchestra had all lost their validity.

It was conceivable that his contemporaries defended themselves against Schoenberg's music. This music destroyed all hearing habits, it seemed to threaten everything that was great and beautiful in music and that belonged to simple life, it was the destruction of an old world of musical conceptions.

Like every big revolution this music was ruinous, life destroying, menacing. The Viennese audience was very quick to recognize the revolutionary in the romanticist Schoenberg.

In 1898 two of the first songs by the 24 year old Schoenberg were performed in Vienna, two lieder from his Opus 1. The audience became as excited and infuriated listening to the declamatory music, as though they were hearing Wagner's "Tristan" for the first time. Schoenberg most certainly was the first musician who did not need to compose an opera or a symphony in order to be booed. Two songs sufficed.

Arnold Schoenberg presaged all this. He knew that the music authorities thought about new music as Gounod did who, at a solemn meeting declared: "Don't let yourselves be taken in by big, empty words like realism, idealism, impressionism . . . all these watchwords are out of the dictionary of that nihilism that is today called modern art." Schoenberg also knew that music audiences thought just as the old organist Scheidt had written in 1651: "Music is now so foolish that I am amazed. Everything that is wrong is permitted, and no attention is paid to what the old generation wrote as composition."

With open eyes he wandered into unknown territory, and he knew that beauty "is not the experience of everybody but at most the experience of a select few." To understand the road that Arnold Schoenberg took, one must understand the era in which we live and, at the same time, a piece of the future.

II

Arnold Schoenberg was born in Vienna. In this city old music traditions were not history and past, but a part of the present. They belonged to the atmosphere of the city and adhered to its soil. Scattered all over the city were houses in which the classic musicians had lived; theatre halls and palaces of noblemen where classical music had first been played; inns where Beethoven or Schubert had taken their evening meals; churches where Haydn or Schubert had sung in the choir when they were boys.

In the woods surrounding Vienna the memories of Beethoven and Schubert, Hugo Wolf and Johann Strauss were alive, and in Vienna's soil rested all great composers who had written classical music. In Vienna classical music, the forms of classical music and the classic harmonies were heirlooms of the past and were carefully preserved, like the old porcelain in the brown mahogany chests and the miniature portraits that adorned the walls in old Viennese homes.

Arnold Schoenberg grew up among these traditions. Like other young Viennese musicians he inhaled classical music with the air. To him classical music meant above all Beethoven, the musician who with iron hand grasped all motives, forged whole movements out of a single theme and, in his grand last string quartettes combined the four voices in free and strict counterpoint.

I can still visualize young Schoenberg at a rehearsal of the Beethoven string quartette in B-Minor, op. 130, listening with enthusiasm to the counterpoint play of the last movement, and enraptured anew at each new transformation of the theme. Being a musician meant already for young Schoenberg being a counterpoint musician.

Only the greatest composers had been counterpoint musicians; tone thinkers, not just tone poets. Bach was one, and so was Haendel who liked to improvise double fugues at the piano; Mozart was one in the ingenious plays of the Jupiter Symphony and in "Requiem"; Haydn was one and likewise Beethoven in his last most important works, from which modern music is descended.

Another counterpointer, a man who thought in strict and logical terms, was Brahms, who belonged to Vienna's present when Schoenberg was young. At that time he wrote his compositions in an old Vienna family parlor, the little windows hung with lace curtains and its brown furniture oldfashioned and sturdy. He would sit at his desk enveloped in dense cigar smoke, growling in his beard, while the goose-quill drew notes on the paper. He would leave his room and, with swinging steps, walk over to the music hall where his new music was played, or to the opera or to the inn. Here the waiters bowed respectfully, and guests would tell each other: "Over there, that's Brahms."

Schoenberg undoubtedly met Brahms quote often, and his teacher, Alexander von Zemlinsky, often talked to him of Brahms who in the "Tonkuentslerverein" had praised Zemlinsky's compositions.

Brahms had transformed his keen critical mind and his logical severity into contrapuntal thinking. Out of three notes Brahms develops the dismal tragic passion in the first movement of the first symphony. A motif of three tones changes into ever new tone figures in the second symphony by Brahms, and a similar motif consisting of three notes holds together the entire first movement of the third symphony.

(This development of three tones must have impressed Schoenberg. One of the songs in his "Pierrot Lunaire" (Die Nacht) utilizes such a three-note motif, which recurs more than a hundred times in the course of the song. That is the Brahms technique in its most concentrated form.)

This Brahms technique was adopted by Schoenberg. Motifs were the material for musical structures. Counterpoint taught how to make such motifs flexible, how to expand and condense them, to reverse and subvert them. For contrapuntal thinking such motifs were crystallized forms, arranged around an axis according to rule, and the motifs could be turned and twisted without the laws of their form being destroyed. That was the doctrine of Brahms music which Schoenberg adopted.

Schoenberg possessed a dialectical talent of the first degree, and dialectics in music means: contrapuntal thinking. In his opus 7, the D-Minor string quartette, the main theme already comprises three ideas which yield ever new forms, and all Schoenberg's other early compositions contain a wealth of contrapuntal work.

In the songs of Pierrot Lunaire this contrapuntal art is enhanced to the boldest "canons," "mirror canons" and "double canons." The inversion of the double canon in the 18th song "Der Mondfleck" is one of the most masterful accomplishments of art. These ingenious plays of musical fancy are musical logic and musical dialectics in their most perfect freedom and boldest flexibility.

It is this logical talent that distinguishes Schoenberg from all other composers of the new era. At the most, Max Reger can be compared with Schoenberg; but Reger was not capable of fully mastering the over-abundance of music within him with intellectual power. In Schoenberg logic and dialectics of musical thinking are creative. His counterpoint is not a Bach copy, as was often the case with Reger, or a Haendel copy as in the "Triumpflied" by Brahms, or a copy of Orlando Lasso and Eckhard, as in the Brahms Motets.

This counterpoint is not a stately wig. It springs from Schoenberg's innermost spirit and is the particular pattern of his spiritual strength.

Schoenberg's logic was the bright light that banished the twilight of romantic art. In this light the romantic symphony looked like a theatrical decoration by day. In this brightness all mixtures of art dissolved like compounds dissolve in retorts when the chemist sends an electric current through them.

The chromatic harmonies detached themselves from the triads when the bright glare of tone thought lit upon them. Logic digested, changed; it made the tone material fluid, pointed out the emptiness of pompous facades and the necessity for constructions; it pressed toward clarity, simplicity, authenticity of material and functional distinctness.

In Vienna, where the young musician grew up, Schoenberg saw a similar trend in architecture. Vienna had a great architect who wanted to build houses that were practical. He expressed this practicality in simple forms, houses in the shape of cubes and prisms and without glued on trimmings. This architect was Otto Wagner who, in 1895 published his pamphlet: "Modern Architecture." Three years later one of his pupils, Josef Olbrich, built the edifice that housed the young painters of Vienna. This was in the shape of a cube topped by a cupola of gilded laurel.

Another of his pupils, Josef Hoffmann, erected modern houses and villas in Vienna and Brussels. In 1896 in Berlin Alfred Messel constructed Wertheim's department store in a new, simple monumental style with gigantic rod-shaped windows. The modern architectural trend pervaded all western Europe. Everywhere one began to build with iron and beton. All over Germany van der Velde had erected homes, museums and factories in block form and with smooth surfaces that did not conceal the inner structure and the material. In 1902, with his museum in Hagen he elevated cement to artistic significance.

Paris had an architect of similar mind in Corbusier, who declared: "A house is a machine to dwell in."

The spirit of this new architecture that became a universal style, was sensible, logical, clear. It was a direct contrast to the romantic spirit in architecture which constructed in ancient styles in the nineteenth century: Greek temples and Renaissance palaces, Gothic houses from fourteenth century Venice or Florence. This was the spirit of the new machine and factory age, of the new practical world; it was a mathematical spirit that opposed romantic fantasy, color luxury and excess.

Schoenberg's logic was descended from this spirit. From the very start of his artistic development there is already present in all the romanticism of the young composer the Schoenberg style of thinking with its inexorable severity and its brightness. How this style of thinking first allies itself with the romantic form and romantic tone, with the romantic fantasy and romantic exuberance, then works its way past them, crowds romanticism into the background, finally destroys it altogether and independently develops new artistic forms, is a spiritual accomplishment of the very first order.

Like every composer of his time, Arnold Schoenberg started out as a romanticist. He knew the moonlit nights of romance, when woods and fields are suffused with a silver sheen, and moonbeams hang from branches and house tops. He, too, watched glow worms flitting through the bushes, their lights blinking on and off; and he knew nights in July when the air is all light blue. Such nights are described in the adagio of his first string quartette and in "Transfigured Night." The second song in the "Gurrelieder" is also steeped in moonlight. White light ripples through the orchestra, and delicate spider threads and wood-wind passages sparkle.

Divergent string flageolets and harp pizzicati right out of Berlioz' magic kitchen evoke romantic nocturnal mood.

In the prelude to this work Schoenberg paints the dusk, the hour in which all objects melt into the darkness, the favorite hour of all romanticists. Evening noises sound promiscuously, the distance drones, there is rustling and roaring, humming and whispering. Hundreds of different voices resound from a single chord.

Additional nature romance is contained in Schoenberg's portrayal of the summer wind that chases across fields, through the reeds of the lake, over meadows and spring flowers.

The narrative of the "Wild Hunt" reminds of the descent into hell in Berlioz' "Sinfonie Phantastique." Bones rattling, the wild hordes rush by, three male choirs sound their "Holla, Holla" into the air, and a roaring tonal mass of calls revolves in the atmosphere.

In "Pelléas and Mélisande" Schoenberg hears the roaring of the ocean, the splashing fountain and the quiet in the dark dungeons of Golo's castle at the same time as Debussy hears these romantic voices in Paris.

Schoenberg could portray as realistically as Richard Strauss and impressionistically like Debussy. In his monodrama "Erwartung" (1909) he proved that he can also portray that which fills the thoughts of man with dread in dark recesses of the soul and that hovers above the thoughts as a gray cloud. He knew "surrealism" long before Andre Breton published his "Manifeste" in 1924. He was acquainted with every type of romanticism existing in Europe between 1830 and 1930.

Arnold Schoenberg expanded the great romantic orchestra to the limits of the possible. His "Gurrelieder" orchestra is larger yet than that of Gustav Mahler in the eighth symphony. Schoenberg uses two more piccolos, one English horn, one e-flat clarinet, one bass clarinet, one contrabassoon, two horns, two trumpets and three trombones above those employed by the titanic Mahler in his eighth symphony. In addition there is a ten and eightfold partition of the strings, three male choirs of four voices, an eightvoiced mixed choir, five singers and a narrator. For this score music paper with 48 lines had to be especially made.

The orchestra for "Pelléas and Mélisande" is smaller; yet with 35 instruments (not counting a heavy string section, percussion· instruments and harps) it was still a giant orchestra. From Berlioz on the romantic fancy preferred this orchestra because it made possible all the transitions from the most delicate partitions of the instruments to a hurricane-like massing, and because it was a gigantic color organ.

In all of Schoenberg's compositions the tone is color, atmosphere, mood; it is a sensual, voluptuous tone, although often quite supernatural, as for instance the iridescent nine-voiced flageolet chords in the first song of Tove in the "Gurrelieder"; sometimes it was grotesque like in the song of Klaus Narr, or fantastically picturesque like the glissando of the trombones that sweeps through the vaults of the castle in "Pelléas" like a death wind.

Until 1906, when Schoenberg wrote his "Kammersinfonie," he belongs to the great modern colorists, to Richard Strauss, Claude Debussy, Dukas and Ravel, to the young Stravinsky, to the masters of brilliant, picturesque, gay orchestra colors.

Exactly the same can be said of Schoenberg the harmonist. His starting point is romantic harmonics that expand the triads chromatically, stretches the chords and pulls them apart. It does not dissolve dissonances and causes basic harmonies to disappear behind colored harmonies that mingle and tangle.

That had been Wagner's harmonics in "Tristan and Isolde": all expression of longing, passionate desire; the whole soul with all its dark recesses, with all its emotions from darkness to light, with the erotic undercurrent and the quest for death into which the restrained torrent is transformed. Arnold Schoenberg adopted this "Tristan" harmonics in "Verklaerte Nacht" and in the "Gurrelieder." It is the language of erotic passion, excited emotion, agitated moods.

Just as Richard Strauss in "Salome" and "Elektra," so does Schoenberg enhance the chromatic media of expression; and just as Strauss lets the great, sublime melodic ties of Salome come forth from strained harmonics, so does Arnold Schoenberg produce out of similar harmonics, and with intensive enhancement, the melodies of "Verklaerte Nacht," of his String Quartet in F Sharp Minor (1907–8) and of his monodrama "Erwartung" (1909).

Schoenberg is not a realist as Richard Strauss had been when he attempted to trace hysterical emotions in the "Salome" melodies. He is what could be called a romantic expressionist. Passionate tension sends the melody soaring. Love becomes exuberance in the melodies. This music glows and flames, and harmonies and melodies become like steel in a smelting furnace, a foaming, seething mass.

The forms of which Arnold Schoenberg makes use in his first great compositions, the poetic programs in "Verklaerte Nacht" and in "Pelléas," the huge orchestra, the painting, portraying tones, the harmonies that resolve chromatically, are all romantic music. Sentiments and moods are romantic. The patterns are romantic. But through this romantic massing of forms, tones, and harmonies Schoenberg's logic works its way. His strict, objective thinking— artistic thinking, the thinking of creative imagination—separates the purely musical from the literary and the picturesque, the tone from foreign alloys.

The programs vanish. The romantic orchestra disappears, as do the color panels and color mixtures. Romantic harmonics disappear. The music shows only a transverse section of moods. All this develops step by step, from one opus to another. No evolution of a composer was more logical than that of Arnold Schoenberg. From "Verklaerte Nacht," "Pelléas and Mélisande" and the "Gurrelieder," from the String Quartet in D-Minor and the "Kammersinfonie" to the String Quartet in F Sharp Minor and the "George Songs" Schoenberg's music develops more and more from the pictorial and poetic to pure material utilization, as though it were on the assembly line, being moved from workroom to workroom.

During this entire work procedure Schoenberg's theoretical thinking remains alert. Nothing is left to chance and to whim. The tools are always re-examined carefully, the material observed minutely.

In the George songs and the five orchestra pieces, op. 16, Schoenberg for the first time cleansed his music of all historic

patterns and expressive media and presented it chemically pure
as Schoenberg music (1909). One year later he wrote his "Harmonielehre" in which distinct boundaries are drawn between the
classic-romantic and the new harmonics. It is a clearsighted book,
ingenious and bright that demonstrates in brilliant form Schoenberg's superior art intelligence.

If, in a revolutionary like Schoenberg, one expects to find obscurity, passionate opaqueness, fanaticism, the "Harmonielehre"
proves one wrong. In this book his intellect is lucid, his humor free,
his sagacity clear. In the book is that kind of humor owned only
by the man who is absolutely certain of his facts and who stands
above matters; and that modesty that always distinguishes the great
man from the ever vain and unsure little people.

With the fascinating intelligence shown by this book, and with
superior humanity, moving calmly from one composition to the
next, Arnold Schoenberg developed his personal music pattern
increasingly bolder and lifted it out of romantic music.

The musical construction waxes stronger from opus to opus,
and Schoenberg's romanticism has a steel frame from the beginning. His "Pelleas and Melisande" does not resolve in impressionistic
mood, but is intrinsically held together and fastened with thoughts.
Themes and counter themes, contrapuntal transformation of
themes and contrapuntal voice-phrasing from the solid foundation,
in which each component part has been put in its place with the
hand of a master.

The D-Minor string quartet and the Chamber Symphony are
akin by virtue of the solid frame into which the four symphonic
movements are fitted in entirely new arrangement, and through
the independence of the voices that go their own way. In the
Chamber Symphony, written during the same period—1906—in
which were formed the giant orchestra of Gustav Mahler's eighth
symphony and the stuffed orchestra of Reger the romantic orchestra had completely disappeared.

The orchestra instruments do not apply color, nor are they
carriers of moods, but parts of a structure. The music is architecture, not painting or poetry. The main theme is a construction of
five quart intervals that can also be folded up to form a single

chord. Each of the 15 voices of the music is a part of the musical scaffold. As was the case with Bach, the sketch of this frame is furnished by counterpoint which, in the scherzo part of the Chamber Symphony performs its greatest accomplishment in free expansion of music's logical powers.

Counterpoint also governs the entire second part of "Pierrot Lunaire." The mood of this composition is still romantic, the figure of the pale Pierrot who imagines visions in the moon beams, is the dreamy figure that Wilette so often painted on cabaret walls in Paris. Still, Schoenberg's music form is not impressionistic, no matter how intensively it draws the fantastic moods of the man in the puffy pierrot costume.

Out of the poetic mood arise the canon feats of "Mondfleck"; the glittering and twinkling of the moon macula on Pierrot's black dress is reproduced with the canon and its inversion and the three-part fugue in the piano accompaniment. Claude Debussy had painted this flickering moonlight with colorful specks. Schoenberg grasps it in the play of contrapuntal lines.

Schoenberg's counterpoint became entirely abstract in the five piano pieces, opus 23, in the serenade for 7 instruments and in the suite for piano in which his tonal thinking found its most energetic concentration. Every kind of romanticism is far removed. The music hovers in bright, thin air in a space in which there are no dreams and no desires any more, no passion and no picturesque designs. The themes are sections of the 12 tone scale, practically geometrical formations of this scale. They are unreal tone figures that are brought to life: homunculi who want to become humans.

Each of these tone pieces is a development of such unreal tone figures. There is nothing else in the tone pieces but the tone figures in ever-new transformations and metamorphoses, in changing positions and arrangements, turned upside down and inside out. The tone figures are condensed to chords and stretched out in musical lines. A uniform development led Schoenberg from Brahms-like counterpoint to the peaks of these musical, logical plays of intellect. This development is as remote from all romanticism as geometry is from dreams.

III

Hearing the name Arnold Schoenberg, the average music listener thinks first, and almost exclusively, of the destroyer of the classic-romantic harmony, and the inventor of that music which is called "atonal" and which is considered ugly or frightening. But then new harmonies were at all times considered ugly or frightening.

Classical music could not escape this fate either. Under date of February 12, 1817 Rossini wrote a letter to his friend Cicognara in which he laments the fact that Haydn had begun "to break up the purity of musical taste by introducing into his music hetero-geneous chords, artificial transitions, bold innovations" and that Beethoven "with his compositions that lack every kind of compact structure and all natural invention, conceived in caprice and odd-ness" had spoiled the individuality of instrumental music.

At all times every new dissonance appeared as anarchism. The beginning of the Mozart C-Major Quartet as much as the beginning of the prelude to "Tristan" which Hanslick called a "chromatic whining."

The fact is that since Beethoven's death the dissolution of the classic-romantic harmony system made incessant progress. Even in the time of early romanticists chromatics were the acid that cor-roded the classic harmonies. The more chromatics expanded during the nineteenth century, the more chords became equivocal and the freer the transitions.

Debussy's whole tone scale is found in Liszt compositions al-ready, just as Debussy's augmented triads can be found in Liszt's "Faustsinfonie." The first Tristan chords can be recognized in Schumann compositions.

In Wagner's "Tristan and Isolde" this development reached its first great climax. The chromatics spread over the entire music and the chromatical harmonies obscure the triad harmonies. In the works of Richard Strauss, Max Reger and Claude Debussy classic harmonics are already in a stage of complete decomposition; Strauss mixes the most varying triads, Reger causes the most modern chromatics to flow into Bach forms and in Debussy harmonics change completely to fluid mists.

If there had been no Schoenberg, then some other young composer of the early twentieth century would have taken the last step toward which the historical development was rushing, and would have removed the last remnants of the classic-romantic harmony system, which had become an historical ruin.

As systematically as he undertook every step forward, Arnold Schoenberg took the step from classic harmony to the unknown sphere in which the triads did not circle around a centre according to ancient rules, but in which new harmony groups formed. "Pelléas and Mélisande" already contains fourth and whole tone chords; in the "Kammersinfonie" the classic third structure of chords is replaced by a fourth structure.

In the last movement of the String Quartet in F Sharp Minor Schoenberg takes the final step: he forsakes the broad classic-romantic path upon which so many great, and thousands of minor composers had wandered, and steps into the unknown tone sphere surrounded by new, glittering ethereal sounds to the words: "I feel the air from other planets," sung by a soprano. Schoenberg must have experienced the same sensation then as Wilbur Wright did when his aeroplane left the ground for the first time and soared into the atmosphere. That had been in 1903. Schoenberg's first free flight into the tone sphere took place five years later—1908.

The contrast between consonance and dissonance had lost its meaning for Schoenberg. Nature did not create this contrast. Consonances were the closer upper tones, dissonances the more distant. The relations of consonances to the basic tone are simple ones; the relations of the so-called dissonances to the basic tone are complicated. The difference between dissonance and consonance is a minor one, not essential. "They are just as little contrasts as two and ten are contrasts."

In this small sentence Arnold Schoenberg's entire aesthetics are laid down. Being an artist, he could give way to his fantasy when he wrote down his new harmonies. "In composing," Schoenberg states in his 'Harmonielehre,' "I decide by sense—the form sense. That tells me what to write, everything else is out of the question. Every chord that I write corresponds to an urge; the urge of my need for expression, or perhaps the urge of an inexorable but unconscious logic in the harmonic construction. I am fully convinced that it exists here too."

It is the systematic instinct in Schoenberg that prompts him to try out in various music forms the new harmonies which are entirely free and arranged according to hitherto unknown laws.

In 1908 he composed his songs "Fifteen poems from Stefan George's 'Book of the Hanging Gardens,' " with short motifs for the voice that is filled with sensitive emotion; and with independent motifs in the piano which, while often a mere breath, are always musical lines, never color spots or illustration. The songs are a type of chamber music refined to the utmost; voices of the soul that vibrates most delicately, like a quiet garden pond brushed by the wing of a butterfly.

In 1909 there followed the three piano pieces, again with totally independent parts; they were completely intrinsic music, visionary tone portraits. The year 1910 brought the "Five Orchestra Pieces" with the solo treatment of an all new orchestra that has nothing in common any more with the romantic orchestra. There is no rustling of harps, the medium range of the orchestra is no longer filled with the soft timbre of the horns, there is no tension created by the roll of the kettle-drum.

The sound of the strings is reduced, the colors are blends of solo instruments in unusual ranges, the wind instruments are often muted; the strings are employed not as a group but as solo instruments, the muted trombones play glissandi and tremoli with loosened "fluttering tongue." In the third piece one and the same chord is struck in various tone combinations; only the tone color changes, it twinkles and shines in varying degrees of brightness.

The morning mood of an alpine lake gave Schoenberg his inspiration for this piece, but the music is neither realistic portrayal a la Richard Strauss, nor impressionistic painting a la Debussy; it is a kind of tone-color poem, scenic mood and atmospheric mood representing unreality and idea.

In the other pieces tone forms and tone formulas are utilized; they wander through the solo voices and appear as melody and as harmony in the unreal light of the solo instruments.

The new harmonies, the new tone, the new type of motifs and their treatment, rhythm, too, and blendings—they all belong together. It is absurd to see in Schoenberg only the man who brews atonal harmonies in his retorts. He is a composer with a new type of fantasy that shapes all the elements of his music. His harmonics and his thematic figures form a whole, just as his tone and his rhythm constitute a whole. Therefore he can use tone scales as melodies and as harmonies simultaneously in the same composition.

His harmonies are a product of contrapuntal voice phrasing rather than a creation of harmonic fancy. Schoenberg's work is a complete unit, and the result of a complete axis rotation undertaken by Schoenberg in the music. Not just the harmonies, but melody, tone and rhythm as well show from a different angle.

This turn of Schoenberg's was chiefly a turn against romanticism that had controlled the music of the entire nineteenth century. It has nothing to do with the realistic turn in which some of the greatest artists of the nineteenth century participated: dramatists such as Ibsen, Bjoernson, Verga, Gerhart Hauptmann; novelists like the Goncourt brothers, Zola, Tolstoi and Dostojewsky; painters among whom were Courbet, Manet and Liebermann, and musicians like Richard Strauss.

Neither has this turn anything to do with impressionism. True, Schoenberg uses naturalistic and impressionistic art means, but they are not the dominating forms of his music. In "Verklaerte Nacht," "Pelléas and Mélisande" and in the "Gurrelieder" he employs naturalistic and impressionistic technical attainments, but he is no naturalist and no impressionist. He is Arnold Schoenberg, the strongest anti-romanticist and anti-realist extant in twentieth century music.

Romanticism is too theatrical to suit his personality; too rigged out, too impure as art; and its gay splendor can not satisfy the era that is suffering under heavy social and economic problems and that expects a cure from rational scientific spirit for the ailments of the age. Realistic art is closer to real life than is romanticism, but it only reflects the surface, not the depth. Artistic development leads Arnold Schoenberg away from romanticism, naturalism and impressionism to an art that is more real than romanticism and, at the same time, adheres less to the surface than realism or the nervous, pale heir of realism: impressionistic art.

His new music is modern music, reality; music uncloaked, unadorned, without false facades. It utilizes the tone material aptly as the ivory carvers of the middle ages worked their material, or like the stone-masons who created the Gothic windows and gargoyles of the big cathedrals from granite blocks.

The musician no longer plays the philosopher or the poet or the painter; he remains musician, a man who lives with tones and thinks in tones.

In Schoenberg's time, but without having any connection with him, an Austrian school teacher, Matthias Hauer, preached the theory in pamphlets and essays that music is a pure treatment of the material in the tones of the twelve-tone scale. A group of tones in the twelve-tone scale that is shaped in various ways by the musician is designated by Schoenberg as a "tone figure." Hauer calls it a "tropos" which is the term it was given by musicians of the middle ages.

Such ideas seem to have been in the air at the start of the twentieth century. Everywhere music has the urge to withdraw from romanticism which had made a mystic out of the composer— a mystic who proclaims God in the terrestrial world. It turned to the new time that gave dignity to genuine material everywhere, be it in art trade, in architecture, houses, boldly arched steel bridges, machines or automobiles.

Thus music turned realistic in a higher sense of the word: it became practical, work, construction. At the same time, however, music turned its back on the gay-colored world surface which Richard Strauss had portrayed in his symphonic poems with such masterful color technique.

It had been Richard Strauss' pride to reproduce musically every sound, every motion and every form of life. His "Don Quixote" pictures a second time the battles of the knight with sheep herds and windmills, Cervantes having done so the first time. His "Alpensinfonie" are the Alps in an illusory imitation of its forests and snow peaks, edelweiss and cascades.

At a rehearsal of "Alpensinfonie" a violinist dropped his bow during the storm scene. "Mister, you dropped your umbrella" the composer-conductor informed him. He was able to say this because the storm scene with its wind machine is realistic.

Debussy's narratives also give only the colorful surface, rain and ocean waves, falling leaves in autumn and Spanish street scenes, in flowing light and trembling colors.

Schoenberg's music penetrates this surface of reality which it had pictured with greatest perfection in the early compositions. It continues into the sphere of the unreal where the forms materialize, and into the solitude beyond the world. That is the cause for Schoenberg's music often sounding so gray, shapeless and thin to the listener. His music is of material that does not belong to the everyday world. Its figures are not physical shapes but spiritual ones, albeit often merely in the embryonic form of thoughts that detach themselves from the unconscious and only begin to take effect in the soul.

The combination of concrete material treatment and abstraction gives Arnold Schoenberg's music its peculiar style. His music comes from the modern world of work and moves into the sphere of unreality. The transition from external nature imitation to a spiritual Hereafter is characteristic of all art before the start of World War I and one of the signs that revealed the deep dissatisfaction of the time. However, the greatness of Arnold Schoenberg's music lies in the union of the urge to abolish realism with the solid workmanship of the tone material.

That which Ibsen's "Master Builder," Architect Solness, proclaims as the highest ideal of his art, and what he wanted to build for man after churches and homes: "castles in the air with firm foundations"—that is contained in Arnold Schoenberg's music.

IV

During the time in which Arnold Schoenberg first approached the ideal that he had in mind, he attempted to grasp his inner visions in pictures. World occurrences had become ghostly to the great anti-realist, and he endeavored to capture their true meaning in colors and shapes. He painted portraits which would show not the outward appearance of the person pictured—among them the composer himself—but their inner being. He painted landscapes that were wholly fantastic and "fantasies and visions": eyes that stared out of the dark; demonic faces filled with fear and terror; dreadful glances out of shadowed eyes.

Also during this time Schoenberg had taken up connections with the Munich painter's circle of Wassilj Kandinsky, Alexei von Jawlensky and Franz Marc which since 1912 had congregated around the periodical "Der Blaue Reiter." The ideas of Kandinsky and his circle were akin to his own ideas. Kandinsky painted only mood inspiring line, surface and color pictures; shapes and colors in free rhythms; surfaces with outlines never before seen. In 1911 he began "absolute painting" with his picture "Composition 4." That was the same year in which Schoenberg wrote absolute music in his "six little piano pieces": sketches of rhythms or unusual harmonies, glances into an unknown land of pure music, snapshots of the motions of sounds.

Similar to Kandinsky, Jawlensky painted his "Variations" since 1907, in which the motif of the picture expanded completely in free play of the imagination. He also painted pictures in which he sought new form laws, for his credo was: "Art is the longing for God" and one must forsake nature in order to find God.

Franz Marc, who fell in the war in 1916 sought space-artistic lines and color play in the portrayal of animals. August Macke, also killed in the war, temporarily joined the Munich circle. His longing for the abstract led him to cubism. His idea of art was pure and noble. His creed was: "High above life hovers the idea, art. There is a conflict between life and art. In your quiet hours, liberate art into the form."

In France Fernand Leger started to paint his abstract pictures in 1913. He called them "form variations." This was a European movement, and Arnold Schoenberg was its first great musician. Like the Munich circle and like Leger Schoenberg sought in music the shape of pure musical forces, the motions of the rhythms, "absolute music," not imitating or displaying music: tones and combination of tones, sounding lines and their variations; a spirit-world of sounding forms.

Arnold Schoenberg first searched for this spirit-world with fantastic compositions: two musical one-act plays and "Pierrot Lunaire." The first of these musical one-act plays is entitled "Erwartung" (1909) and is a song scene with large orchestra. Only one figure is on the stage, a woman searching for her lover in the forest. The composition begins at the edge of the woods. Streets and fields are suffused in moonlight. The forest is a tall, dark mass.

The second scene takes place in the forest, the woman groping her way through. Out of the dark the woman finds her way to a clearing, more and more fearful; from out of the woods she steps onto a broad moonlit street, where she finds her dead lover. With the woman's scream: "O Du bist da . . . Ich suchte . . ." the play ends. Like in a nightmare one feels the throat contracting more and more. The play is concentrated like a dream, colorful like a dream and as unreal as a dream.

The white gowned woman who wanders through the forest until her clothes are torn to shreds is not any specific personality. It is the loving woman per se who has lost her lover to another woman and who remembers the hours of happiness and the parting after a night of love. Her reminiscences, her sentiments of love, her fear and her grief constitute the substance of the opera which consists simply in the woman's monologues.

Eugene O'Neill's "The Emperor Jones," written eleven years after Schoenberg's "Erwartung" (1920) is a similar play consisting of monologues. Like Schoenberg's woman Brutus Jones wanders in the woods and his fear increases from scene to scene with the rhythm of the beating tom-tom that becomes ever quicker and more menacing.

It is Schoenberg's music that places the whole play into the realm of unreality. His music is not intensified declamation, it does not paint situations or events. It does not strengthen reality, but the Beyond of moods. The tones have a life of their own. The sound is spiritualized, the tone blends are precious, unusual and

never reminiscent of earthly matters. The tone concentrates the
intensity of emotion and is somewhat visionary. The many blendings and crossings of harmonic circles emphasize the impression
of the incorporeal.

The action of the play: the woman's search, her memories of
love and happiness, the moods of the night in the woods, the
finding of the dead lover—could all have been portrayed naturalis-
tically. But this realistic world is not Schoenberg's world. What
he set to music is a vision, a dream-like poesy, a world behind the
real world.

The second of these fantastic Schoenberg operas, "Die glueckliche Hand," also has a dream-like character. It begins as a nightmare: in the first act green glowing faces stare out of the night
at a man, prone on the floor, who is being pressed to the ground
by a green glowing mythical animal. The green ghost heads talk in
a singing tone, or sing in a talking tone. Their voices are unearthly
and sound like groaning and moaning.

Ghostly voices and unreal tones are heard in the orchestra too,
where above an arrested chord of seven tones individual short
phrases vibrate like sighs of a shackled soul. What we hear the
green ghost chorus singing are the voices of the inner being. What
we see is the deepest abyss of the soul itself. Night and horror have
become tone.

In the period before the war started many artists visualized
such nocturnal ghost-like faces. Lasar Segall painted such faces.
His picture "The Eternal Wanderers" (in the municipal museum
in Dresden) consists almost entirely of these heads with big staring
eyes; heads that glow in the dark like masks; phosphorescent heads
like those that sing in Schoenberg's music—that is, if one can call
the moaning, whispering and hissing singing.

The other scenes of "Glueckliche Hand" are also visions: the
man whose face and chest are covered with bloody scars. This
man drinks from a gold goblet which flies from the hand of a
beautiful woman into his hand. A bloody sword in hand, he climbs
a cliff and, in a cave where laborers are working in realistic workmen's clothes, he demolishes the anvil with a hammer and lifts a
tiara from out of the cleft. At the end of the play he is again

held down by the paws of the mythical creature and the green ghost faces stare at him and whisper in pity: "Du Armer."

Color and light visions unite with the music. When the woman appears in the second picture and stands alluringly on the stage in a light purple dress, glaring yellow sunlight is supposed to come through the slit in the light blue canvas of the background and strike the pale yellow draperies at the side of the stage. These lighting plays are accompanied by the delicate voices of solo instruments and gentle celesta tones.

In the workmen's cave the dark purple light has to run into brown, red, green and yellow tints. Later, during a storm, the illumination changes from reddish to brown-gray, dirty green, blue-gray, violet, dark red, blood red, orange and yellow. Simultaneously the music increases in volume. A motif consisting of three tones is intensified more and more, until it is resounded by the trumpets.

Arnold Schoenberg was probably inspired to this combination of colors and music by Scriabin, on whose "Prometheus" the Russian music author Leonid Sabanjeff had given an explicit report in the magazine "Der Blaue Reiter" (of which Schoenberg was a collaborator).

Pictures, lights, colors and figures melt with Schoenberg's music and form a unit that appears as a dream and a play of symbols, as an opera from the fourth dimension. In this music expression is compressed until it reaches its greatest intensity, and nothing real is being traced. The music is not an illustration of true events evolving on-stage. It has a life of its own. The figures on the stage are symbolic; the colors and forms of the scene, the changing light—in one instance said to be emanating from the main figure—are hallucinations.

The music resounds from the unconscious where are rooted the nerves of emotional impulses and where man connects with elemental life. The text of the opera may well be termed Freudian, for Freud defined the "action" of a dream as abridgment and concentration of impulses, memories and thoughts that have been repressed into the unconscious and that radiate from there.

The music, though, is Schoenbergian: music that is only music, motion of tones and musical voices; fantastic blends of tone colors, sounding music figures in which moods are reduced to the shortest formula.

Arnold Schoenberg remained in the realm of fancy with his "Pierrot Lunaire" (1912). The speaking voice, accompanied by a small instrumental group (piano, flute, violin, clarinet and cello) is as unrealistic as the poems of Albert Guiraud themselves. The rhythm and tonal range of the speaking voice are indicated by the composer, and the voice rises from unaccented whispering to all tone shades of an exalted language. It is neither declamation nor song, but something between the two: a spiritual voice without sensual tone, the naked soul without melodic styling; unreal and yet deeply touching.

The instruments combine their tone with the ghostly timbre of the soul, and change from song to song. In one of the songs: "The sick moon," the pale sound of a flute melody unites with the sighing tone of the speaking voice and forms a dialogue of ghost voices.

Of the two Pierrot figures in modern music: Stravinsky's "Petrushka" harlequin and Schoenberg's moonstruck harlequin, both composed at the same time (1911, 1912), Stravinsky's puppet is grotesque and witty; Schoenberg's harlequin touches the human soul, he is a dreamer, a poet whose fantasy is set in motion by the moonlight.

One would be inclined to employ impressionistic means for the moon settings: moonlight tones, diffused silver light, twinkling spots. However, Arnold Schoenberg is already far removed from that. He does not paint moon moods in a real world. He portrays the Pierrot soul, Pierrot's fantasies, the suffering of the pale man in an imaginary moonscape. The music has everything: the pale light of the moon, and the magic of the glittering light. But no longer does the composer paint with flickering tones the surface of the world during a moonlit night. His patterns are solid, distinct and determined. The lines are entwined artistically. Each of the "seven times seven" songs is a crystal-like formation.

One gets the impression that music, having charmed, painted and composed with tone colors for a whole century, finally remembered its own nature: the tones which are nothing but tones, and the forms which are merely the natural arrangement of tones. Such forms and tones hover beyond the world in a spiritual sphere and all they took along with them out of the real world is the composer's soul with its wings of sorrow and longing. This longing is symbolized by Schoenberg in his Pierrot.

Schoenberg composed Four Orchestral Songs, opus 22, before the war and during the first year of the war. Each of the four songs —one composed to a text by Ernest Dowson, the other three to poems by Rilke—has its own orchestra with new sound combinations. The singing voice has the Schoenberg intensity, widely arched lines, a spiritual expression that grips almost physically. The tone colors are unusual. In the first song six clarinets are supported by strings, trumpet, three trombones, cymbal, xylophone and tamtam. The groupings of the solo instruments are very unusual and provide the musical lines of the tone poems with a fantastic lustre. They strengthen the soulful expression of the lines and place the bleeding heart in a gold and jewel encrusted pyx.

By the time war broke out Arnold Schoenberg had so far intensified and perfected his artistic evolution that he guided music out of a romantic realm into a sphere in which every tone and every combination of tones, every musical line, every expression of soul had been brought forth from a hitherto unknown fantasy place in new and personal shape.

Every single part of his art production had to be newly created. Each step was an exploring trip, every new work was progress along an unknown path. Although in his great works that were composed between 1909 and 1914 Arnold Schoenberg moves in spheres which no other composer had ever set foot on before, he is nevertheless certain of himself and conscious of his power. There is nothing unclear in his music, nothing that ferments and nothing opaque, such as is generally found in revolutionary epochs of art after all barricades have been torn down.

There is nothing in this music that could be considered reminiscent of the wild shapelessness of the German "Stuermer und Draenger," or of the emotional storm of young Schiller or of the extravagant fantasticality of Hector Berlioz or of the pleasure with which Richard Strauss created street noises with his music.

Every one of the new and unaccustomed tones, and every tone blend; the singing voice that neither sings nor speaks and that is nevertheless intelligible; the orchestra with its unusual light refractions—all are handled with an assurance and superiority which, after great new art has become old is generally called classic.

The virtuosity of the counterpoint alone, which plays artistically with new tone material, proves the clearness of Schoenberg's imagination. Compared to the shining light in which Schoenberg's musical thoughts move rapidly and lightly, Max Reger's masterful counterpoint appears dull and muddy.

The four compositions that constitute the climax of Arnold Schoenberg's work in the period before the war could easily be taken for artistic creations of a fantasy that retires from the real world into the ivory tower of imagination, like the poems of Browning, Keats or Stefan George, or the pictures of Burne Jones or sketches by Blake. The two music poems that Schoenberg wrote for the stage, "Erwartung" and "Glueckliche Hand," are as fantastic as hallucinations. "Pierrot Lunaire" is an artistic, poetic world with unusual and precious sentiments.

The four orchestra songs are a musical setting of poems of which the poetic expression has been styled and the word-pomp of which reminds one of Byzantine mosaics. This artistic world can easily recall the world of an artist who likes artificial things; however, Schoenberg is neither decadent, nor is his a morbid mind with cunning inclinations. His "Harmonielehre" proves him to have a clear, logical, keen mind, and to be a man of humor and kindness, very human and very deliberate.

Following his exploring trips into the unknown, he tried out the new elements, the new forms and expressive means of his music first in works that seem to move in a fourth dimension of imagination and sentiment. His reasons for that were exclusively artistic ones.

His new music that renounced all classic and romantic art media was especially suited to the reproduction of a world beyond, because it does not call to mind the usual surroundings. Its new tones appeared as music from a sphere in between the dark of the unconscious and the brightness of the conscious. The music itself, like every new artistic creation, came to light from the dusk of the unknown. Its roots were still in the lower stratum where new pictures, forms and sentiments originate. Thus this music was especially suitable for portraying an unreal world.

Not until 1930 did Schoenberg adapt his new music to the salon comedy when he wrote the one-act opera "Von Heute auf Morgen." In this opera the people live in up-to-date apartments, the women wear mundane clothes and, at the end, the child asks inquisitively: "Mama, what is that, modern people?"

Schoenberg's twelve-tone scale was at that time already so developed that it fitted in splendidly with steel furniture, cupboards and electric bed lamps as a part of modern furnishings. However, in 1912 Schoenberg music was more at home in a spiritual sphere than in a modern metropolis, and it harmonized better with a moonstruck Pierrot than with a woman who lets a tenor court her in order to arouse her husband's jealousy.

The perfection of Schoenberg technique was completed in the period after the first world war and will be discussed in connection with music trends in the postwar period. But Schoenberg had accomplished the most essential and difficult part of his work before 1914. He had left the classic harmony behind him, as well as all artistic forms that are supported by this harmony. The romantic timbre, the romantic orchestra and the romantic mingling of the arts had become a thing of the past.

A new music had formed in him; music that was nothing but tone and combination of tones, self-propelled, shaped only by musical laws. The musical construction was no longer determined by poetic, pictorial and idealistic inspirations but by the tone substance. No more were harmonies finished triad designs handed down to young musicians by old practicians in conservatories everywhere as a model. They were a new creation, an act of fantasy. Replacing the development of musical thoughts in length and breadth, the cross-section had stepped into depth. And all this forming and shaping took place not in that old, intimate tone sphere that was divided by the seven-tone scale, but in a space of twelve tones where the composer's imagination had to search anew for tones, tone combinations, themes and thematic treatment.

This was the path along which Arnold Schoenberg had progressed up to 1914. He had gone this road with the boldness of an explorer and the moral courage of one searching for the truth; he had gone slowly, systematically and with a keen, critical mind. He was not afraid of hissing audiences and the advocates of public taste, nor was he intimidated by the ridicule and sneering of the men of yesterday. He was the greatest musician of the twentieth century who made the stride from an old era into a new age like a man crossing a big bridge above a menacingly swelling torrent.

11

Before World War I

I

THE CLOSER EUROPE came to the fatal year of 1914, the larger waxed the spiritual tensions in which were reflected the social and economic tensions. A new generation of musicians was growing up all over Europe and had reached the age of 20–30 when war broke out. Honegger was 22 years old; Georges Auric 15; Francis Poulence 25.

Milhaud at 22 was still attending the conservatory and was just composing his "Poème" which was performed in 1915 at the concert Colonne. Paul Hindemith was 19 years old, Ernest Krenek a mere 14, Alban Berg 29. To this war generation of young musicians Richard Strauss at 52 was an old man and even Claude Debussy, likewise 52 at the start of the war, belonged to a past era. Eric Satie, to whom young musicians in Paris flocked like chicks to the mother hen, was already 46. Time seemed to pass more quickly in this agitated epoch. One aged rapidly. The world revolved faster. The pulse of the time was feverish.

Standing between the old generation of fifty year olds and the young generation in their twenties were Igor Stravinsky, a man of 32; Arnold Schoenberg, 40 and a revolutionary, and Maurice Ravel, 39 years of age.

Stravinsky had just completed "Les Noces" and was preparing to write mechanical music. Schoenberg turned to constructive music. About this time Ravel and Stravinsky had become fast friends, and Ravel had just become acquainted with Schoenberg's "Pierrot Lunaire."

The great turn of the times is also distinctly noticeable in these

musicians. Stravinsky's "Three Pieces for String Quartet," Schoenberg's "Four Orchestra Songs, opus 22" and Ravel's three Mallarmé
poems for voice and small orchestra—two flutes, two clarinets,
strings and piano—are all music in new style, and a definite
approach to abstract music.

In the years before the war painting and music undertook the
same turn from the portrayal of reality to the portrayal of unreality, and from the colorful surface of objects to the abstract forms
of the Beyond. The naturalistic portrayal that was introduced into
modern music by Richard Strauss with great daring appeared just
as superficial as Debussy's impressionistic representation of clouds,
ocean and gardens. The qualities that made such music new and
bold were hardly understood any more. The expansion of harmonies was taken for granted, and the lustre of the Richard Strauss
orchestra was considered a heavy mass of material tone.

As early as 1904 the English music author Ernest Newman
spoke of Richard Strauss, whose greatness he had often described
with wonderful perception, as "the man who once was a genius."

Pleasure in the world's beauty had changed to a deep dissatisfaction with the world; enjoyment of lustre and color to hate
against the displaying side of matter. Out of this discontentment
and hatred grew a sadistic destructiveness. The world—or at least
the outer shell of the world—was torn to shreds. It seemed as
though the metaphysical instinct which had always considered
nature and world only illusions, in a fit of despair was trying to
invade the realm of ideas and was determined to use force in order
to get to the bottom of things.

Around 1910 the geometrization of figures and objects was a
typical art form employed by painters and plastic artists. Matisse
had termed the new art trend in painting "Cubisme." André Derain
—a year older than Stravinsky—wanted to use colors and phenomena of nature the way poets use rhyme and rhythm: for the
construction of forms that contain a mathematical formula. In 1907
he cut his stone sculpture of the cowering woman in cube form.

Also in 1907 Georges Bracque began to geometrize his landscape visions. The Andalusian genius, Picasso, who had hitherto
painted with plastic grandeur the heavy figures of peasants and

circus performers, began around 1910 to dissolve the world into mathematical forms.

Faces lost their roundness, and intense emotional expression was condensed with angles, triangles and quadrangles. A girl playing the mandolin was composed of geometrical figures that slid above and beneath one another. The head of the artist facing the easel was compressed entirely out of straight lines and angles and set against a background of lines, planes and cubes. The light of thoughts gave it an intense brightness, and triangle eyes and triangle mouth radiated inner life.

The sculptor Alexander Archipenko had been toying with arched abstract forms since 1913, and Rudolf Balling worked the plastic picture of a triad out of stereometrical masses. Oswald Herzog aspired to "absolute sculpture" and freely invented forms just as Kandinsky had tried for "absolute painting" and Eric Satie for "absolute music."

In every branch of art the same revolt broke loose against naturalistic portrayal of world phases. Towards 1910 art everywhere turned anti-materialistic, anti-realistic and anti-rationalistic. The profound dissatisfaction of the time in pre-war years revealed itself in this turning from the illusion of a phasic world.

In Italy this revolt against the world turned to "Futurism," preached by Filippo Tomaso Marinetti in 1909. In 1910 this "Futurism" proclaimed his theories from Milan in the journal "Poesia." In the same year "Figaro" in Paris brought Marinetti's infamous appeal that called for arson against historical art: "We will destroy the museums and the libraries. Let the good arsonists come with fingers that smell of carbolic acid! Set fire to the libraries! Divert the canals that they may flood the museums!"

Futuristic poems became a chaotic sequence of words. Mallarmé's symbolism of dark pictures and mystic word sounds, from which are descended Marinetti's "Parole in libertà," was entirely dissolved into the illogical. In the theatre the logical sequence of scenes was also dissolved. In pictures by Severini past and present, close and distant, small and large impressions were intertwined. Giorgio Morandi counterpointed the objects in his pictures without any concession to naturalness.

Giorgio de Chirico composed objects out of machine parts and shaped Hector and Andromache as puppets, calling them "Metaphysical Essences." Boccioni painted the inside and the outside of objects simultaneously—"Simultaneous Visions." He painted a laughing woman whose laugh makes the whole environment of the room dance. Another futuristic painter, Carlo Carra, painted a hackney-cab in rapid motion and included everything seen by the passengers as well as the passers-by.

The program of futuristic music was explained in 1912 by Francesco Pratella in the preface to his "Musica Futuristica." He turns against the preponderance of the technical and the fabricated: "We have to destroy partiality for well-made music, which is merely rhetorics and impotency. We must destroy doctrinal and academic prejudices, and we have to declare as contemptible, stupid and common the phrase: 'let us turn to ancient art.'"

The positive demands are: 1) Harmony and counterpoint are to be united in the creation of an absolute polyphony. 2) The usual, traditional, obsolete and buried stencils of the symphony are not to be taken for the essentials of symphonic art. 3) A stage work is to be conceived as symphonic form. 4) All new accomplishments of nature are to be introduced into music that is subdued by ever new scientific discoveries. One is to reproduce the musical soul of the multitude, of the large industrial workshops, of the trains, transatlantic voyages, of traffic, automobiles and aeroplanes, and to combine with the chief themes of musical poems the domain of the machine and the victorious kingdom of electricity.

Pratella's program was adopted by the Soviet composers. Mossolov's "Iron Foundry," the factory noise in the second symphony of Shostakovitch, the symphonic description of the steam engines in "Dnieprostroy" by Julius Meltus, and the ballet portrait of an industrial age in Prokofieff's "Pas d'acier" (1925) are among the music that glorifies the "domain of the machine." Shostakovitch did not fail to include a factory whistle among the instruments in the second symphony. George Antheil introduced the noise of the aeroplane propeller in his "Mechanical Ballet." That too corresponds with Pratella's program.

In Soviet Russia the ground had been well prepared to receive futuristic ideas. In Moscow a group of poets had already formed in 1912 (Mayakovsky, Hlebnikoff, Burlyk, et al) and proclaimed that it is up to the poet to formulate his own language which should free the words from the chains of logic and use them only as tone and as a symbol. "Artistic norms" should be "banished from the steamboat of modernity."

After 1917 Boris Pasternak and Vladimir Mayakovsky temporarily made this the official school of communistic art. The futuristic school of Igor Severyanin, founded 1911, extolled the Ego, man as quintessence of the universe and God as the shadow that man throws into Eternity. This, too, is part of the school which united in its poems pictures that dispersed like clouds and rhythms that hovered loosely. In France the symbolists had done that, the ancestors of futuristic, non-realistic art.

The Soviet government dissolved all these artist groups in 1932 and pronounced Maxim Gorki's "Socialistic Realism" the sole sanctifying church. Shostakovitch, who had an open mind for modern spiritual trends, absorbed symbolistic and futuristic ideas. For that he was placed under interdiction as a "partisan of the decay and disintegration of bourgeois culture."

Of the futuristic art ideas constructivism remained the most fertile in Russia too. The machine spirit of the new age of steam and electricity had attracted Italian poets and painters, and the founder of futurism, Marinetti, had written "Novelle Elletriche." In 1915 Prampolini had painted constructivistic decorations for Marinetti's stage plays. Futuristic painters repeatedly painted aeroplanes circling in the air, and the futuristic revue "Novecento" glorified poetry and art that had their roots in sport machinery.

In 1924 a group formed in Soviet Russia that attempted to bring fiction into accord with the character of modern technical development and strove for "speed, economic energy distribution and efficacy" after the example of modern machinery. Art should be: "the maximum development of a theme," according to the theory of K. Zelinsky.

However, futuristic ideas — anti-romantic and anti-realistic everywhere—were not confined to Russia. They were propagated in England and in the United States of America as well. In London in 1914 the painter and writer Wyndham Lewis propagated manifestos by Ezra Pound and the French sculptor Henri Gaudier-Brzeska which opposed naturalism and impressionism. As far as Gaudier-Brzeska was concerned, Greek sculpture constituted naturalistic art and belonged in the garbage pile. Wyndham called this new art trend: "the new vortex plunging to the heart of the present" —vorticism.

In the United States similar movements went by the firm name of imagism. The adepts of this school considered the material of poetry as visual pictures which, loosely connected, emerged from the rhythmic current. In 1912 Ezra Pound was the leader of this group; he was succeeded in 1914 by Amy Cowell. Here, too, was an irrational, symbolistic anti-realistic art movement.

At the extreme left wing of these groups that obtained their watchwords from futuristic headquarters marched the little troop of Dadaists from 1917 on. This group, followers of Tristan Tzara, restrains all logical association between thoughts and expression and proclaims absolute freedom of form and substance.

After the war all these movements flow into the sur-realism of André Breton. They all have the same aim: art not as reflection of nature and man, but as portrait of a higher sphere; liberation of unrational and unconscious spiritual forces in the artistic act.

Even where art glorifies the modern machine age, it employs its constructions for the portrayal of unreality, and the steel machinery for the picturization of an unreal world. All these artistic trends oppose romanticism as being an untrue and phrase-like emotion. "Uccidiamo il chiaro della luna" (Let us kill the light of the moon) Marinetti called to his followers.

Realism no longer satisfied the young generation which, unlike Zola, did not find greatness and strength in the real world, but only inanimation and dissatisfaction. Playing the fool, one searched for a new intrinsic value and a new meaning of the world, ample proof that this young generation of pre-war years found the present unsatisfactory despite all its technical marvels.

The abstract arts, the geometrization of world phases, and the futuristic trends spread across the whole globe, and every important art of the present was tied in with these universal movements. Even the grotesque scions of the futuristic movement have some import yet as protest against romantic sentiment and against realistic portrayals. They reveal the moods of despair, revolt and destructiveness that come to the surface even before the start of the war, and that increase during the war, flooding the entire globe after the war.

In music the anti-romantic mood turns to glorification of noise music as proclaimed by the Italian painter Luigi Russolo as music of the future in his manifesto "L'arte di rumori." Among other things this manifesto declares: "It is necessary to penetrate the limited circle of pure tones and to gain the unlimited diversity of 'tone sounds.' We will intone those various sounds and arrange them harmonically and rhythmically." This idea of noise music also played a certain part in the music of the period between the two world wars—particularly in the compositions of Edgar Varese— and Stravinsky was as great a pioneer in the field of tone sounds as he was in many other fields.

Noise music is the anti-pole of romantic music. The romantic timbre was sensual and gay-colored. In noise music it is practically faded and withered. Its poetical mood and picturesque coloring have turned to primitive harshness. One stands on the opposite bank of the river that separates the land of romantic forests from the present. Noise music proclaims: Romanticism is dead.

II

The generation of young musicians growing up in European countries shortly before and during the war have common traits. As many different tongues as these young musicians speak, they nevertheless form an intellectual unit. None of them is interested in romanticism any more. For them the Wagnerian music drama, or the Liszt symphonic poem, is no longer a model for their work. The young artist generation is minus every pathos, suspicious of all great gestures and all pompous art, of the rustling orchestra in the operas, color play in music, of symphonic work with leitmotif, of the precious brocaded cloak that draped romantic music.

The old artistic values: splendor, lustre, pathos, had become theatrical tinsel for the young musicians, and did not correspond to the present: neither to the social needs and social conflicts, nor to the important factors of the present—the tendency for facts, exact science and the technical spirit of an extremely capitalistic era. This era had covered the face of the world with factories in which every machine was a wonder of exact thinking.

Igor Stravinsky, who understood this phase of European intellect better than anybody else, analyzed especially well the pomp of romanticism and particularly of the romantic orchestra. He speaks of "the unhealthy greed for orchestral opulence of today. It has corrupted the opinion of the audience. We have had enough of this orchestral dappling (Stravinsky declares as spokesman of the war generation of composers) and these thick sonorities; one is tired of being saturated with timbres and wants no more of all this overfeeding, which deforms the entity of the instrumental element by swelling it out of all proportions and giving it an existence on its own."

However, it was not just the grand romantic style of Wagner and Liszt that had become meaningless to the war generation, but the super-fine romance of the symbolists and impressionists as well. The precious dreams in words, colors and tones seemed just as empty to the young musicians as the pathetic declamations had become. One was ashamed of every sentiment, every emotion, and considered any emotional effect of art to be effeminate.

Again I will let Stravinsky speak for this young music generation: "Most people like music because it gives them certain emotions, such as joy, grief, sadness, an image of nature, a subject for day dreams or—still better—oblivion from 'every-day life.' They want a drug—'dope.' It matters little whether this way of thinking of music is expressed directly or is wrapped up in a veil of artificial circumlocutions. Music would not be worth much if it were reduced to such an end."

Stravinsky opposes "sentimentalism" in music: "the sentimental twaddle so often talked about Chopin, Beethoven and even about Bach: tedious commentaries on side issues of music." He opposes "sentimentalism" of musical expression and maintains that it "always gives precedence to the purely sonorous scheme over elements of an emotional character."

The war generation expends a large part of its artistic energy in removing from music all emotion, all subjective sentiment, all delicacy which the Rousseau epoch put into the music. Werther's tears, the sentimentality of Klopstock's and Lamartine's era, the emotional revelry of Rousseau's time had been just as unfashionable as the dreams of the romantic period. Into the place of the emotional stepped the motorial, the motion of tones per se, music as sounding machine with purring wheels. One barricaded oneself behind the glaring and the bizarre, in order to conceal sentiment, and soft emotions were ridiculed. One preferred to play clown, rather than display one's grief.

This escape of young musicians to motorial, blaring or mocking music led them to jazz in the last war year. The jazz that came to Europe in 1918 was "anti-waltz" music. The waltz that invited Europe to the dance after the Napoleonic wars was romantic, sentimental and emotional. Jazz was ironic, vital, without any sentimentality, and blaring. In the waltz the sensitive melodies sang and tempted the dancing couples to embrace. In jazz the wind instruments shrieked and cut grotesque faces.

Clarinets and saxophones sneered with grinning passages. The trumpet projected shrill, extremely high tones into the air. The double-bass threw rattling pizzicati into the raging and bleating. Trombones quacked strangely with muted sounds. And the percussion instruments were being worked by a Negro, showing his white teeth in a laughing face. He hit the timpani, large and small drums, wood-blocks and cinellas, grinned and made a lot of noise and imparted an exciting primitive rhythm to the music.

This animal music, filled with vitality, had reached New York and Chicago from the saloons of New Orleans and now was in full swing at the elegant hotels and night clubs of London, in the bars of Montmartre and Montparnasse in Paris. Its brutal rhythm, its grating sound conquered the war-tired European world.

The first important composer to adapt jazz to serious music was Igor Stravinsky. He himself described the effect of jazz on his imagination, and in his autobiography he talks about "the passion I felt at that time for jazz, which burst into my life so suddenly, when the war ended. At my request a whole pile of this music was sent to me, enchanting me by its truly popular appeal, its freshness and the novel rhythm. . . . These impressions suggested the idea of CREATING A COMPOSITE PORTRAIT of this new dance music, giving the creation the importance of a concert piece. . . . So I composed 'Rag-Time' for 11 instruments, wind, string, percussion and an Hungarian cymbalum."

This music of Starvinsky's was first heard in 1919 at the Paris Opera during a Koussevitsky concert. In the same year Stravinsky completed the "Piano-Rag-music" which was dedicated to Arthur Rubinstein and was to try out all "percussion possibilities of the piano." Following the model of the jazz piano, the piano is treated as percussion instrument, as drum and xylophone.

In "Histoire d'un soldat" Stravinsky's princess dances in addition to the waltz a tango and ragtime; and this was only 1918. Even before the era of jazz the romantic waltz had become a subject for ridicule in Stravinsky's eyes. In the "Easy Pieces for Piano" that were composed 1915–1917 and that later were transformed into the two Suites for Orchestra, a kind of Strauss waltz gets an ironic parody treatment. Here the waltz becomes half abstract, half grotesque. In the orchestral arrangement the irony with which the waltz is treated becomes heavier yet. The waltz melody is not played by the sentimental waltz violin; the flute and the shrill piccolo blow it, while clarinets and bassoons play the accompaniment.

Everything sounds distorted, giving the impression of a sweet dessert spiced with cayenne pepper. The witty waltz caricature is dedicated to Eric Satie, the great ironicist.

As of Stravinsky, one can speak of Darius Milhaud and his jazz epoch. In 1919 Milhaud heard an American Negro band in London and, after overcoming his first repulsion, he was enthused. "Every evening I sat close to the orchestra to watch how it was done. In 1920 when I came to New York, I went to Harlem. I read books, I bought discs—the Black Swan records—and I brought them home and studied them and made use of special effects."

The "Shimmy for Jazz Band" and three "Rag Caprices" for piano are documents to prove Milhaud's jazz enthusiasm. In 1920 Milhaud's "Cinema-symphony on South American Airs," "Le

Boeuf sur le toit" was first performed, in which jazz and tango rhythms accompany the grotesque figures of the American speak-easy. In 1923 Milhaud's ballet: "La creation du monde" that included percussion music and jazz rhythms was taken on tour through Europe and America by the Swedish Ballet.

Tango music is also contained in the ballet with voice by Milhaud, entitled "Salade." The composer had studied this rhythm at the jungle source in Brazil.

After this jazz epoch, though, Milhaud no longer sought inspiration in the syncopated rhythms, blaring tones and the drums of jazz. "Jazz after that (Milhaud explains later) never interested me at all, but from it a rhythmic freedom remained." This is the way one disowns a mistress of whom one is ashamed and to whom one owes beautiful memories.

Milhaud's friend and fellow-combatant, George Auric, also paid homage to jazz with a foxtrot entitled "Adieu New York," and Ravel included the "Blues" in his violin sonata, and other jazz patterns in his ballet "L'enfant et les sortilèges."

The jazz rhythms danced across the Rhine and into the music of Paul Hindemith—in the "Klaviersuite 1922." They inspired the versatile Ernst Krenek. In his "Toccata and Chiaconne" for piano Krenek places the classic-solemn fugue and the new profane foxtrot side by side. The adagio of the fugue begins with "most profound expression" and "very soulful" and the foxtrot ridicules the fugue theme "vulgar."

Krenek's opera "Der Sprung ueber den Schatten" (The jump across the shadow) is constructed on a foxtrot foundation. Another Krenek opera, the sketch "Heavyweight" (1928) draws a caricature with blues and tango milongas of the dictator Ochsenschwanz, who is a boxing champion. In the opera "Life of Orestes" (1930) jazz is even combined with the marble pillars of the Acropolis, and the marble girls of the Erechtheion have to listen to these modern rhythms. Street singers with monocles, and a hero in knicker-bockers promenade through the portals of the Propylaeum and the classic age learns jazz dances instead of Pindar hymns.

Since 1927 Krenek's opera "Johnny Spielt Auf" had been played all over the globe. In this opera an animal-like Negro violinist and a sensitive composer are rivals, and the jazz fiddler conquers the elegant white woman and the whole world. On stage one finds hotel lobby, automobile, film, streamliner; and in the modern world vacated by Nibelungen gods the jazz tunes of an up-to-date composer make themselves at home—a composer who replaces "Donna e mobile" with "Swannee River" as a hit tune.

Three years before Johnny and his jazz made music for the entire world, New York witnessed the first performance of Gershwin's "Rhapsody in Blue," the date being February 12, 1924. One year prior Aaron Copland's concerto for piano and orchestra had been peformed.

After having set the fantasy of modern musicians all over Europe in syncopated rhythm, jazz had returned to its native country where it was introduced into serious music by Gershwin, Copland and by John Alden Carpenter (in the pantomime "Crazy Cat" and in the symphony "Skyscraper"). After a period of impressionistic languidness, the strong, vital rhythm of jazz was adopted greedily.

The war generation of musicians was not captivated just by the rhythmic vitality of jazz. Something of the magic effect that the dance produced among primitive tribes had remained in jazz music. The dance of primitive peoples conjures up the clouds in the sky, it lures the wild animals and it increases fertility when the drums begin to sound and the primitive man goes into a frenzy and dances in mystic enchantment.

After four years spent in a blood bath, the world needed this stimulation, the intoxication and the elemental fascination. The music of this world required the strong rhythmic incentives for the revitalization of its worn-out nerves. The young musicians had grown tired of the fine nerve moods. This trend was best characterized by Milhaud who wrote: "I sought a robust music, I wished to avoid the mannerisms of outworn idioms, of pastel shades and sentimental harmonies. I had a horror of useless detail and of unnecessary developments."

The young French composers as much as the German Paul Hindemith sought in music more vitality, more aggressive force than Claude Debussy's super-refined art possessed. In this state of mind the rhythmic liveliness, the energetic noise and the harshness of jazz considered a new stimulating art element. After 1918 jazz acted like a fertility charm for serious music.

The new war generation was unromantic, and so was jazz. One grew tired of the large orchestra dressed in ermine and purple, and the jazz orchestra was minus adornments. Each instrument went its own way. There were no blends and no transitions. Woodwinds opposed brass instruments, and percussion instruments led their own existence. Clarinets and saxophones sounded sharp, trumpets and trombones shrill. The violins that had danced like elves in the romantic orchestra of Mendelssohn, that glowed like fire and rustled like the forest in Wagner's orchestra—they almost vanished behind the noisy, grimacing wind instruments.

There was no tone area in this orchestra and no expanded harmonies; only spasmodic, gesticulating, forcefully drawn lines. It was no coincidence that Igor Stravinsky, having become familiar with the jazz orchestra, composed his "Histoire d'un soldat" for an orchestra that consisted of only four wind instruments (clarinet, bassoon, cornet and piston trombone), two string instruments (violin and counter bass) and percussion instruments (1918). The wind instruments are preponderant, as in the jazz orchestra, and the percussion instruments play the same important part as they do in the jazz band.

The soldier is accompanied to Hades by the percussion.

Stravinsky's orchestra is not a jazz band, but it is inspired by the jazz orchestra. It is something of an idealization of the jazz orchestra, and as such it is employed in the following Stravinsky compositions, in which again the wind instruments are preponderant: the symphonies for wind instruments (1920), the octet for wind instruments and the concerto for piano and wind instruments (1923/24).

Before Stravinsky, Richard Strauss and Arnold Schoenberg had approached the chamber orchestra from an entirely different side. The small, artful orchestra in "Ariadne on Naxos" (1912) is a romantic chamber orchestra. It serves color and delicate light play. Arnold Schoenberg's chamber orchestra in "Kammersinfonie" (1906) serves a definite artistic purpose: the portrayal of thought constructions. The chamber orchestra of Stravinsky in "Histoire d'un soldat" wishes neither to produce costly colors, nor to concentrate the ideas. It wants to provide the story of the soldier with a wood-carving style. It wants to be hard, primitive. The tones are not supposed to blend and melt, but to stand directly next to each other. The orchestra should resemble those sketches that are sold at village fairs in wooden shacks: shrill, coarse, with rough lines and undiluted, loud colors.

When the soldier at the end of his story is accompanied to hell, one is reminded of the strong outlines of mediaeval danses macabres. The orchestra is an unromantic orchestra, a type of circus music of the jazz age.

The chamber orchestras of Milhaud and Hindemith are also descended from the jazz orchestra. The hammering and drumming, the thrashing and rhythmical noise-making of jazz was adopted by the war generation of composers as a means of unromantic expression. In Stravinsky's music percussion already plays an increasingly important part. In contrast to Strauss and Mahler, it does not serve coloring purposes. It is brutal rhythm, elemental life, it releases primitive forces in music.

Even the piano, used by Chopin and Schumann, Liszt and Scriabin as an instrument for expressing romantic dreams, is transformed into a percussion instrument by Stravinsky.

Right behind Stravinsky follows Paul Hindemith, as usual, with his "Klaviersuite 1922." He provided the last movement of this work with the following instruction: "Don't take into consideration what you learned in your piano lesson. Don't ponder too long whether you have to strike the key with your fourth or your sixth finger. Play the piece very wild, but always strictly in rhythm, like a machine. Consider the piano here as an interesting sort of percussion, and handle it accordingly."

Next to Stravinsky, though, all the other composers appeared poor in percussion fantasy. Within him is the Russian primitive force of rhythm. In his "Sacre du printemps" is a mythical grandness of rhythm, in "Les Noces" popular primitive power.

Even in songs Stravinsky's rhythmic effects are grand. In the "Four Russian Songs," composed in 1918–1919, the same piano that in the romantic period often sounded like a mandolin in

Schumann works, and like a harp in Liszt compositions, is a kind of kettle-drum.

Next to Stravinsky Darius Milhaud is most inventive in the exploitation of the timpani and the drums. In the stage music that Milhaud wrote for the Claudel adaptation of Aeschylus' "Oreste," the percussion instruments describe the sinister menacing fate, the wild passion, the destructive force of the tragic. The first piece of the triology, "Agamemnon" (1913), he titled: "Drama with support of percussion instruments"; the second part, "The Choephores," was: "Drama, chorus, percussion and orchestra"; the third part, "The Eumenides" (started in 1917, completed in 1923), was composed for large orchestra with sixteen percussion instruments and chorus. Dull drumming and hammering gives Milhaud's declamatory choruses a frightful background of storm clouds laden with tragic forces. In the ballet "Salade," too, Milhaud accompanies the spoken words with percussion rhythms, and, similarly, he accompanies the recitation and choral singing with percussion instruments in his opera "Christophe Colomb."

Richly tuned percussion instruments drone in Milhaud's music to the ballet "L'Homme et son désire," drums, tambourine, triangle, tom-tom and castagnettes. Milhaud is not imbued with the elemental force of Stravinsky, whose rhythmic sense is derived from the primitive power of the Russian people; he is a clever man who seeks and finds primitivity where all primitive music originated in jungles and in caves: among drums and timpani, whence the voices of demons resounded terribly.

The jazz drummer of today is the successor to the primitive witch doctor who used the drum to conjure up spirits. The drums and timpani of today are descendants of primitive drums that brought dancers to a frenzy with their magic tone, and the composers who let the percussion instruments rumble around 1918 wanted to banish demons like their predecessors in the African bush. Jazz was the magic dance of a profoundly stirred, frightened world.

Around 1918 the effects of jazz were felt in serious music everywhere. The contrapuntal independence of the voices was promoted by jazz music, in which saxophone, trumpet and clarinet went their own way side by side and each of these instruments attempted as blaringly as possible to assert itself. The so-called "polytonality," whereby each voice plays in its own key, most certainly was inspired by jazz. Since 1913 Milhaud first developed polytonality systematically.

Music making with smaller tone steps than the half-tones was also advanced by jazz. But most particularly it was the travesty in jazz music, the glare, distortion and grimacing of the tones, the parody-like laughing and grinning of the music that was welcomed as an anti-toxin against romantic exuberance. The young generation no longer believed in lofty sentiments, and was suspicious of sweet phrases. It grew up in a world that tore itself to pieces despite a lot of big talk.

These young people were surrounded by death and destruction, and complete bankruptcy of all declamations of human dignity and humanity, progress and culture. Such experiences could only produce an aversion against everything that was emotional in music. Thus music after 1918 was driving closer to the mechanical, to inanimation, to rattling tone movement and to music as objective figure, not as subjective mood. In no composer did this turn produce such intelligent and individual music as in Igor Stravinsky.

III

All the composers who developed in Europe during the first world war were united in their credo that music is the pure art of tone motion. In France this credo had first been proclaimed by Eric Satie. He was lauded by Stravinsky for having played a meritorious part in French music: "By opposing to the vagueness of a decrepit impressionism a language precise and firm, stripped of all pictorial embellishments." The group of "Six"—Honegger, Auric, Poulence, Tailleferre, Durey and Darius Milhaud—adopted this gospel with enthusiasm.

Each of them utilized it in his own personal manner; Milhaud with brilliant, robust, easy flowing invention, Auric and Poulence with polished French esprit, with wit and irony; Honegger with objective energy that shapes sparsely and forcefully. His half impressionistic work "Pacific 231" already has an energy of rhythm that is usually alien to impressionism. In this orchestra piece Honegger portrays the myth of the modern locomotive; the breathing and storming advance of the machine, the rhythmic motion of the pistons, the rolling of the wheels, the hissing, steaming steel monster of the industrial century and the iron dragon "three hundred tons heavy, roaring through the night at 80 m.p.h."

Honegger's oratorios ("Le roi David") are not endowed with biblical pathos, but they have constructive force; the people of the biblical age are modeled hard and sharp, and action and dialogue have the urgency of a modern fact report.

Among the "Six" Milhaud was most affable to literary inspirations. Authors and poets gave his musical creation an intellectual background. First it was the poet Francis James who influenced Milhaud and of whom Milhaud says with praise: "He led me out of the symbolists' fogs and revealed to me a new world to be captured merely by opening one's eyes."

There followed Paul Claudel who, according to his own words led him "to the threshold of an art alive and sane, ready to submit to the influence of those powers which shake the human heart." In 1913 he set to music Claudel's satire "Protée," not as an archaeological imitation but as play of modern intellect and circus humor.

In the same year he began the composition of the Claudel translation of "Oreste" by Aeschylus. The peak of collaboration with Claudel was reached in the opera "Christophe Colomb" (1930).

After his return to Paris from Brazil in 1919, Milhaud was as much influenced by the intelligent paradoxons of Jean Cocteau as were all the other members of the "Six" group. Milhaud composed Cocteau's sketch "Le Boeuf sur le toit" in 1920. For use by the Russian Ballet Cocteau wrote for him the text to "Train Bleu" with gigolos, golfers, and tennis players at the Riviera (1924) and for the Opera Comique he wrote the text of a gloomy opera of one hour's duration: "Le Pauvre matelot" (1927). Only four persons appear in this opera, and the action is strong and forcefully concentrated.

The opera is a sketch-like nocturne wherein the returning sailor, unrecognized by his wife, is murdered by her and her lover. The orchestra is chamber orchestra. The music is sparse, popularly primitive, like a wood-cut. All new impressions are registered by Milhaud with great sensitivity, whether it was the Brazilian dance music or jazz, the clouded tragedy of Aeschylus or the buffo mind of Aristophanes, naturalistic or fantastic sketches or short operas.

Milhaud is a lively, mobile mind who loves to experiment. Poulence and Auric are finer and show better taste, but Milhaud is more powerful.

It was of great significance for the development of music in France that the French writers, painters and composers found a focal point and a common toiling ground since 1908 in the Russian Ballet of Diaghileff. The modern trends in the various art fields met in the performances of the Russian Ballet, and modern artistic ideas streamed out of the art studios in Montparnasse into the work rooms of the musicians and poets.

Diaghileff had a sixth sense for the important artists of tomorrow. He had discovered Stravinsky whose collaboration with the Russian Ballet began in 1906 and lasted to 1929. Diaghileff had heard "Firework" and the "Scherzo fantastico" by Stravinsky at a Siloti concert in Paris and immediately engaged the young Russian composer for his Ballet.

In 1908 he was commissioned to orchestrate two pieces in a Chopin ballet which was danced by Pavlova, Karsavina and Nijinsky (Les Sylphides). From then on Stravinsky composed a number of his greatest works for the Russian Ballet: in 1910 "Firebird" with Karsavina in the title role; 1911 "Petruschka," 1913 the "Sacré du printemps," 1920 "Pulcinella" and "Chant du Rossignole," 1922 "Renard," 1923 "Les Noces," 1928 "Apollo Musagetes."

There was of course opposition to the new music: Karsavina refused to dance in "Firebird"—the "horrible thing"; in Monte Carlo the Russian colony, headed by a general, requested that "Petruschka" no longer be presented; the orchestra in Vienna found the "Petruschka" music unplayable, and the first performance of "Sacré du printemps" at the Theatre Champs Elysée in Paris was a giant scandal.

Still, the performances of the Russian Ballet sent Stravinsky's fame spreading across the globe. The Russian Ballet was also the

starting point of Stravinsky's friendship with Picasso, who painted
the decorations for "Pulcinella," for Diaghileff had also acquired
this genius for the Ballet. In 1917 Picasso painted the decorations
for "Parade" by Cocteau-Satie. Dances, action, music and colors
all contained the spirit of the present.

Picasso also designed the scenery for De Falla's "Le Chapeau
tricorne"; for "Cuadro Flamenco," and for Satie's "Mercure," and
he painted the curtain for "Le train bleu" by Cocteau-Milhaud.

Poets, painters and musicians got together at rehearsals and discussed the artistic problems of the day. New art theories, new
formulas, new watchwords rose up in the air like cigaret smoke.

The modern artists of all Europe made the Russian Ballet their
headquarters: Frenchmen like Ravel, Satie, Milhaud, Poulence,
Auric, Sanguet, Florent Schmitt; Russians like Stravinsky and
Prokofieff; the German Richard Strauss who wrote his "Josefs-
legende" for the Russian Ballet in 1914 and whose "Till Eulen-
spiegel" was presented in 1916 with decorations by R. Edm. Jones.
There were also the two Spanish artists De Falla and Albeniz; the
Englishman Lord Berners and the Italians Respighi and Rieti.

If one reads off the names of painters who designed costumes
and decorations for the Russian Ballet, one seems to be reciting the
captions of a history of modern painting: Matisse, Derain, Bracque,
Picasso, Roualt, Chirico.

The whole evolution of painting from the late-impressionists to
surrealism, cubism and constructivism took place on the stage of the
Russian Ballet. In this intellectual atmosphere Stravinsky grew up,
and here he received his strongest inspirations.

But the Russian Ballet was also a source of artistic inspiration
for the group of "Six." When Karsavina, Pavlova, Fokine, Nijinsky and the other artists of the Russian Ballet danced in the Paris
Opera, that gala house became the center of European modern arts.

IV

The European withdrawal from romanticism, from the great
romantic orchestra and romantic color art found a particularly
vigorous exponent in Germany in the person of Paul Hindemith.

Hindemith was musician, and nothing but musician. He does not have the intellectual education of Milhaud and is not associated with literaries, painters and ballet dancers such as Jean Cocteau, Picasso and Diaghileff, the way the Paris group of Satie followers was. Neither did he live in a metropolis, as did the French composers, where the spiritual trend of the time was felt in every cafe.

Hindemith emerged directly from the orchestra. His instrument was the viola which is no primadonna like the violin that is always in the foreground. At the viola stand he fiddled right in the center of the orchestral tones. All around him sounded violin melodies, woodwind passages, droning bass tones of the counterbasses, the smashing sounds of the trumpets, and all these sounds were a whole ringing world to his ears, like the noises of the forest to the hunter who knows every bird call and every animal sound in the woods.

Old Bach, playing music with wife and children in his home of a Sunday, loved to sit at the viola. One sits so nice "in the midst of harmony," he would say. And so Hindemith, too, sat "in the midst of harmony."

The roaring and promiscuous sounding of tones was the music he understood. Music to him meant: creation of tones, formation of sounding figures; nothing else. For a musician of his type there is nothing nicer than to invent tones and to unite them. To make verses in music, or paint with music, would never occur to such a man.

For a viola player who played his own voice in the midst of sounding orchestra parts, music was not chiefly an art of harmony motion as it was for impressionistic musicians. For Debussy and composers of his school the chords had been the carriers of mood. The world melted in mist, the air was the shadow from which objects emerged, the sky was covered with clouds. All exactitude of musical lines dissolved like writing on a blotter. But a viola player like Hindemith wove his musical lines at the loom of the orchestra right into the colorful design.

He knew the value of such determined, clear lines. For him music was above all a play of lines. In the music were entwined expressive, characteristic, lively lines. The means of joining these lines was called counterpoint. Therefore to Hindemith counterpoint became the import of music. His contrapuntal knowledge is great and can only be compared to that of Max Reger. But Reger's counterpoint was in the German style, heavy, massive, oftentimes bloated. Hindemith, however, was no clumsy Bavarian but a sanguine Rhinelander who came from a district where German and French blood were intermingled strongly. His counterpoint is masterful, light and playful. He treats the contrapuntal binding of musical lines like a tennis player the ball. His technique is that of a sportsman who is accustomed to overcome difficulties with a firm, light hand.

The musical lines that he interweaves in counterpoint fashion are not bound by triad harmonies, they are entirely independent and free. They have keenly drawn contours and in all of them there is fresh, temperamental, fanciful life. Sometimes their freshness possesses a bit of the street-arab quality, something new in music.

Into this fresh music Paul Hindemith draws everything that was created or attempted in present-day music in the way of new forms and new techniques. Atonality, motoric music, the jazz-like chamber orchestra, the "objective" opera, the so-called "utility music"; all modern art programs and watchwords stimulate Hindemith's composing. It was Stravinsky in particular who always urged him on to new experiments.

All these new techniques, forms and styles or style fashions are wood for Hindemith the musician, which is burned in his fireplace and crackles merrily.

Hindemith has lively appreciation for the present and for modern life. He felt obviously comfortable in the bustle of this modern life. Street and machine noise, crowds of people in the new cities, rapid traffic, cars, electricity either running through wires or floating through the ether, are all contained in the background of his music. The composer himself designed the cover page for "Klaviersuite 1922": a city of today, illuminated by arclights; cars, buses, bicyclists, trolleys, human throngs.

In Hindemith's opera "Neues vom Tage" the typewriters rattle in the office of a marriage broker, the chorus sings the praises of a modern bathroom while the heroine is sitting in the bathtub, and the big love duet pokes fun at the ecstatic style of Wagner.

Hindemith was not led to modernity by any intellectual inclinations, but solely by his lively disposition. He has the true talent of a raconteur who can retell every new story and every new event with spirit and gusto. He is interested in odd objects and stories from near and far because he enjoys combining such stories with his own inventions and because, like all lively people who are young inside, he needed new material all the time for entertainment and conversation.

Paul Hindemith experienced only a brief period of romantic youth during which he preferred rare colors, precious chords, select orchestral tones and strong emotional expression. All these qualities can be found in his two expressionistic one-act operas: "Moerder, Hoffnung der Frauen," composed to a text by Oscar Kokoschka, and "Sancta Susanna," written to a libretto by Stramm. He soon transferred his affection to music of contrapuntal lines for which the various patterns of chamber music were the natural reservoir.

This music had the rhythm of a new age that was no longer dreamy, but active. Hindemith's lines had a motor like automobiles, and were set in motion by it. Right in the first string quartet by Hindemith, by which he first became known in distant circles, the first theme plunges "lively and forcefully" into the fill of life. The four instruments dash forwards unisono. The rolling tone figures have life, vitality, energy. Strong rhythmic chords strengthen the freshness of the music.

Under the influence of Stravinsky's music the rhythmic liveliness increased even more in later compositions of Hindemith's, and music changed completely into an art of motive energy. However, the joy of rhythmic motion had been inherent in Hindemith from the start. It is absolutely natural in a violinist whose fingers slide over the strings.

Unlike other musicians of his age, Hindemith had never experienced an impressionistic period. Debussy never influenced him; not even when he set to music Rilke's "Marienleben" poems, the dark mysticism of which seemed to demand music in the Debussy style. He composed these songs in a pure line style. The lines of the solo voice move completely independent of the piano lines. There is something architectural in this lineal construction of music that is reminiscent of Gothic chapels with the flowing lines of the pillars and the massive work of the windows. The portrayal of Maria in the temple is reproduced in the strict form of the passacaglia which builds the temple arcs like architecture in the frescoes of Fra Angelico.

Hindemith's enjoyment of music expends itself in independent voices. In his "Concerto for Orchestra" opus 38, each of the string parts has its own theme, each theme is of the strongest vivacity, everywhere the rhythm is keen and the rhythmic motifs run through the parts, emerging once here, once there, always fresh and forceful.

Polyphonic music, which is given so much vitality by the marked rhythmic motifs and by the roulades and trills, is not studied but invented naturally, as though contrapuntal phrasing were not work but pleasure. The music abounds in joie de vivre and is written by a man to whom music is as natural as breathing is to other people.

The greatness of Hindemith's musical talent can best be judged by comparison with that other composer who also stands actively in the bustling throng of the present and always brings merchandise in the most up-to-date style to market: Ernst Krenek.

The development of Krenek goes parallel with that of Hindemith. Like Hindemith, he adopts new intellectual vogues and utilizes them. Again like Hindemith, he is productive in many fields, in chamber and orchestral music and in the opera. He has an open mind for innovations, for music without literary or artistic background and without the gay lacquer of orchestral tones; for contrapuntal lineal style; for atonal harmonics; for the small concert orchestra, and for the objective "Concerto Grosso."

In opera especially he is always in the "avant garde," and he changes his materials and styles in conformity with the changing modern watchwords. In "Zwingburg" he wrote a cantata of extremely strong revolutionary mass mood, in "Orpheus and Eurydice" a symbolistic opera, in "Sprung ueber den Schatten" the first foxtrot opera. He wrote opera burlesques and the jazz opera "Johnny Spielt Auf," and his latest work was the grandly plotted "Karl der Fuenfte."

And yet, how much richer is Paul Hindemith in music. How much intellectuality is missing in the far more narrow talent of

Krenek, how much dryness. With Hindemith it is always a genuine musician who writes music, whether it be operas or chamber music, or music for a flute or songs with viola accompaniment, whether a cantata on Lindbergh's flight or a piece for children: "Wir bauen eine Stadt" (We are building a city). He always composes in fullness with good, mediocre and insignificant ideas, but always equally joyous and equally fresh. He resembles those good German drinkers who early mornings have their glass of beer, stroke their beard gayly, gulp down the blond beverage with gusto and, at sunset, sit down before another beer with the same enjoyment.

Such is the temperament of Paul Hindemith and, in an age of intellectual artists, it is an especially refreshing trait. The doctrine of music that should be naught but music certainly had more ingenious exponents in Schoenberg, Stravinsky and Bela Bartok than in Hindemith. But how convincing this Hindemith music writing is! How natural! How little touched by modern doubts and modern lack of sensuality! Whatever Hindemith wrote in unimportant music had as much vitality as his good music. His talent consists of his musical temperament and his liveliness. He is never tired, and never persists in routine.

The impression made by Hindemith's music was never better characterized than by Stravinsky, who wrote: "The appearance of Hindemith in the musical life of our day is very fortunate, for he stands out as a whole one and an illuminating principle among so much obscurity."

V

In Italy D'Annunzio's art also governed the work of composers before and during the war. The splendor of D'Annunzio's word tones, the marble lustre of his verses, the glorification of art as a solemn, quiet temple area outside of life, the cultus of unusual sentiments had a strong influence upon most Italian composers between 1910 and 1914.

These symbolistic ideas, derived from Huysmans and Baudelaire, from Stephan Mallarmé and Verhaeren, from Dante Gabriel Rossetti and Ruskin, were joined by the national ideas of D'Annunzio, by his praise of the Italian past which had left its mark in all Italy in cathedrals and palaces, in marble pillars and statues, and by his glorification of the Italian landscape and the Italian sea.

Composers such as Montemezzi and Zandonai and, especially unique and pensive, Ildebrando Pizetti, set D'Annunzio's verses to music between 1914 and 1918. During the same period the impressionism of Debussy came from France and was adopted eagerly as a new art of fine, subtle color. Even the robust Rimsky-Korsakoff pupil Ottorino Respighi mixed into his rich colors the delicate, diffused impressionistic shades and with them produced fine coloristic effects in his symphonic description of the fountains of Rome (Le fontane Romane).

The D'Annunzio circle, which included musicians like Pizetti, Perinello and Malipiero, at first showed interest in the other modern trends also. Francesco Malipiero employed free harmonics, and Alfredo Casella became the center of all modern musical ideas in Italy. The first to influence Casella's work were Gustav Mahler and Richard Strauss. Casella was an ardent admirer of the creative work of the titanically aspiring Jewish man who might well have reminded him of Leone Ebreo, the Italian predecessor of Spinoza.

Later he adopted the ideas of Debussy, Ravel and Schoenberg, and he united all these modern inspirations with the forms of old Italian concert music. His "Partita" uses the forms of the "Sinfonia" and "Passacaglia," and the chamber music instrumentation with several wind instruments, piano and strings is constructed after the instrumentation of Italian chamber music in the seventeenth century. The method of composing with the varying tone groups, the solo instruments, the rattling of lively figure work, is a part of Italian Baroque; the themes are stylized Vivaldi music; but the middle parts are voices of the Stravinsky era.

This modernist is Italian, and the noise and tumult of the Italian street inspires his music every bit as much as Vivaldi's and Corelli's Baroque music and Stravinsky's modern music. The rushing strettas of Rossini and the Italian folk song sound into his music. All these various elements are blended in his music, and the pleasure in pure music-making keeps them together.

In Italy, too, modern music, tone play and tone motion in

harmonic freedom, had gained a foothold, and in Italy, too, it was the composer generation that had been born around 1880—Respighi 1879, Pizetti 1880, Zandonai 1883, Casella 1883, Malipiero 1880—who assumed leadership before the war. The year 1880 was a turning point in the evolution of music.

In 1881 Stravinsky had been born, likewise Bela Bartok; Alban Berg in 1885. In all Europe it was the generation of 1880 that liberated music from the last remnant of romanticism.

From France the new tendencies of music reached Spain. As in Italy, it was first Debussy's impressionism that fascinated Spanish musicians by its color play, its modulated harmonies and its atmospheric moods. Isaac Albeniz moved to Paris in 1893 in order to be closer to Debussy, and Manuel de Falla also traveled to Debussy's city in order to enjoy the company of Debussy and Ravel.

In his "Nocturnes for piano and orchestra" (1916) de Falla portrayed the Spanish gardens in the twilight of impressionism. In the stage play "El Amor Brujo," which pictures gypsy life and combines dance, pantomime and song harmonically, he employs the modern chamber music orchestra. He employs the same orchestra in the ballet "Le Chapeau Tricorne" that was first performed in Paris by the Russian Ballet in 1919 with decorations by Picasso. During the war the young Spanish musicians introduced into Spain's music the Milhaud mingling of scales, the Schoenberg atonality, the Stravinsky rhythmics.

In Poland Karol Szymanowsky, a poetic, artful composer who mixed fine tones, turned to free harmonics. He too covered the road from Chopin and Scriabin to Richard Strauss and Debussy and from there to Stravinsky. A subtle musical intellect, he was a cosmopolitan composer with sensitive nerves and a curiosity for all new artistic experiments.

During the war Schoenberg, Scriabin and Stravinsky had increased their influence in England. The music of César Franck made a big impression, and the Russian Ballet regularly brought the modern French composers to London.

A new generation of musicians continued to attract more and more attention. The oldest in this group was Gustav Bolst, whose free treatment of dissonances and unusual rhythmics were as fascinating as his intellect and his philosophical, mystic inclinations. His "Jesus Hymn" treats a Greek Gnostic text with powerful harmonic means; the suite in seven movements, "The Planets" (1919) has a mystical ending.

Arthur Bliss is an experimental mind who likes to blend the solo voice that sings textless syllables with his orchestra. This orchestra is also employed as a chamber orchestra (in "Rout") and in the piano concerto it is spiced with Stravinsky-like percussion instruments. Lord Berners, a pupil of Casella, was accepted by the Russian Ballet into its roster of modern composers on the virtue of a performance of his ballet "Le triomphe de Neptune" (1928).

VI

Until the revolution of 1917 broke out, Russia was under the powerful influence of the romantic national school which had its headquarters in Petersburg. Here, from 1871 on to the year of his death in 1908, Rimsky-Korsakoff had instructed whole generations of young Russian musicians in composition. Glazounoff, Liadoff, Tscherepnin and Stravinsky and, for a while, Prokofieff were his pupils, and his pupil Glazounoff became his successor in 1909.

Rimsky-Korsakoff handed down to his pupils the magic tricks of coloristic fantasy which in his case was endowed with gorgeous oriental colors, the colors of Persian rugs and gayly glazed vases. The orchestra technique of Wagner, Liszt and Berlioz was taught in the Petersburg school, and in addition the romance of Russian folk songs, the gospel of a music in which the Russian landscape and the Russian nation are suffused with colorful orchestral light.

During the same time, from 1877 over a period of forty years Tanejeff taught in Moscow as successor to Tschaikowsky. Nikolai Medtner and Reinhold Gliere had graduated from this school and Scriabin had been Tanejeff's most brilliant pupil. The tendency of the Moscow school was a strong conservatism. Nikolai Rubinstein who had founded the Moscow Conservatory and was its first director until 1881, would have nothing to do not only with Liszt and Berlioz, but with Borodin, Rimsky-Korsakoff and Mussorgsky as well.

Tanejeff also declined Liszt, Wagner and Berlioz, and of the Russian "Five" he appreciated only Rimsky-Korsakoff. His Russian composers were Glinka and Tschaikowsky, whose friend he had been.

Instead of decorative color gloss as it was taught in Petersburg, passion, emotion and subjective experience were demanded of music in Moscow. That was Tschaikowsky's legacy that was preserved at the conservatory in Moscow.

In the pre-war period an artistic trend was coming to the fore in Russia's art life which in France was called "symbolism" or "decadence"; in Russia it was known as "formalism." This artistic school comprised all non-realistic tendencies from symbolism, that reveled in strong pictures and dark words, to futurism. Nietzsche, Maeterlinck and Baudelaire began to influence young poets and musicians. Balmont, Bryussoff, Vyachesleff, Mierezhkowsky and other poets expressed abstract thoughts and mystic ideas in words that were tone rather than figure.

In an article "Art as Medium" Schklovsky set forth the ideas of formalism as though it were a manifesto. According to him art was a system of artistic methods and means, form is the aim of art, and the more difficult the form, the greater the art. The artificial form renders comprehension of art works more difficult, thereby prolonging the artistic effect. "A work of art is equal to the sum of the processes used in it."

In music formalism meant a shifting of interest from musical portrayal and musical soul expression to technical problems. Formalism led away from romanticism. It turned as much against Scriabin's subjectivism as against Tschaikowsky's passion and Tschaikowsky's struggle against death and destruction of the individual. It contradicted the illustrative music of Rimsky-Korsakoff and the naturalistic expression of Mussorgski. Music that copies nature, as that of Richard Strauss and Debussy, had no more in common with the essentials of art than music that stormed in Byronic fashion.

With these ideas, which make the form the essential value of art and all details of a work of art a "grip" or "hold" in a large construction, (according to Schklovsky, Zirmunsky or Eichenbaum) music changes from subjective expression to objective formation.

Thus the intellectual movement in Russia goes parallel with the trends in France and Germany that diverged from romanticism, and is identical with the tendency that took Arnold Schoenberg and Igor Stravinsky to objective constructions.

Russian formalism has several interesting music personalities in its midst. One of them is Vladimir Rebikoff, whom the Russian musicologist Leonid Sabanejeff calls the "Satie of Russian music." Rebikoff had been a pioneer of modern music in Russia. Half joking, half in earnest, Rebikoff spoke of Scriabin and Debussy as "his successors."

He was the first of the Russian composers to end compositions on dissonances and to write chords in fifths and fourths. His opera "The Abyss," libretto by Leonid Andrejeff, is constructed entirely upon second chords, and his psychological portrait "Alpha and Omega" upon augmented triads. In his psychological pictures ("Slavery and Freedom," "Impulse and Act," etc.) Rebikoff tried to portray abstract thoughts, the way philosophical ideas are presented in small piano pieces, and psychological portraits in mimic ballets.

Rebikoff's songs are set to music after lyrics by Russian symbolistic poets (Balmont, Bryusoff, et al.). The unique musician for whom music was "a language of feelings, and feelings have neither form, nor laws, nor rules," died in 1922 during Russia's revolutionary wars.

Aleksey Stanchinsky (born 1889), a pupil of Tanejeff, turned from romanticism and impressionism to the objective forms of music material, just as formalism demanded. In his sketches for piano Stanchinsky combines the multiple-voice forms with the new harmonic forms of polytonality. Like Schoenberg's piano compositions, his too are hallucinations and, with Stanchinsky's increasing mental illness, they become more and more hypothetical. Geometry penetrated his fantasy. The musical constructions became increasingly abstract. His death has remained a mystery: it may

have been suicide or he may have been a victim of crime. When
the Bolsheviks came to power, the government published Stanchinsky's compositions.

New theories were handed down to the pupils by Boleslav
Jaworsky (born 1880) who surrounded this bizarre mystic. The
same gravity which, according to Newton, governs the fall and the
motion of heavenly bodies, works for Jaworsky in the groupings
of tones into scales. Tones gravitate to other tones according to the
rules of gravity, and gravitation forms musical systems just as it has
shaped world systems. Thus for Jaworsky too the weight of music
shifts to the structural, to shape and pattern.

Nikolay Roslavyets, who was born in 1880, the decisive year in
the development of modern music, also considers music mostly as
"organization of tonal matter." According to his doctrine there is
nothing chaotic behind the tones, no massing of sentiment, no
flowing of moods. Everything in the tones is simple and clear. They
are material for the composer who must work them as the watch-
maker or jeweler works his material. Music has to express not soul,
sentiment and passion, but thoughts. It should become organization, a "happy medium between an ornament and a chess problem."

Another work of organization are the chords, and like Schoenberg, Roslavyets sees no difference between consonances and dissonances. Dissonances are merely "sharp consonances."

A searcher of new, rare, different tones was Arthur Lurye
(born 1889) who was one of those musicians that experimented
with quarter tones. For him music was the portrayal of "forms in
the air" and akin to the art of etching since its lines form graphic
designs. During the revolution Lurye became "Musical Commissar,"
but he left Russia soon thereafter and fled to Paris.

Russia's most powerful musicians went abroad when the Soviet
Revolution broke out in 1917. Among them were Sergei Rachmaninoff and Nikolai Metner, Sergei Prokofieff and Igor Stravinsky.

Until his recent death in America, Rachmaninoff remained
faithful to a noble romanticism. His stars were Chopin, Liszt and
Tschaikowsky. He was the greatest master of the piano in the
present time, and to him it was still the old romantic instrument

that had tones for ecstasy, for radiance, for singing of the heart and for gleaming spirit.

Metner, a philosophical musician who set Nietzsche to music, composed almost exclusively for piano. A severe, austere and pensive musician, Metner saw design in music rather than colors. His fantasy inclines toward Gothic lines and formulas, a kind of Russian Brahms.

Prokofieff renounced impressionism and romance under the influence of Satie in Paris. The Liszt arpeggios that ripple like harps, and Chopin's melismata that gleam like a string of pearls were not to be found in Prokofieff's music as they still were in Rachmaninoff's. Prokofieff is neither ecstatic nor dreamy, but clear and forceful. Chromaticism, used by Chopin as musical expression of poetic-mellow emotions and by Debussy for the tone of hovering or melting mood, disappears and is replaced by simple diatonics.

All of Prokofieff's music contains clear rhythms and simple melodies, lively tempo, often humor and laughing. He is witty and alive, a musician without solemnity and without attitude, a composer with a fantasy that has no dreamy corners and no dark recesses and that lets the light stream in through many windows.

In opposition to romanticism Prokofieff placed a modern classicism such as Busoni had proclaimed. "There is a return to classic forms which I feel very much myself," declares Prokofieff. "I want nothing better, nothing more flexible or more complete than the sonata form, which contains everything necessary to my structural purpose."

In such classic forms it was that Prokofieff composed his "Classic Symphony" in 1917 during the Russian revolution. This was witty, lively, melodic music in which a modern composer imitates at least Haydn's serenity, if not his great soul.

When the colossal masses of Stravinsky's "Spring Rites" were invading Paris, the influence of Stravinsky's rhythms and barbaric percussion was very strong and dominated Prokofieff's "Scythian Suite" (1914). However, that influence had completely vanished. One is in a playful tone sphere in which there is neither seriousness and passion, nor soul; only spirit.

For the Russian Ballet Prokofieff composed the ballet "Chout"

(1919) and "Le Pas d'acier" (1927). In 1934 he returned to Russia. Here, in contact with his native soil, he found popular greatness and a strong, simple ballad tone in the music for the "Alexander Nevsky" film. The music of the picture "Lieutenant Kije" is imbued with flashing intellect, the music to "Peter and the Wolf," composed in 1936 for the children's theatre in Moscow, with easy humor.

Prokofieff's music has no transcendental background. He does not travel through the land of music laden down with trunks. He is wholly unencumbered and can easily get from one place to another. His whole secular music consists almost entirely of lively lines. The tonal quality, the magic of color, the poetic mood of the instruments have no particular role in this music. The poetic of the harmonies that was still great in Debussy, holds no interest for Prokofieff. He has technical spirit, and the simplicity of his music is a product of education. His classicism is not the creation of a classic imagination, it is the idea of an artist. It is the reaction of a modern musician toward the style of the impressionistic epoch. The classic forms are used for the facade of a modern house, the walls of which are smooth and minus ornaments and in which resides a brilliant man.

VII

Milhaud, Hindemith, Krenek, Casella, de Falla and Prokofieff are talents. They are all brilliant composers who are at home in their era and are stimulated by all spiritual and artistic trends of this era. They are technical talents who try out new forms and new expressive means as soon as these new technical media appear on the market. They are all great intellectuals, versatile and mobile, and thus the suitable composers for an epoch in which the last remnants of a magnificent classic and romantic past had been removed and where in several places excavations have been made for new music houses.

Next to so many vital, clever composers is the Hungarian Bela Bartok, a true genius, and, side by side with Arnold Schoenberg and Igor Stravinsky, the third great creative composer in the early twentieth century. His music absorbs less from the era than he places into the time out of his own fantasy. Composers like Milhaud, Hindemith and Prokofieff require continuously stimulation from their time in order to create. Milhaud is influenced by the literary trends in France; Hindemith by Stravinsky's new style forms; Prokofieff by the spirit of art in Paris.

Bela Bartok lived in a solitude, and went his own way. His mind was not mobile, but it was strong; it was not like wax that absorbs the impression of strange forms with ease, but rather like a signet ring that puts its own mark on every note. Era: for most talented composers before and during the world war that meant the summation of spiritual, literary, artistic movements in Europe. For Bela Bartok the same word meant the age in which he was living and working. For the talented composers the time is some-thing flowing, that carries ever new forms along. For Bela Bartok it was something permanent.

Bela Bartok is not to be considered a genius only because he has a spiritual pattern of his own and because the particular type of his musical imagination cannot be compared with any other type. He possesses not only the fantasy of a genius, but the lucidity of a genius as well. The music forms that Bartok created, his harmonies and his rhythm, were studied with intelligent keenness. His artistic world is not just a sphere of fantasy, but a world of logic. Bartok's artistic development like that of Arnold Schoenberg is without any arbitrariness, clear and sure. And again like Schoenberg, Bartok deserves praise for the moral courage with which he pursued his path into unknown regions of music without being deterred by ridicule and repudiation. Imagination, intelligence and morality are united in Bartok's work, as they are in every great art.

Bela Bartok's road led from Lisztic romance and impressionistic neo-romance to new music, which is motivated only by musical forces and which shapes objectively its sounding contents. Music without color decoration, without literary facade, without illustrat-ing tricks, without theatrical attitude; music that did not dissolve in subjective moods but was form and figure; music in which the sounding lines were not harmonically bound: that was the goal aspired to by the musical geniuses and, following them, by the musical talents of the pre-war era in diverse ways. That was the goal that Bela Bartok, fine and quiet, sought to attain in his own manner.

His path led through the Hungarian plains and across the Rumanian mountains, through poor peasant villages strewn along dusty highways with their gayly painted houses. In all these hamlets Bela Bartok collected folk songs and folk dances. The romanticists too had collected such folk songs and dances, and had included them in their art production. They were attracted to the folk song by the exotic quality of it, the naive mood, the simplicity of sentiment. When romantic composers introduced such folk tunes into their music, they covered the primitive music with the gay colors of the new era, with rustling piano or luxuriant orchestra tones. Franz Liszt had done that with the gypsy music in his "Hungarian Rhapsodies."

But Bela Bartok was no romanticist. He was not interested in the national quality of the folk song and folk dance, nor the primitivity, nor the local coloring of a definite landscape, but by their melodic and rhythmic qualities which will not be subordinated to the design of art music.

Within the folk song which he gathered in Hungary, in Roumania, in Slovakia and in Tunis there was a very strong and characteristic melodic line that was constructed differently from the art melodies which arose from a basic tone and returned to the basic tone and which, in classic music, had always been a circumlocution of harmonics. Many of these melodies were based on the ancient five-tone scale. Others circled around one or two tones. In most instances it was impossible to accompany these melodies with the usual major and minor chords. They belonged to a different system, were much richer and more individual melodically. Most important was the ever expressive and concentrated melody and, above all, the rhythm which was free rather than regular. The harmonic quality was less important; it resulted by itself out of the melody and out of the connection of horizontal lines.

In 1915 Bela Bartok published his "Roumanian Folk Dances" for piano, and his Hungarian peasant songs, in 1920 his Improvisations on Hungarian peasant songs. In the Roumanian folk dances the harmonies are colored in such a manner that the melodic structure becomes distinct. There are always only a few colored spots and lines, like the drawings and ornaments on the wooden chests of the peasants. Or the stamping rhythm is underlined, like in the "Roumanian Polka." When a melody is repeated, the accompanying chords alternate, thus placing the melody in a different light.

Bela Bartok found in folk songs and folk dances a primitive music with free melodies, harmonics and rhythmics, the basic elements of which had to be artistically developed and enhanced in order to attain new strong character music. Bela Bartok's entire musical creation may be considered an artistic re-formation of Hungarian folk song elements. He is the only one among the modernists whose music despite boldest innovations remains tied to folk music. Unlike romantic composers, Bartok does not consider the folk song a primitive form to which the educated composer stoops and which he adopts, feeds and clothes as though it were a foundling. It is the source of his strength, the great nature whence all forms are descended. Elemental life, the elementary force of the world.

Above all it is rhythm, in which all elemental life finds its most intense enhancement, that fills Bartok's music with energy. In "Allegro Barbaro" (1911) this elemental rhythm is wild and rough; it is like an invasion of mystic forces into the modern world, just as the noisy, ecstatic Bacchus march had been an invasion into the ancient world. All nervous reveries of impressionistic music scattered in fright before this outburst of brutal rhythmic element. Not until two years later did Stravinsky, in his "Spring Rite," roll such rhythmic masses into the orchestra.

Bartok used the popular rhythm not only in its wild original form; he animated it to grotesquery and irony (in the scherzo of the second string quartet, 1915/17). In the "Suite for Piano" opus 14 it is folk dance rhythm in the first movement; in the second movement it is witty play with a pounding motif that is always turned anew. Just like Stravinsky, Hindemith and Prokofieff, Bartok makes a game of rhythmic rolling and mechanical tone motion; but only in Bartok's works can the connection with the rhythm of folk music be proved.

However, Bela Bartok did not develop just the rhythm in Hungarian folk music. He also had the boldness to formulate the singing in his one-act play "Herzog Blaubarts Burg" after the melodics of folk songs. The voice repeats the musical phrases like the Hungarian folk song does. It has something of the concentrated expression of folk ballads. A passionate dramatic language is developed from the melodics of the folk song. That which used to be musical expression of primitive emotions now becomes modern intense declamation.

Bela Bartok learned something else from folk music. In collecting and utilizing folk songs, his sense of keen, weighty expression increased. All the Hungarian folk tunes that he had gathered from the Hungarian steppes or out of Roumanian forests, in Slovakian villages and Balkan dance halls, had a characteristic outline, even if they were just a few bars of music. They were concise and full of expression. They compressed grief, lament and longing into a musical form that lent eternity to expression of the soul.

Once it was a melodic turn, another time a rhythmic figure, then again an unusual harmony that condensed the contents of these songs so that they resembled a face marked by the years, by experiences, by sad and joyful fates. When the folk music was polyphonic, every single musical line was fixed solidly in its form. This polyphony could not be based on any major or minor harmonies. The melody governs the polyphony, not the harmony.

The accompanying voices are not ornamentation either, nor external color; they are essential and necessary. It was the keenness of musical motifs that Bela Bartok learned from folk music; the conciseness and concentration of forms, the reduction of musical content to the essentials.

The same composer who, in his one-act play "Herzog Blaubart's Burg" and in his ballet "Der holzgeschnitzte Prinz" (1917) created an orchestra that equals the orchestras of Richard Strauss and Ravel in wealth of colors, in freedom of harmonics and in lustre—that composer is capable of compressing the content of his compositions with spiritual force so that no tone of the work is mere ornament and stimulating decoration.

The smallest piece is like the concentrated essence of larger forms. In each of them there is the work of motif transformation, each is thoroughly organized, enhanced; fantasy work in its strongest concentration. Each of the 135 little piano pieces in his "Mikrokosmos" (1935) is in itself a large composition in a nutshell.

Bela Bartok is a constructive mind. In the development of plastic, objective forms he was far ahead of his time. His "Herzog Blaubart's Burg" is constructed like a suite which, in each of its seven movements develops a special musical mood tableau, elaborates and enhances it.

The music to "Holzgeschnitzter Prinz" is shaped in musical sections, and when the decked-out wooden figure of the prince is revealed as a puppet, the music has the form of an "altered reprise": the music of the prince in grotesque shapes in mechanical, inanimate repetition. This work was composed in 1914–1916, long before Alban Berg's "Wozzeck" (1922) wherein the music is patterned in symphonic sections.

Bela Bartok adopted form principles from Hungarian music, but whatever developed out of this music in new art patterns, new harmonies and new rhythms has no national tightness. The symphonic music of Smetana, Grieg, Tschaikowsky and Sibelius that is associated with the folk song always has a background of national scenery. The music of Bela Bartok always rises to a sphere of general thoughts. His music does not resound in the region of abstract tonal thoughts in which Arnold Schoenberg was at home at the peak of his creative work.

Bartok's music knows pain and joy, but the human quality in this music is the common human quality, not humanity in national confines. There are moments in Bela Bartok's music in which he writes Beethoven-like music. There is no music in later times that approaches so closely the spiritualized music of Beethoven's adagios in his last string quartets as some of the elements in Bela Bartok's music.

The great lento that closes Bartok's second string quartet, with its grievous laments and its sighs emanating from a bleeding heart; or the "Sostenuto" that ends the Piano Suite opus 14 with its fervent complaints—both are great music written in the spirit of Beethoven.

Like most sensitive souls, Bela Bartok often conceals this sensitivity behind grotesque humor and ludicrous derision. His rhythm then becomes thorny, his temper aggressive. Wild chord beats and glaring dissonances have to drown out the secret laments of a wounded soul.

In Bela Bartok's music is a rich humaneness. The mechanization of music as found in Stravinsky, and the constructivism of Schoenberg in later years, are equally alien to Bela Bartok. No matter how new his music, no matter how far he ventures into the unexplored tonal sphere, his music never loses its intrinsic warmth. His keen mind, forming clearly and surely, did not chill the emotion and did not allow the soul to freeze, as does Stravinsky's intellect.

Regardless of how much Bela Bartok condenses music and reduces it to the very essential of tone and rhythm, and even when he seeks heights where the atmosphere becomes thin and cold, music remains an art of the soul, of its grief and sorrow. The songs of the people, from which Bela Bartok is descended, still resound into the lonely spheres in which the spirit of a great composer seeks a new truth and the light of a new beauty that glows at the edge of the far-away.

VIII

Thus in all countries of Europe before the outbreak of the world war, composers of the most varying types are headed for the same goal: a new music for which the forms and expressive media of the classic-romantic music are a grand and shining past, but no longer the artistic tongue of the present. The great turning point of history, recognizable in the most terrible wars of modern history and in a series of revolutions, coincides with the great turning point in the history of music. In one as in the other it is a question of dissolving old forms. In one the destruction of political and social forms, in the other the disintegration of spiritual forms. The concussions in the realm of states, society and economy are just as serious as the shock in the sphere of music.

When war broke out in 1914, it was the old political and social powers that first collided. The great crisis of European life came

to a boiling point, and contemporaries saw in the bloody events
the destruction of an old world.

In the revolution of music, however, it was quite apparent that
in all the turmoil it was not just a matter of the end and dissolution
of old forms, but at the same time a question of the start of a new
evolution. The young music generation developing in all European
countries before and during the first world war had the same
aims. They were a unit. French, German, Spanish and Russian
musicians strove for the same things and worked for the same
future in the same frame of mind.

For all these young musicians romance was dead, just as feudalism was dead in political history. A thing of the past was the
rustling, brilliant orchestra that painted and portrayed, philosophized and play-acted. A thing of the past was all magic of tone
and all transformation of tone to color. A thing of the past were
literary programs in music. A thing of the past were rhetorics in
music, all emotional exuberance, all grand pose.

In the middle of the eighteenth century Rameau, I. I. Fux and
Marpurg had surveyed the gigantic foundations of classic harmonics. Now they dissolved and with them those forms which
rested on the giant foundations, such as the symphonic form. The
chromatic harmonies expanded more and more during the nineteenth century and pressed into the seams of the blocks of classic
harmonies. From Chopin and Liszt to Richard Strauss and Debussy
the resolution of classic harmonics continues to progress.

Schoenberg, Stravinsky and Bela Bartok forsook the quaking
foundation and boldly stepped into new spheres of harmonics, and
the young musicians of 1914 went along with them and followed
them. They all ventured into the free tone sphere. Many of them
experimented with unaccustomed intervals, some with very small
intervals. Haba experimented with quarter tones and in 1931 even
wrote an opera, "Mother," all in quarter tones. Busoni experimented
with one-sixth tones and the Mexican Julian Carillo even with one-
thirteenth tones. They all consider the harmonic space as something infinite rather than something limited, and in it they search
for new intervals and tone combinations.

For all the young musicians music was no longer, or not chiefly, an art of emotions in sounding form. Since the middle of the eighteenth century, when Rousseau preached the might of free sentiment, emotional masses found their way into music; they were great and strong emotions in the classics, intimate and dreamy in the romanticists, erotic emotion in Richard Wagner, intellectual sentiment in Liszt, religious feeling in Bruckner. Finally the epoch of released emotion came to an end with the nervous moods of Debussy.

The young musicians distrusted great and beautiful sentiments. For them music was pure tone and musical beauty was beauty of tone and tone combinations. Tone was material that had to be utilized. Composing was an intellectual work. The type of romantic musician who considered music as a kind of religion that would help him to rise above real life, had become antiquated. The musician as dreamer, as magician, as poet, as saint and as posing actor, had disappeared.

Romantic music had retired to the north-east corner of Europe. Here, in the "land of a thousand seas" Jean Sibelius wrote music since the end of the nineteenth century; music in which the landscape and the history of his country live, romantic music as it originated in all North European countries since the middle of the nineteenth century. Norway, where Bishop Landstad and Sophus Bugge collected folk songs ("Norskefolkeviser," 1852–1853, and Ganle Norske Vokeviser 1858) had its Grieg, who introduced the melody of the Fjords into serious music.

Denmark had its Gade who included in the symphony the dismal Northland tone and the nordic folk dance. And Finland has its bard in Sibelius who transformed the sagas and legends of the Finnish Kalevala epos into art music.

At the age of twenty-five, Sibelius wrote his first great work on Kalevala motifs, the "Kulervo" symphony, consisting of five movements. He always returned to the myth world of the old epos, and Tuanela and Lemminkaeinen became orchestral frescoes. The orchestral work "Finlandia" became a monumental portrayal of the Finnish landscape with its gloomy spruce and fir forests, its foaming whirlpools and defiant granite peaks.

This was the landscape that forms the background in the symphonies of Sibelius. There is a wealth of nature moods in these symphonies which are joined by the moods of the hard struggling composer. The romance in this music is not soft and dreamy as usual, but hard. The symphonies are like rock in their form, in their broad contours, in their sharp lines. There is a mystic and symbolic quality in the tones, as in all romantic tone, but the atmosphere surrounding the music is all real; it is the distinct air of a real landscape which, with its mountains and forests, is constructed in the symphonic forms.

The symphonic content of the Sibelius works, like those of Tschaikowsky, Borodin and Glazunoff, consists of the emotional conflicts of the individual, the clash of fate and individual personality, the battle of the soul with tragic forces. It is the latest form to which the subjectivism of Lord Byron turned.

Another romantic corner in northern Europe existed in England. At the turn of the nineteenth century the "Society for Folk Songs" was founded in London, its mission being the collection of English folk tunes. Composers went to the countryside looking for old songs among the peasants and shepherds. Others frequented the old pubs and, surrounded by tin tankards and ale jugs, listened to old ballads and dances.

Lucy Broadwood, the singer; the critic Fuller-Maitland, and the author Cecil Sharp became the leaders of this movement which spread across all England and which was sponsored in particular by pupils of the English composers Parry and Stanford, themselves friends of the poet Tennyson. Simultaneously, from Oxford and Cambridge Universities interest was spreading among the young musicians in music of the great English composers of the Elizabethan era, Byrd, Bull, Morley, Tallis and others, in whose works were found the ideal English popular tone and rhythm.

Ralph Vaughan Williams became the most forceful composer of this English romance, and he utilized English folk songs in his orchestral works. ("Norfolk Rhapsodies," "In the Fen Country," "London Symphony," etc.) Folk tunes give his music the colors of the English landscape, of the meadows and rivers, and folk tunes fill the "London Symphony" with the rhythm of national life in the big city.

A special kind of romantic movement came forth from the Jewish people toward 1900 and received its vital strength from the desire for a homeland where tortured, persecuted Jewish life could concentrate. In 1900 Joel Engel, music critic of "Russkija Wjedomosti," gave his first lecture on Jewish national music at the Imperial Ethnographical Society. He was to devote his whole life to that subject. He arranged concerts and lectures on Jewish music in all large cities in Russia. Stimulated by Rimsky-Korsakoff and Balakireff, Engel had collected the music of the Jewish ghetto that had accompanied the Jews in their wanderings through many European countries with laments and joy, grief and dance.

In 1908 Engel founded the "Society for Jewish Music." Young Jewish composers such as Achron, Gnessin, Milner, Krejn, Rossowsky and Ssaminsky gathered around him and began to seek in their compositions a special Jewish melos that was inspired by the old formulas of synagogue singing and Jewish folk music. Engel himself elaborated on ghetto melodies, wrote songs to Yiddish or Hebrew texts by Perez, Bjalik, Tschernichovsky, and beggar dances for the "Djybuk" performance of "Habima." In 1924 Engel went to Palestine, and died there in 1927.

In all European countries the romantic music trend originated with the collecting of folk tunes. In northern Europe and in Tzechoslovakia and in Russia the composers attempted to recognize the soul of their nation in the folk song. After this start came the composers who, adopting the folk music, created art music in national style and augmented melody and rhythm of the folk song to the proportions of great art works, as for instance Smetana, Dvorak, Glinka and Dargomyisky, Grieg and Gade. That which had been nature in the folk tune now became conscious great art.

The Jewish composers who had been taught by Joel Engel to recognize the soul of the people in the ghetto song no longer remained arrangers of folk and synagogue melodies, but let their musical fantasy be stimulated to free art creation by songs of the ghetto and synagogue. These composers were attempting to formulate an ideal melody of the Jewish people.

The pathetic songs in which the Jews in the synagogues of Asia, Africa and Europe poured out their hearts in prayer became

an inspiration to magnificent music for such composers as Josef
Achron, Michael Gnessin, Salomon Rosowsky, Michael Milner and
Alexander Krein. The ornaments that decorated the prayers and
that, like the gold embroidery and silver bells of the Thora rolls,
are the jewels of biblical words, echoed in the motifs of artistic
musical works, and mingled with the technique of Scriabin, Ravel
and Debussy.

Chassidic melodies, wherein child-like souls serve God with
serenity, gave the tunes dance rhythms. All this music obtained its
intrinsic power of emotion from the Zionist movement that had
filled the houses of the Polish and Russian ghetto with lustre and
light. From here Jews young and old wandered back to the ancient
country where once at the sacrificial altar of the Temple in Jerusalem the Levites sang the psalms of David, the silver trumpets
pealed and the priests spoke the blessing of Aaron over the people.

The greatest composer to come forth from this movement is
Ernest Bloch, born 1880 in Geneva. In 1913 Bloch composed his
"Hebrew Melodies." He himself describes what he wanted of this
music: "It is the soul of the Jew that interests me, the multifarious,
glowing, agitated soul that I sense out of the Bible; the freshness
and simplicity of the patriarchs, the vehemence that is expressed in
the books of the Prophets; the ardent love for justice, the despair
of the preacher of Jerusalem, the pain and profundity of the Book
of Job, the sensuality of the High Song. All this is in us, all this is
in me and is my best share. And that is what I want to transfer to
my music: the holy agitation of a tribe that slumbers in our soul."

That is the kind of music Bloch wrote in such works as "Three
Psalms," or in his cello rhapsody "Shelomo." His proud pathos and
the lustre of his music really contains something of the spirit that
created the pictorial splendor of the psalms, the noble emotion of
a prophetic soul and the rapture of a people that was first to see
God of the Universe as a sun of justice.

All these romantic trends were the last stragglers of the great
romantic movement that spread across all Europe from France and
Germany during the entire nineteenth century, and that satiated
one country after the other with its ideas.

This movement pushed forward in large waves until it had set in vibration all European states—the northern countries and Russia last. Everywhere romanticism meant an awakening of national ideas, and in music a new interest in folk songs and folk dances, whence serious music fetched melodies, harmonies and rhythms. Everywhere romanticism was an awakening and rising of a people to new wanderings.

The English musicians who visited the countryside in the early twentieth century to collect old ballads and songs wanted to create a national music in England as had existed strongly and peculiarly in the Elizabethan era. Sibelius included old Finland, that had created the folk epos of the Kalevala poem, in the European cultural world. The Jewish composers want their music to join the future of their people with the present and with the past. All these romantic trends are in restrospect of ancient times, seeking new strength therein for future creating.

The big general movement in Europe that set all arts in revolutionary motion was hostile to romanticism. It did not glance back, but advanced like pioneers who don't think of the home they just left but of the day's work and of the houses of the future. Geniuses like Schoenberg, Bartok and Stravinsky, and talents such as Milhaud, Hindemith or Prokofieff were united in the idea of creating unromantic music and cultivate new land. While tensions in Europe wax ever larger, and the contrasts between and within the states ever deeper, the young musicians joined and formed a unit. They represented a new Europe, or, inasmuch as they were also joined by the young musicians in America, a new world.

12

The Faces of Stravinsky

As an artist, Igor Stravinsky has many faces. He is a Russian and bound to the Russian nation as strongly as all great Russian artists. And he is a Parisian who, together with Cocteau and Picasso, with Derain and Bracque, with Bergson and Proust shapes the spirit of Paris in the pre-war era. He is a man of elemental rhythm and at the same time a man of gleaming ingenuity and wit. He is driven by strong impulses, and yet he is an intellectualist. He has an ingenious foresight for the future, but does not lose interest for passing artistic fashions. He stands above his time, and simultaneously within his time, which stimulates him and which he depends upon.

When I met Stravinsky, I saw before me an elegant, dainty man of the world who spoke Russian, French, English and German with equal assurance. He wore the most up-to-date dress-coat like somebody born and bred on the boulevards of Paris. His hands were carefully manicured like those of a man who moves in elegant society. His social attitude was adroit, cultured and smooth and one could easily imagine this man moving with the grace of a novel hero in the international society of Nice, Monte Carlo, Paris and London. At the same time, though, his body underneath the fine dress shirt is covered with holy images and amulets. That is the real Stravinsky. A Russian turned Parisian who nevertheless has not forgotten to wear holy images and amulets. A modern intellect with strong primitive instincts.

Stravinsky differs from Arnold Schoenberg in the admixture of stylishness and a touch of intellectual dandyism. Arnold Schoenberg was never associated with the things that were unessential motion and superficial breeze of the day in his time. He had an open mind for everything that was new and valuable in the arts; for the strong lyrics of Richard Dehmel, for the refined rhyming art of Stephan George, for Maeterlinck's art of mystic mood, for Kandinsky's painting. But only to the extent that they mirrored his own artistic world.

Schoenberg was never affiliated with modern art trends because they were new or sensational, as for instance Richard Strauss was associated with Oscar Wilde's art, or Stravinsky with surrealist painting. Schoenberg had no interest whatsoever for modern art per se, that causes a momentary stir and is a topic of conversation in salons. He himself never drew the attention of the salons and was never the sensation of the day, as was Strauss as composer of "Salome"; not even Schoenberg's failures and scandals were sensational, as the failure of Stravinsky's "Spring Rite" had been in Paris. Like Bela Bartok, Arnold Schoenberg stood outside his time, in a zone of solitude, misunderstanding and hostility within the time.

Stravinsky was at home in his era and by his association with the Russian Ballet, he was already in the center of the present. Stravinsky is unthinkable without the "Café de la Rotonde" on Montparnasse, where the progressive artists of Paris before and during the war created the new spiritual fashions and discussed them before a glass of Pernot. He is in the midst of the throng of intelligent radical artists; he is always in the present, in Picasso's studio, in a restaurant with Diaghileff who designs new ballets while enjoying oysters and Chablis; at the "Ball Nègre" where the jazz band plays for elegant Parisiennes seeking the latest sensation in the arms of Negroes.

Arnold Schoenberg has nothing in common with the world of today that searches for tomorrow as a gourmet tries a new pastry. He and Bela Bartok are really the only modern musicians who do not for one single moment let jazz rhythm pound into their music as it does in works of Stravinsky, Milhaud, Hindemith and Krenek. Their rhythm is derived from a loftier sphere of the mind.

Naturally Stravinsky's true greatness has nothing to do with the moods of the day or Parisian nights. But they touch his music, they stimulate and they tint his work. They give his personality a special character. Stravinsky's modern tie that shows the latest color and newest design of Paris distinguishes him from the other modern musicians. This interest of Stravinsky for new currents of the day lends a flexibility to his artistic development that is not inherent in Arnold Schoenberg or Bela Bartok. Both of them walk straight ahead, without taking their eyes from their distant goal, along the path to an unknown territory that is not associated with the present and which is unknown in the artist cafes and in the conventicles of modern artists.

Stravinsky is not only a great musicial who wrote great, lasting works; he is also an intelligent musician, filled with the curosity and inquisitiveness of a lively intellect, full of interest for the age in which he lives, full of lively interest for everything that is new, latest fashion and the very latest whim.

In 1910, the year in which Stravinsky wrote his first great ballet music for the Russian Ballet in Paris,—music that was endowed with delicate colors and with the magic of the Hector Berlioz and Rimsky-Korsakoff orchestra—Arnold Schoenberg was already composing his three piano pieces opus 11, the figures of which soar through atonal space like spirits. Schoenberg had preceded Stravinsky that far into new four-dimensional regions of music, where the tones lost sensuality and became all spirit, and where the forms lost their material shape. In that same year Schoenberg wrote his F-Sharp Minor String Quartet, music from a "higher planet."

Painting had begun then already to turn anti-realistic, and Picasso's geometrization of reality, Kandinsky's free color visions, Leger's variations of forms were abstract art when Stravinsky was still writing romantic music. Stravinsky's artistic evolution furthered his progress from romantic beginnings, but this development rarely evinces the magnificent logic of the Schoenberg development and the strict necessity expressed in the progress made from work to work. It contains much more liberty and much more chance, whim and intellectual curiosity. In many instances the composer's development has a literary character. Occasionally one has the impression that Jean Cocteau is prompting Stravinsky in what to say and where to go.

The rudiments of Stravinsky's art are to be found in neo-romantic color play and in the colorism of the orchestra. His teacher had been Rimsky-Korsakoff, who had written some of the most dazzling scores of modern times and had illuminated his symphonic music with the lustre of Byzantine-oriental cupolas and church mosaics and with the gayness of oriental fables. Rimsky-Korsakoff and Debussy were the composers who influenced the twenty-one year old Stravinsky, son of an opera singer, when he began composing at the Petersburg conservatory.

One of his first orchestral compositions was "Firework" (1908). The theme is truly impressionistic: rockets shooting upwards, hissing fire wheels, Roman candles that disperse into fiery stars. One wonders that Debussy was not the first to compose such fireworks music and that his "Feux d'artifice" did not flash from the piano until after Stravinsky's composition. (1910–1913). Debussy may even have been inspired to his work by Stravinsky's creation; it is quite possible that he heard it at a concert in Paris in 1909.

Stravinsky's impressionistic nocturnal portrait is a brilliant orchestral piece with its lights flashing in the night sky, with its chromatically circling wheels, its fire balls, its whistling and hissing. It is very short, of only a few minutes duration. It is this brevity that distinguishes it from Debussy's impressionism, the moods of which expand in a dreamy artist fantasy. Unusual, too, is the rhythmic energy of Stravinsky's music.

Stravinsky's association with the Russian Ballet of Diaghileff brought new and greater tasks. His most important compositions originated in connection with the Russian Ballet. He found a wealth of stimulation in associating with Diaghileff who searched for new things in art; a pleasure-seeking, temperamental, extravagant genius who was comfortable only in the company of modern artists and who knew only one fear in life: the fear of growing old.

Only an artist of Dostojewsky's rank would have the power of properly describing such a genuine Russian as Diaghileff had been. His enjoyment of life was childlike; he was always surrounded by dancers, poets and musicians; in elegant restaurants and at the Lido he sparkled with esprit, and he stormed through life carefree and extravagant. A Maecenas and impresario, speculator and worldling, tears would roll down his cheeks when, after a Paris première he drove to the Champs-Elysees and recited Puschkin.

What a novel this man and his group of artists could inspire: his great primadonnas, Pavlova, Karsavina, the gaunt, dark-eyed Ida Rubinstein, the magnificent dancers whom he discovered and who were his friends: Nijinsky, Lifar; the painters Bakst and Benois and Fokine, the choreographer, who first brought the dreams of his glowing artist's imagination to the stage; the hordes of the most modern poets, musicians and painters whom he inspired with new ideas and with whom he discussed new ballets as though there were nothing more important in the world than a new ballet form, lines and colors on the stage and the body expression of beautiful women and handsome men.

Diaghileff moved in an atmosphere of sensation, and his premières in the Châtelet or at the Paris Opéra were attended not only by the beautiful ladies and elegant gentlemen of high society, but by all the artists in Paris as well. Stravinsky spent years in this artist circle, and his musical genius obtained from here the stimulation that he needed, the slogans that inspired him and the formulas that he transformed into music.

In 1910 Karsavina danced his "Fire Bird" which was decorated by Bakst and staged by Fokine. This music too is romantic music in the style of Rimsky-Korsakoff, and it is Russian in the themes and in the orientalism of the coloring. The lyrics are Tschaikowsky at his gentlest, the tone delicate in misty strings and in woodwind instruments, filled with modulated nuances. The middle parts of the orchestra, too, are pure song and a web of singing voices. Stravinsky has special colors for the sinister demon sphere of the magician Kastchei, and in the arrangement in which the music is now heard and which only was created in 1919, these colors are intensified.

Here, rhythm and tone are already genuine Stravinsky rhythm. There is something elemental in the rhythm, in the short motifs that are whirled around again and again, in the accentuations against the time, in the jolts and lashes of the rhythmic motifs. To that end the drums are beaten with hard wood drumsticks, piano and harp and xylophones symbolize the tone of bells and gong beats. The chords are shrill, stinging, hard. The brass instruments yelp like infernal dogs. The contrast between light, bright fairy world and the dark realm of the demons is worked out with force, and the rich, full timbre of the big orchestra closes with one of those enhancements with which the romantic composers put the crowning touch to such apotheoses.

With this music Stravinsky is on a level with Rimsky-Korsakoff, Franz Schreker and Ravel. Only in the gripping music of the sorcerer and his demons there is something wild, archaic, uncontrolled such as is not available to any other composer. This music with its glaring colors, its throbbing rhythm, its hammering blows is not the romantic theatre of the Berlioz fantasy. In it there is an outburst of wild earth powers, and underneath Stravinsky's fashionable shirt one hears the Russian amulets jingling.

Stronger yet is the Russian feeling, the elemental quality and the powerful rhythm in the next ballet that Stravinsky wrote for the Russian Ballet: "Petruschka" (1910–1911). Here, too, the orchestra is the large orchestra that produces romantic colors, with fourfold woodwind instrumentation, with 12 brass instruments (4 horns, 4 trumpets, 3 trombones and 1 tuba), and strings. In addition there are harps, piano and plenty of percussion. However, in spite of the many color tubes it is not quite the romantic orchestra any more which, with its broad color canvas, its many nuances, transitions and blends, was an orchestra created for tone painting and sorcery of sound.

The Stravinsky orchestra is no longer exuberant, but hard. Above all it accentuates the rhythm, lets the contour of the themes protrude distinctly and intensifies the accents of the music. The timbre of the orchestra enhances the intensity of the music. The music is no longer colorful atmosphere, but the earth proper. Even where the woodwinds play around the themes with passages and trills and the music resolves in a web of runs, in a rustling and whirring, the rhythm is forcibly indicated by wind and percussion instruments.

This rhythm is always the rhythm of the Russian folk song and folk dance. It is not a spiritualized rhythm, but primitive, strong as peasant soil, wild as untamed nature. It stamps as with rough high boots, it whirls, it circles. Russian composers before

Stravinsky included this Russian rhythm of Cossack dances in their music, and in Borodin's "Polevetzer Dances" this rhythm rotates in a circle.

But how tame this rhythm is in the works of other composers, compared to the elemental force that it possesses in Stravinsky's compositions. Only his rhythm is no longer connected with the Russian landscape, with steppes and forest, with the wooden huts of the peasants and with the streets; it is bound to the depth of the earth itself, where primitive rock forms hard masses.

The people's hustle and bustle at the fair, and the puppet play are the substance of "Petruschka." The dances of the people, crowds and mass movement are set in contrast to the performance of wooden puppets where love, jealousy, despair and death become theatrical play. There is always very strong motion in the folk scenes. The harmonies paint the turmoil. Triads glide up and down, harmonies are piled up, chords placed against each other, chromatic tones set in circular motion. From this underground of moving harmonies short themes arise, shaped of just a few notes, like primitive music, and are whirled around with ever new rhythmic accents.

Familiar Russian folk tunes, such as the song "Along the Petersburger street," or the "Song of the Plain," appear in the dances of the nurses and coachmen. Mostly, though, only typical versions of Russian folk music appear in endless repetitions. Rhythmics are completely free, and often different rhythms collide. Stamping rhythms, such as those in the coachmen's dances, are intensified to orgiastic proportions. Everything in this music is strongest life, tumult, reality. Not in one instant does the rhythmic energy lose its strength, and the orchestral timbre increases this vitality with shrill colors, with distribution of rhythmic motions among various instrumental groups, with rhythmic thrusts of the brass instruments, the piano and percussion instruments. One is just as far removed here from the over-cultivated impressionistic orchestra as from the gay-colored naturalistic orchestra. It seems almost as though a big mechanical apparatus were set in motion that transforms the music into rhythm.

From out of the mass commotion emerges the play of marionettes. The music changes here completely to mechanical motion. Sharp, clinking, porcelain-like tones preponderate. The instruments are either percussion or fretted instruments; piano, harp, xylophone, triangle and drums come to the fore. When Petruschka is repelled by the blackamoor with a kick, the orchestra sounds like breaking glass. The dances have an extremely harsh rhythm and the woodwinds, that sound somewhat mechanical anyhow, stand out.

The telescoping of different keys makes the harmonies sound rigid. Petruschka's collapse is veered to the grotesque by tone and instruments; the piano passages sound scurrilous, and the desperation scene (the climax of the puppet play), with its promiscuity of keys and abruptness of breaking off, sounds completely marionette-like, and the end of the scene gives the impression of a china doll falling to the floor and breaking.

The scene "At the Moor's" also sounds puppet-like. The oriental mood is transformed to the mechanical; delicate pizzicati of the strings imitate the tone of plucked instruments in the Orient, soft cymbal and drum beats duplicate Oriental percussion. The ballerina dances to the tunes of a small trumpet that smacks of the nursery.

Petruschka's struggle with the Moor becomes all marionette action. In the death scene of Petruschka its themes are folded together in ten bars, like the figures are placed in a box when a game is finished. Altogether new, bizarre tones at the end produce the ghostlike apparition of Petruschka. It sounds spookishly bizarre, and the short finale of the string pizzicati is extremely fantastic. This ending proves in a grand manner that there was life in the marionettes, and above the puppet play rises Russian mysticism, which finds a soul even in wooden puppets, and old Oriental faith that saw in the play of marionettes an image of an exalted life.

Everything in this music is new and personal: rhythmics, harmonics, melodics and tone. Everywhere the roots of the music are to be found in primitivity and in folk lore. The keys that it employs are no longer the major and minor keys of art music; they are derived from the lower strata of music's historic development. The old five-tone scales are used, as well as old church keys. In this ingenious music one re-discovers the very primitive formation of melodies as groups of tones that rotate around one tone in the narrowest space.

The rhythm is likewise that of primitive music; the quart and quint passages that Stravinsky often uses in the harmonies belong to the oldest assets of music. This rooting of music in the elemental and the prehistoric is certainly Russian. Just as ancient Byzantium lives on in churches, the old Orient in Tiflis and in Samarkand, so does age-old primitive music live on in the villages of the Caucasus and Ural. Although an intellectualist, Stravinsky is nevertheless bound to the Russian earth, to the mighty elemental forces emanating from this earth that are more powerful than transitory millennia, to the native soil where in dark depths the patterns of national life are molded.

In the third ballet that Stravinsky composed for the Russian Ballet, "Spring Rites" (1911–1913) he ventured into this very depth and brought forth the greatest music written by him.

In this music the strange spirit of prehistoric times is conjured. Everything here is mystic, vast and massive, like one of the ancient relics of the Bronze era that were discovered in northern Europe, with their rock-plate settings and symbolic designs on granite blocks. There is not one tone in this music that would remind us of the time in which we are living. The music consists of tone blocks. Its motifs ring in the primitive sounds of an age in which singing was still a magic means of conjuring spirits. Its rhythm has its roots in a past era, in which human life was still a part of nature.

The religious awe that befell primitive man when winter's ice melted and new life grew out of the earth is reproduced in this music with ingenious means that are entirely novel. Here the music itself is re-united with the earth which in olden times was something alive, abounding with sacred powers; the gigantic mother whose mighty womb was worshipped already by the cave man and at whose breasts the animals sucked, as portrayed by statues in the temples of Asia Minor.

Divine service of prehistoric times is presented in this music, not as an exotic oddity the way Verdi portrays worship in Egyptian temples in "Aida" or as Bellini presented Celtic druids and priestesses in "Norma," but as an imitation of the spirit of that time. The

myth comes to life in this music. The awe experienced by man
2000 years ago in conjuring the fertility of the earth. The symbolism that makes the life of the earth into an image of human life,
and the sacred union between man and earth. The ecstasy of the
dance that subjugated the powers of the earth with magic means,
and the solemnity of human sacrifice.

No music that sounded like the music which surrounded
Stravinsky could portray that. None of its tones could reproduce
such mysteries as those that filled prehistoric man with fear and
awe when he danced the corn into the soil, conjured the spirits of
his ancestors and spilled the blood of a sacred virgin, letting it flow
over the soil so that it might bear fruit.

Stravinsky first had to create the orchestra which was hard as
the soil after a long winter, a mighty mass, a huge deity. He
employed the big romantic orchestra, but it turned into something
new. In this orchestra the woodwinds were used in groups of five
instruments (5 flutes, 5 clarinets of different types, 5 kinds of oboes,
5 bassoons), and there was a broad tone mass of brass instruments:
13 horns and trumpets, and 5 trombones and tubas. This made
possible rigid boulders of tone, the contrasting of many tone layers
and the overpowering of the soft string sounds by harsh wind
tones.

The chords also remind of stone and earth. A massive heaviness is in them. Chromatic tones are compressed into the chords
and heighten the tone. A motif in C is accompanied by the motif
in D-sharp; tone figures are brought into thirds by two instrument
groups, and the thirds move in second intervals. Basses in G-sharp
and F-sharp are thrust against a motif in F. In this manner the tone
becomes as compact as a dry mass of earth, the tone masses hard
and weighty. Seventh, fifth and fourth parallels make the tone
shrill, sharp, primitive. In the orchestra tonal masses in strange keys
flow beside or against each other. They harden like cooling lava
masses, or they curdle to tone lumps.

Often the music only turns to beats, to stamping chords of the
whole orchestra in which two different chords are driven together.
In the section: "Ancestral Rites of the Eldest," the orchestral
accompaniment becomes entirely noise consisting of piled seconds

and syncopes of drums and tambourine. Thus the orchestra becomes an elemental mass that appears to be created by volcanic earth movement.

Ancient too is the formation of music from motifs that move in the smallest sound spaces and are very short and mostly syncopated, and horrible are the fanfares of the wind instruments that sound in primitive whole steps. The tubas of the priests may have sounded like those found portrayed on the "Kivik monument" in Norway in a stone hollow of the Bronze Age. Priestesses are standing around an altar here, all veiled. Prisoners are led to the sacrificial pit and priests blow on "lures." (Lures are big horns of bronze, found in Nordic tombs.)

It was the spirit of this age that Stravinsky revived in "Spring Rites." When, in the "Procession of the Eldest" four fanfares sound simultaneously, each in its own key, all of them powerful and solemn, accompanied by the various rhythms of percussion and surrounded by the trills in the orchestra as by sacrificial smoke, one is transplanted to an age of long ago. The rhythms, too, lead into this age, these elemental beats of the whole orchestra in dissonant chords which, toward the end, in the dance of the girls, sound shrill and pain-racked, as though conjuring the labor pains of procreative spring soil.

There is a special metre in almost every bar, and from two-sixteenths to five-sixteenths the movement in the end dance is changed; it becomes convulsive when the priestess wants to become one with the elements, with the deep strata of the earth. Trombone glissandi, small and large drums, kettle-drums, cymbals and fanfares intensify the excitement that is to bring the earth in an uproar. The barbarism, the savagery, the ecstasy, the hysteria of longing for death possess mystic grandness in this music.

This barbarism is also Russian. It originates from one of those sects in Russia that mix pain and erotic emotion to create the great ecstasy wherein man and the Hereafter fuse. The free rhythm comes from Russian folk music. Likewise the short motifs within the range of a quart. No Russian melody is used any place, as it had been used in "Petruschka," and yet the melodics are Russian in their mood. The orchestral nature scenes, too, with which both parts of the music begin and in which are described the awakening of spring, the swelling of the sap in the earth, and the rustling of spring in icy air, have Russian mood.

The use of mediaeval church keys, the free polyphony, the harmonic blendings of Major and Minor can all be traced to folk music in Russia, in which is preserved so much primitive and antique character. And where could the symbolism of spring be sensed more profoundly than in Russia where the transition from the ice of winter to the reviving breezes of spring is felt much more strongly than in other European countries that have shorter and milder winters? This spring symbolism transplanted Stravinsky into a long past world, where it was still celebrated with religious ceremonies: with the roundelays of the young maidens who conjure the sun; with the dances of young men who plant the corn in the earth and stamp on the soil; with the prayers of the old priests who kiss the earth, and with the ecstasy of the priestess who with her blood weds the earth. It is an ancient, wild, prehistoric world that embodies in the dance rhythm the rotation of the stars, the rhythm of the divine forces in life and the tempo of the erotic. Therein lies Stravinsky's greatness: that he was able to reproduce all this with his music, which condenses orchestra timbre, melodies and harmony to rhythm.

The smallest motif has its rhythmic form, the voices of the orchestra that flow freely side by side have their own rhythm, and the whole composition has its great, elemental, whipping, exciting, barbaric and ecstatic rhythm. It is the rhythm of "Magna Mater" which the ancient people celebrated with intoxicating sounds of the cymbals, with the sacrifice of priests and the erotic surrender of virgins in the temple.

Within a period of five years Igor Stravinsky had traveled the road from impressionistic romance and Debussy-ism to a music which, with its timbre, its rhythmics and harmonics had severed the connections with classic-romantic music. This music was a big enhancement of the primitive forces of Russian music. It seemed as though within this music a great revolution of popular feeling had pierced all art forms of the present, and as though Russia's instinctive life had invaded modern civilization.

A new myth of this elemental world had been created in "Spring Rites," grand and powerful as a myth of ancient times, bloody like all religions of prehistoric time, and abounding with the rhythms of symbolic dances; with solemn procession that transforms men to gods, and with demoniacal dancing that joined man with earth and heaven.

The present era has seen no greater creator of myths than the small, graceful Russian. Friedrich Nietzsche had created a new myth in "Also Sprach Zarathustra," Boecklin filled groves, ocean and islands with new mythical figures, Max Klinger had created mythical figures. But Igor Stravinsky had returned to a prehistoric age which no artist of the present had portrayed, and to the rudiments of civilization where all thinking was still symbolic and earth was the maternal womb, filled with sap and blood, from which life emerged.

This myth of earth and fruit, of new life that forms in dark depth, and of spring's powers that awaken new life, was brought to life by Stravinsky with the ancient religion that sacrifices lives in order to propagate life, and that, with the rhythms of the dance, conjured the fluttering of new life.

II

Following this grand work, Igor Stravinsky wrote his "Three Pieces for String Quartet" (1914), and this was a different Stravinsky.

In this music everything living had become a shadow. The music had changed into mechanism. The tones had become noisy. The rhythm devoured all music and left only bones. The second movement resembled a machine. The instruments screeched like sirens. The third piece, with the voices colliding in icy air and with the many high, peaked, emotionless violin tones, sounded eerie, as though all shaping forces had escaped from life. Later, in 1928–1930, Stravinsky orchestrated these three pieces as well as the "Etude for Pianola," written in 1917, and published them in orchestral arrangement as "Four Etudes for Orchestra."

The Etude for Pianola was entitled "Madrid." However, the

Spain that Stravinsky describes here is not the romantic Spain as it was last portrayed in music by Debussy and Ravel; not the Spain with its glowing nights and the fragrance of orange groves, with the clicking of the castanets and the rhythms of women's white bodies. This is a dead and mechanized Spain. Street noises movement of the people on the street and gestures are reproduced, not colors and sunshine. Nothing remains of life in Spain but the machinery of life.

The same thing takes place in the "Easy Pieces" for piano duet, composed in 1915 and 1917 and later (1925–1926) arranged for orchestra as "Suite 1 and 2." Some of the pieces are landscapes. "Neapolitana" and "Espanola" are music of the south minus the color of the south. They too are merely noise and motion of the south. The tarantella and bolero and seguedilla rhythms are sketched. Their sensuality is practically withered, their melody completely turned to noise. The music becomes a gesture, hand motions and body rotations, as though music were to be made for deaf mutes.

Even the "Balalaika" that follows is not a Russian melody, but mostly dry rhythm, humming repetitions, whirring motion. The music is completely rigid. In the "March," the "Waltz," the "Polka" and the "Gallop" we also find only rhythms, noise, machinery wheels.

From this music of Stravinsky everything had fled that had made the works of the composer great so far, the alliance with Russian lore that had put life into the smallest musical phrase in "Petruschka" and which in mythical greatness had made "Spring Rites" a colossal fresco of Russia's past. What did the transformation of music into movement and machine noise signify? What was the sense in thus mechanizing the tones? What did the alienation of Stravinsky from mother earth mean?

Stravinsky's turning, the new face, signified Stravinsky's association with the artistic trends that were growing stronger in Paris in literature and painting before the war, and that were separating the arts from life and reality, from nature and man. Anti-romanticism, hostility against impressionism and, simultaneously, hostility against naturalism led to the alienation of the arts from reality in

Paris around 1910. The deep dissatisfaction of the time expressed itself in the dissolution of the real world, in the destroying and shattering of naturalistic forms, in the escape to a Hereafter that gave mathematical forms and mechanical proceedings the severity of laws.

Among the modern poets with whom Stravinsky associated, no one represented the mechanization of the world more intelligently than Jean Cocteau. He considered the world one big automaton that re-formed all happenings into a mechanism. Mechanical too was the fate of man. Even God intervenes in life as an apparatus. Angles (according to Cocteau's description in his poem "L'ange heurtebise") are spontaneous automata. Art, which is a simile of life, must be a mechanism, not a photograph of external life.

In Cocteau's film, "Le sang d'un poète," for which Georges Auric wrote the music, all reality is changed into a sur-realist world wherein figures and events enter into new associations and a new mechanism moves all happenings. The film was the "tenth Muse" for Cocteau, but this muse of an automatized world was unknown to the Greeks. The phonograph also belongs to the automatized world. Cocteau himself recorded two poems (Le Camarade and "Les voleurs d'enfants"), not as a photograph of his voice but as "listening objects." This voice should sound "new, hard, unknown"; it should have nothing human.

With the text of "Oedipus Rex" which Cocteau wrote for Stravinsky, he wanted to create the stone monument of a Greek tragedy and transform the myth into an apparatus the mechanism of which produces tragic fates.

Another artist had a part in Stravinsky's transformation, which begins around 1914: Pablo Picasso. Nobody executed with greater intensity the mechanization of the world, as preached by Cocteau, than did Picasso on the canvas. People and objects change to unreality, to surfaces and lines, to geometrical figures, as though mechanical forces had taken possession of the world and had distorted all figures there.

The shattering of the world, the destruction of its forms as though a bomb had torn a life to shreds, found fertile ground in Stravinsky, ground that was prepared for this type of nihilistic art.

What else was the rhythm that bursts out so vehemently in Stravinsky's compositions if not a power that conquers life and reality? When, in "Petruschka," Stravinsky turns a love tragedy into a puppet play and the music into something mechanical, into wooden figures that flounder on wires, into china faces, is that not a mechanization of life as Cocteau demanded it?

But without Cocteau and without Picasso Stravinsky's artistic development would have been accomplished less intellectually and less in conformity with new artistic slogans that floated on the shining surface of intellectual life in Paris. The doctrine of mechanizing the world, as proclaimed by Cocteau, and in addition Cocteau's other tenet that music should be a "plastic phenomenon in magic distance" which one should listen to objectively, influenced the whole future work of Stravinsky.

Stravinsky, whose brilliant mind was set in motion by art trends in Paris and constructed ever new intelligent apparatus of mechanical and motoric music, from time to time returned to his native soil, to the fertile fields of Russia: in 1918 with the "Story of the Soldier," 1919 with the "Russian Peasant Wedding" (begun in 1914) and with the four "Russian Songs"; 1921/22 with the opera "Mavra" and 1930 with the "Psalm Symphony."

The aforementioned works are distinctly different from the other compositions written by Stravinsky after 1918. They are not only clever, they are strong; not only dazzling but gripping; not mere technical accomplishments but inventions that are as Russian as Dostojewsky's novels, or Mussorgsky's "Boris Godunoff" and Tolstoi's writings.

The "Story of the Soldier" is the greatest work of the theatre produced by the pre-war era and bound to the spirit of that time. Its text is popular, popular the form with a narrator and a small orchestra consisting of six instruments and percussion; popular the melos with the primitive small intervals, the turning and twisting of the musical motifs and the tone figures such as popular fiddlers use in their improvisations.

Popular, too, is the wood-cut design of the music, the conjunction of independent musical lines; popular is the mysticism of the choral and the ending with the percussion instruments that accompany the soldier to Hades. This small piece of art is not: "Plastic phenomenon in magic distance" according to Cocteau's program; it stands in the midst of life and treats all timely questions of the age: Stock exchange, industry and, above all, militarism which marches stiffly through the music with mechanical drill motions and automatic obedience. The "March of the Soldier," into which are thrown commando fanfares and alarm signals as into a military machine; the dances of the princess with their free tango, waltz and ragtime rhythms; the grotesque dances of the devil are all genuine folk art despite all the wealth of musical work. Russianism is inherent in every motif and in every little piece of rhythm. It is the atmosphere by which the piece of art is surrounded, and the earth upon which it stands.

The "Four Russian Songs" that originated in 1918/1919 are also rooted in popular Russian soil. In two of these songs a large part is sung without indication of time. The last song is a Russian sectarian song with old-Russian prayer formulas. The piano accompaniment, like the accompaniment of a percussion instrument, is hard and arid.

The same type of accompaniment is used by Stravinsky in his masterpiece "Russian Peasant Wedding." Originally Stravinsky had composed this choral work for an orchestra consisting of a mechanical piano, electric harmonium, percussion instruments and two Hungarian cymbals. The orchestra was to be a mechanical orchestra that would propel the singing action with a steel engine of rhythms. Later Stravinsky reduced the orchestra of his choral work to four pianos, cymbals, bells and xylophone. The chords are hammered and beaten. The description of the wedding is executed by the choruses which, like church choirs, often sing responsively or are grouped in soli and choir.

The lines of the musical design are hard. Voice hits voice, each going its own way. This lends the music a primitive and ancient quality. Mediaeval scales, preserved in church litanies, give the melodies something rigid. The wedding celebrants are peasants, earthborn, strong, simple people.

In no other work did Stravinsky approach reality as closely as here. One is transplanted to the wooden hut in a Russian village.

Icons are on the walls, and above the towering bed hangs a picture of the Virgin Mary in glaring colors. In the tile oven burns the fire from the wood of the forest. This is where the wedding and the wedding feast take place. The saints are invoked when the bride is given to the groom. The blessing of the Holy Mother is implored. The aged parents stand guard before the room of the newlyweds. New life is created while the old life ends.

All this is described in chorals which, like Russian folk songs, condense all moods, from the blunt to the solemn, into keen rhythms and short phrases. Without being a naturalistic portrayal, the work is full of life.

In the Buffo opera "Mavra"—'dedicated to the memory of Puschkin, Glinka and Tschaikowsky'—the spirit of the Russian small town comes to life. The loss of a cook is bewailed, the neighbors gossip, a hussar, while being lathered for a shave, sings sentimental ballads. All this is grotesquely formed, and small town gossip gets an orchestral base of wind instruments and five solo violins that draws all the burlesque into a rattling mechanism.

Above town and village rises the dome of the church, and Stravinsky's Russian landscape would be incomplete without the lights at the altar and the choral singing in the church, which in Russia is the Byzantine church with gold trimmed cupolas, mosaics on the walls, picture walls before the Holy of Holies and the mournful, dark head of the Saviour that looks reproachfully down at the sinners.

With his "Psalm Symphony" in 1930 Stravinsky entered the Russian church, a devout and penitent man who crossed himself on entering the portal to take part in the religious service. Three parts —supplication, response, Halleluja—in the Latin language of the Vulgate, proclaim divine law.

There is a tremendous inflexibility in this music. The tone is dismal, inasmuch as the high voices of the choir were filled with rough boys' voices and the high strings were missing in the orchestra. Two pianos, harp and drums ring into the music as church bells, powerful and heavy, in lawful severity. Solid formulas of the basses support the entire music as pillars carry the church. Church scales, Oriental pomp of coloraturas, harsh chord tones, monotonous recitation of prayer formulas and, chiefly, the solemnly proceeding or threatening motifs of the basses stamp the music with the character of a divine service in a cathedral in Constantinople at the time of Constantine or Justinian. When emperor and empress and the court dignitaries and the people prostrated themselves upon the floor, the trumpets resound and the lights flicker.

There is something grandly severe and hard in this music that crushes man and fills the soul with awe. It proclaims the power of God with the solemn mysticism of the intervals that embody the eternal law; with the chords that compress small and large thirds, major and minor sevenths, major and minor seconds, thereby resembling harmonies of metal; and with the tone formulas and tone steps which, like clergymen in their flowing, embroidered robes proceed slowly through the door of the altar room and sing monotone litanies.

Life, reality and humanity appear unimportant when the bells ring, trumpets and drums resound and the choir preaches in solemn unison: "Laudate Dominum."

As seen from this work, the mechanization of music that is associated with the name of Stravinsky, appears as a kind of mysticism, as does the transformation of the music into sounding motion, the stifling of emotions and the inanimation of life. Just so the world appears empty and hollow before the mournful glance of the Byzantine Son of God, motion without spiritual meaning. High above life is the divine law. In the clouds beyond the world is the truth that is heralded with trumpet sounds and before which all humanity kneels in the dust. Between man and God is a sharp separation. Above everything is light, all lawfulness, all eternal values; below is the dark, senselessness motion like the rattling of a mill in which there is no wheat.

When Stravinsky removed the sensual tone from music together with human emotion, and made music a mechanism of sounding forms, he turned all living powers of music into rhythm. In great moments such as are contained in "Spring Rites," this rhythm was an elemental force, something superhuman that bursts from the depths of life. That was all that was left in the world of the divine and the eternal.

Just as it had been for the man of prehistoric times, rhythm again became a great god. All other divinity had fled the world which had become empty, meaningless, activity without sense or aim.

A deep pessimism fills Stravinsky's music in the period before the war. After 1910 his music becomes ingenious music of an intelligent man for whom life and world have lost their purport, and who can sense a super-worldly power only in the wild, whipping, crushing rhythm. This power reaches out of the clouds with a strong arm and presses man against the earth with a hard hand.

The god to whom Stravinsky prays in "Psalm Symphony" is the spirit to whom this arm belongs. It also presses man against the earth. It appears in the rigid rhythms, in the rigid chords, in the rigid melodies of this music. It walks on dark clouds in the heavy basses of the music. Its trumpet voice rings out like a voice of ancient times into a despairing world that goes from one blood bath to another. It is the old Christian God of Byzantium to whom Stravinsky prays. The mournful man who in the church of Cefalu looks with large black eyes and threatening hand from the golden sky to the nave that is enveloped in clouds of incense. The God who punishes mightily and before whom the world sinks into nothingness. The God who considers all mortals sinners. A god without mercy, without forgiveness, without recognition of the divine in all human lowliness and even in all human sin.

13

The Russian Revolution

ONE YEAR BEFORE the world war ended, red flame signals rose in the east. On March 10, 1917 a general strike was declared in Petersburg. Laborers, students and soldiers joined forces in the capital of the Czar's empire, and the attempt to quell the rebellion with violence failed. In March 12th the victory of the revolution was definite. It spread over all Russia and sucked workmen, peasants, students and soldiers into its bloody vortex in which Czardom perished.

From these battles Lenin and Trotzky rose to power. In struggles that extended over a period of three years—from 1917 to 1920 —the new labor and farmer state was fortified. No external intervention and no internal counter-movement could disturb the organization of the Russian workman and farmer regime in which the state arranged the entire economic, political and spiritual life of Russia according to great plans, and developed and governed it.

What was the significance of this development for music and the artistic development described thus far?

It meant above all the subordination of all musical life under the new state and the ideology embodied in this state. No similar attempt had ever been made previously, and it has its merits. Most certainly it is audacious and significant when musical life in a country occupying one-sixth of the global surface is completely organized by the state as an important part of its mission. The cultivation of music in factories and clubs, concert and opera performances in all sections of the country, the expansion of musical development and education, the encouragement of musical talents, support of music-scientific research work, publishing of new compositions, the lively discussions on music—all this created a music life in Soviet Russia that filled the whole width of the new state with vitality and prepared the ground everywhere for new musical seeds. The organization of music life in Russia by the government may be considered as one of the great positive accomplishments of Russia.

Much more complicated is the question as to the significance and purport of the social and economic development in Russia in regard to creative composition. A regime like Soviet Russia, that originates out of a definite ideology and that converts this ideology to reality in every phase of life, must subordinate the work of musicians to its aims. The creation of musicians has to serve a certain idea block that was perfected by the thinkers and politicians of socialism from Marx to Lenin.

There is a possibility, of course, that some day, when the Communistic regime may have been completely developed and established and other forms of life can no longer exist beside it, these ideas will fill the whole atmosphere above the state, just as Christian ideas filled the atmosphere above Europe in the moyen âge, and that the artists would then digest these ideas and inhale them with the air that they breathe. The artists would then work in the spirit of the communistic state, as Giotto and Duerer, the Dutch composers of the fifteenth century, the Mosaicists and the ivory carvers and the architects of Roman or Gothic cathedrals created in the Christian spirit.

The philosophers and scientists would then take the communistic principles as much for granted as the mediaeval scholars the ideas of the apostolic fathers. In the meantime, however, the government in Russia attends to the maintenance of communistic ideas, and communism has its popes who express its orthodox opinions; its Jesuits that are "like a rod in the hand of their authorities"; and its Dominican friars who punish heresies and, although they do not burn the heretics, they assist them in other ways into the old heretical heaven that is of a certainty rich in strong spirits from all ages.

For the time being at least artistic work can come in conflict with the ideas that the architects of the Russian socialistic state consider necessary and correct—as among musicians Shostakovitch found out. Inasmuch as the power of the state that regulates all life is great, and even without secret police would be great, it cannot be stated that artistic creation was active in a free atmosphere.

Spiritual conflicts between state, society and industry and creative artists must lead to the defeat of the artists, as is always the case in autocrat states, even though in Russia a certain amount of free artistic discussion is undoubtedly not only permitted but even encouraged. The "intelligentsia" has a certain amount of elbow space in the Bolshevist regime, but the authorities reserve the final decision as to where to draw the lines of this free space.

They are without doubt aware of their responsibility in building a new society and new economy that increases the security of life for many millions and makes cultural and spiritual life a common possession. Their autocratic rule serves an ideal condition of society that is to be attained, and the measure of freedom that is granted to artistic activity is decided by the problem of forming state and economy, not by personal discretion and lust for power.

However, the same could be said of the people of Athens when they allowed Socrates to drink the cup of hemlock; of the popes when they banned Giordano Bruno and incarcerated Galileo; of Calvin when he caused Servetus to be burned at the stake. Man is always ready with the finest speeches when he wants to kill or otherwise show his power.

Since the outbreak of the Russian revolution there existed the possibility that the ideology of the socialistic state and the ideology of the rest of Europe would come in conflict as far as they are documented in art. Art never develops in empty space, and the evolution of music since the early twentieth century is a part of the intellectual collective work of the time.

The destruction of the classical system and suppression of romanticism, which in all European countries had set in motion so many musical talents, was not an accomplishment of individual countries in Europe. It was a movement that traversed all Europe and to which Russia had contributed with Mussorgsky and Scriabin.

This movement had produced great works of art in the field of music and brought about countless experiments, and innovations that kept music in lively activity. Its intellectual background was the movement of philosophical, economic and political ideas in a Europe in which the old forms of life were disintegrating, and in a serious crisis that was at the same time political, economic and spiritual and in which the future sought its way to freedom.

The arts, including music, had all become abstract insofar as there was young life in them. The tie with life that had been so strong in the great naturalistic art before 1900 had been severed. The old ideologies that had given shape to program music had lost their purport. The purely emotional and the subjective, mood and expression of soul were repressed. One sought objective forms in abstract tones in new tone spheres. The rhythmic motion, the mechanical quality, noise and sound found in Stravinsky's music were signs of a new active disposition following mollusk-like impressionism.

The Schoenbergian constructions in an unreal space were a longing for the metaphysical beyond reality, as it seized all the arts after the war. Abstract art; anti-naturalistic art; art that dissolved the present and the world into lines, planes, stereo-metrical bodies, into motive energies and rhythms: that was modern European art in the period before the first world war.

Russia was not opposed to this art following the outbreak of the revolution. In the destruction of the fundamentals of classic-romantic music one might even recognize a revolutionary art that was comparable to the destruction of the fundamentals of bourgeois society. Even the transformation of music into material work, and the elimination of philosophical ideologies from music could be considered suitable to the realistic spirit of a laborer state.

One thing is certain: after the establishment of the Soviet regime in Russia the entire modern evolution of European art, from French symbolism to Italian futurism, was digested in Russia. Russian "formalism" that stressed chiefly form and technique, the tonal and rhythmic charm of words, the stimulating force of pictures, symbolic significance and surrealistic values, is akin to the French symbolism of Mallarmé and Rimbaud. The intellectual atmosphere in which Russia's "formalistic" poetry developed had been created by poets, by Rilke, Stefan George, Verhaeren and Oscar Wilde and D'Annunzio.

In music Debussy, prepared by Scriabin, left his mark. The transition of music from Debussy's impressionism to Satie's objective tone figures also found receptive minds in Russia, as did the renunciation of the picturesque and the poetic in music. A composer like Nikolai Roslavyets ridiculed "emotion" and "soul of music" as Jean Cocteau had done, and claimed music was an "abstract perfection," which would have delighted Stravinsky. After the revolution broke loose Roslavyets brought his idea of music as "organized tone material" in accord with the idea of the communist society without any difficulty. To be sure, the songs that Roslavyets wrote for the workers after the outbreak of the revolution are simple in structure. ("Songs of the labouring professions"; "The Songs of the Revolution.")

Of all the modern abstract art trends none had a stronger effect in Russia than Italian futurism with its enthusiasm for modern machinery. The effect of futurism was especially great upon the Russian stage. Meyerhold's and Tairoff's scaffolds, mobile platforms and stairs that made the action of a play visible at various levels were the greatest and permanent gain of constructivism, which shot out of Italian futurism—to express it in constructivistic fashion—like the piston out of a locomotive.

Nevertheless there existed some contrast between abstract art and a labor state that had established the structure of society and economy upon rational foundations, and it was bound to come to the surface in increasing strength. Abstract art—to which belongs Stravinsky's music that dissolves in motion and rhythm, as well as the music of the older Schoenberg that forms tone constructions in a four-dimensional space—is life-remote. The suffering and conflicts of man lie far beneath it. Its forms and figures are similes and symbols.

Art of this type has little in common with reality that is a strong power in a revolutionary state; with the enthusiasm of the society that plans and elaborates on this state, or with the great present that is filled with work. It is naturalistic art that belongs to a mechanical-technical world and society and to rationalistic life phases. Symbolistic art is anti-naturalistic. It is modern mysticism: art of an age which is no longer satisfied with the reality of the world which surrounds the people and that searches for a new meaning of existence in a Hereafter of forms, pictures and tones. The Russian state, however, was the present itself, that believed in itself and was convinced that with work and science it could provide man with a new home in which he could live safely.

The mass of peasant and workmen songs and revolutionary chants of the army that were composed after the outbreak of the Russian revolution and were sung in factories and workingmen's clubs, were certainly mostly primitive music that borrowed everywhere: from the Russian folk song, from Mussorgsky, from noble and lowly music. Still, it was associated with everyday life and with the revolutionary ideology, and therefore it was possessed of reality. The great compositions that were written for definite purposes, such as Richard Kastalsky's "Agricultural Symphony" that was to promote the gathering of the harvest; or the musical glorifications of the Soviet Union such as Mossolov's "Iron Foundry," or Maximilian Steinberg's musical description of the Turkestan-Siberian railway in the symphony "Turksib," or "Dnieprostroy" by Julius Meltus, or the "Lenin" symphony by Shostakovitch or Alexander Krein—all of them possess in addition to their artistic values the atmosphere of Russian reality, which gives them strong life.

The wish of composers to describe in music the new forms of life in the Soviet state and to glorify the communistic principle and the leaders who had created this state led to naturalistic portrayal and to music with ideological and programmatic background—music which in other European countries had long been abandoned.

During the second world war the urge to reinforce the battle against the Hitler hordes with music produced a mass of descriptive or programmatic or ideological music. The young Armenian Khatchaturian composed a "poem about Stalin" during the war; Boris Mokrussof an opus for orchestra, chorus and military band, "Anti-Fascist Symphony." Even the aging Gliere wrote a marching song: "Hitler's end will come."

The laudable cultivation of music of the various nations in the Soviet Union (the ten day festival of Buriat-mongolian art in Moscow in 1940, or the music festivals of the art of Azerbaijan,

Turkestan, Kirghizia and Soviet Armenia, and others) united music in the Soviet with the earth and with reality. Between music of this sort and esoteric music that wove patterns out of abstract tones and plunged from a real world into a sphere of pure spirit, there was an inner contrast that nothing could bridge. The one type of music was editorial, panorama and illustration. It was at home in political gatherings and in mass meetings or in the political clubs where the news of the day was discussed. The other music sought the loftier purport of the world in the solitude in which the individual hears voices that are not of this world.

As early as 1929 the "Russian Association of proletarian musicians" formulated an "Ideological Platform" that was to establish laws for music, music science and music critique from the proletarian viewpoint. According to this manifesto all modern music was a reflection of the general disintegration of bourgeois culture. It stated further that "bourgeois music" (all new music which was ardently declined by the bourgeoisie was termed thus) cultivated sensual and pathological erotic moods and let itself be influenced by the music of primitive colonial tribes. It was filled with mysticism and with premonitions of the coming social catastrophe and the end of the capitalistic regime. It described the motion of modern capitalistic cities, and this naturalism likewise is a symptom of the decline of the bourgeoisie.

The manifesto continues: bourgeois music chooses primitive, common materials as means of "fighting the proletariat." Its characteristic art media are: 1) Hypertrophy of the harmony. Vertical harmonic concepts, weakening of the rhythmic design and vanishing of the melodic invention. 2) Hypertrophy of the polyphonic principle, accompanied by a complete disavowal of the key base of music. 3) Illogical, spasmodic rhythmics. The aspiration to independent "constructive music" and mechanical forms. Rejection of the heritage of a classical past, and striving for "novelty," "seasonable art" and "progress" in a narrow, formal, technical sense . . . a sign of the "psychological despair of bourgeoisie and the direct result of its decline and disintegration."

It is evident that this anathema is directed against all modern music, against Stravinsky's as much as against Schoenberg's music.

Like every church anathema this too is tyrannical, harsh and unjust and hits just the strongest and the independent and revolutionary minds and the great personalities that take new paths with moral courage.

The most reactionary bourgeois critic who represents modern music as being ugly, illogical and immoral can sign the above proclamation: Max Nordau, the fat bourgeois who was the first to fight modern art as a sign of the degeneration of modern life and modern society. Another was Eduard Hanslick who saw only morbidness in all modern music.

In banning Hindemith, Goebbels too was thinking along the same lines as the Soviet musicians of this group. All inquisitors and all chief of police in all countries possess the same traits of cruelty, hatred and tyrannical violence and, when they wish to impede free movement of spirit, they use the same phrases draped in morals and decency.

Although the "Russian Association of Proletarian Musicians" was dissolved by government decree in 1932, its spirit went on. In 1936 it came to the famous anathema against Shostakovitch. With his opera "Lady Macbeth of Mtzensk" he had caused the annoyance of a Russian grand inquisitor who considered the music of Shostakovitch as a "return to bourgeois ideals"; in other words, as a lese majesty and assault upon the spirit and the idea of the Soviet state. One should think that a state that can prove so many great accomplishments as the Soviet regime and that has done as much for education and national culture as Russia, would not quake in its foundations simply because a talented composer wrote an opera that displeased the authorities. The fact that in the history of this state there was only one case Shostakovitch does not make the case any less significant. Such contrasts and collisions could happen daily and the possibility always exists that a Pobjedonozew of the Soviet state might mobilize the police force of the state against artistic ideas, motivated by the "higher interests of the regime."

Nor is the importance of this conflict lessened any by the fact that Shostakovitch accepted the verdict, because he is a skilled and adaptable talent, a versatile musician without the strong inner "must" of a genius. The fact remains that a regime that supervises the entire spiritual and artistic life of a gigantic territory, encourages and directs it, just as it plans and directs economic life, must make mistakes, in the face of the weakness, vanity and narrowmindedness of humans, when it interferes with the field of intellect.

The ban against the opera of Shostakovitch was contained in an article of the central organ of the Russian Communist Party, "Pravda," in the issue of January 28, 1936. The opera is essentially a naturalistic work that fills the emotional narrowness of a small Russian town with primitive passions, with erotic love and murder. Says "Pravda": the music is a "leftist mess" instead of human music; a product of that leftist art "which removes from the theatre simplicity, realism, intelligible pictures and the natural tone of speech." "It is the extension of Meyerhold's most objectionable to the field of music." "The composer evidently did not set himself the task of conforming to the wishes and expectations of the Soviet audience. He mixes tones promiscuously to make them interesting for formalist-aestheticists who have lost all good taste."

The success achieved by the opera of Shostakovitch among foreign bourgeois audiences, continues "Pravda," is based on the fact that "it tickles the perverted taste of the bourgeois audience with its brandishing, screaming and neurasthenic music."

The comical thing about this rejection of the Shostakovitch opera, which employs modern technique quite skillfully, is that Goebbels called the same modern music which the Russian grand inquisitor termed "bourgeois music"—"Marxist music." For Russian art police modern music was a symbol of the decline of bourgeoisie; for the Nazi art police a decline of the "individualistic-liberalistic art principle." What the Russian grand inquisitor and his German colleague actually feared was the freedom of the artistic mind which for them was the same as the devil had been for their mediaeval colleagues in the Dominican cowl and in the Jesuit robs.

The imprecation called down upon Shostakovitch and to which he submitted as a sinner in the moyen âge who has been banned from partaking of the communion of the beatific church and now, with ash on his head, seeks atonement upon the church stairs —this imprecation was merely a part of the bans that thundered down upon "formalism" in 1936. In poetry as in music formalism had been in spiritual association with the collective trend of European art. In poetry it was anti-naturalistic. Poetry was the development of technical methods for formalism, and the product of a perfected form. Music was a structure of tones and the lawful arrangement of tone material. In both arts the accent was on material and form.

According to the theories of the leading aesthete Shklovsky, even Hamlet was nothing but the product of theatrical technique and only a "side product of technique." Such art conception, which only recognizes as artistic the formal quality in the arts, is aristocratic and thereby opposed to the spirit of a state wherein not the individual but the masses are the principal figure.

In addition there was the "Prolet cult movement" that advocated a specifically proletarian art, although Trotzky was of the opinion that following the transition period of dictatorship the proletariat would disappear and under the dictatorship the proletariat would be too busy to create new art.

Thus the battle against formalism increased in acuteness, and in 1932 the Soviet government acknowledged only one of the many literary groups: "socialist realism," the aims of which were formulated by Maxim Gorky. It was the old realism which had made great Russian art in the nineteenth century, the realism of Dostojewsky and Mussorgsky, of Tolstoi and of Gorky himself. To be sure, the social critique had to vanish from this Russian realism, and that was what had made realism strong and an instrument in the fight against the Czar.

The individual was no longer presented in his battle against society, as Dostojewsky and Tolstoi had done, but in harmony with society. The great human questions of the moral and religious struggle of man vanished from Russian realism. The state had devoured man, but it permitted him to be happy in the belly of the governmental monster—which is what Shostakovitch did after the Russian dinosaur swallowed the score of his opera.

The great music of the nineteenth century was founded on subjectivism. Classical as well as romantic music represents moods of the individual person, the suffering and joys, the conflicts and divine services of the individual being which had been freed and made self-reliant by the French revolution. Above the individual there was only God and the idea of humanity; not a collective idea as was the religious idea in the middle ages, but rather something that the individual should have to struggle for just as Faust, erring and aspiring, gained heaven for himself.

This titanic sentiment was transformed to a new collectivism by the communistic regime. The individual was merely a wheel in a large machinery that was to serve progress, the common welfare, the prosperity of the people and enlightenment. The music that conformed to this manner of thinking could not be subjective, it had to be objective. The evolution of European music had led to objective tone patterns and tone constructions and to that "formalism" which the Russian state rejected for its art.

The foundations of Soviet music remained the classic and romantic music forms which had received form and substance from the subjectivism of great musicians and which had been developed in new personal style by great Russian romantic musicians, in particular by Tschaikowsky.

Mussorgsky's courageous act of dissolving the classic forms by a powerful naturalism, Mussorgsky's popular strength, the gigantic primitivity of this musician who plows his field with Tolstoi's plow, found no imitation in Russia. The many strong talents who wrote music in Soviet Russia were not strong and not independent enough to create new music forms. They all made use of the traditional forms. The sole Russian musician who could be called a real genius, Stravinsky, lived abroad and had no direct influence on the musical development in the country that was isolated from European intellectual life until the second world war.

Prokofieff had returned to Russia in 1933 after an absence of fifteen years and wrote film music ("Alexander Nevsky"—1939; "Partisans of the Ukraine"); he wrote the fable "Peter and the Wolf" for the children's theatre in Moscow; the opera "War and Peace," and patriotic music of the present, such as the suite "1941" and the "Ballad of the unknown boy." He certainly was the most original among the composers in Russia, the most individual and technically the most brilliant. However, Prokofieff was never more than just a clever talent. He digested inspirations. His hand is skilled in the elaboration of the things that the mood of the day brings to him. With his neo-classicism he followed the trend of the time. In spite of all intelligence, in spite of his technical assurance, in spite of his form talent, Prokofieff was no leader and no stimulator, whereas even the technically weak Satie was a stimulator because, unlike Prokofieff, he understood not just the Today, but the Tomorrow.

True, there were several original and independent musicians in Soviet Russia who experimented, such as Roslyavets, Ryebikoff or Stanchinsky, but their influence was not big. Most of the new Russian composers used the old forms, and the state that owed its existence to a revolution and destroyed the capitalistic pattern of economy and life, was conservative in the realm of music forms.

In no country of Europe and across the Atlantic were there composed as many symphonies in classic-romantic style as in Soviet Russia since 1917. Old Nicolai Miaskovsky alone composed twenty-three symphonies up to 1942. When the Russian revolution broke loose he was writing his sixth symphony. In the final movement a poem of the orthodox about death is sung, while revolutionary songs sound in the orchestra. During the war he wrote his twenty-second symphony in an air raid shelter. The twenty-third symphony was written by Miaskovsky in a city in the Caucasus which both the Russians and Nazis were fighting for. Thus Russia was the only country in which the old symphonic form marched to war.

Next to Miaskovsky stands Dmitri Kabalevsky modestly with only three symphonies (he was born 1904) which in their strong philosophical force appear Brahmsic; and Leo Knipper (born 1898) with only seven symphonies the last of which was meant as a solemn warning that Russia is prepared. It was performed in Moscow in 1939.

Chamber music and concerts in classic-romantic style also found rich cultivation in Soviet Russia. Among the composers of this music the Armenian Aram Khatschaturian (born 1903) is a particularly rich talent. Flowering and exuberant romance fills his piano concerto; there is singing in all the voices, and with the lyricism of the music is blended a timbre of the Orient that tints life in Tiflis, the native city of the young composer. An oratorio "Heroic Moscow" and the "Poem about Stalin" demonstrate Khatschaturian's ties with the Russia of today.

Abroad the talent of Dmitri Shostakovitch was quick to be appreciated. Not just the proscribed opera "Lady Macbeth of Mzensk," but also his first symphony and the Quintet were soon rated abroad as temperamental, clever and personal music. During the war the Seventh Symphony of Shostakovitch achieved sensational success in America. He was the man of the day and the topic of conversation in the most elegant parlors of New York's Park Avenue. Conductors like Toscanini and Bruno Walter fought for this music and publicity, which in bourgeois society is the diligent helper of capitalism, was offered free of charge to the talented composer of the communistic state.

Among the musicians of today Shostakovitch surely has the lightest hand. He enjoys writing music. It flows from his pen without restraint, and it is always music that has something to say and possesses a face of its own. This ease of invention and technique makes Shostakovitch appear chiefly as a brilliant composer whose skill in absorbing new techniques is great, at any rate greater than his ability to shape new artistic substances. This does not mean that Shostakovitch had no personal ideas, or that he was banal in any way. He is always full of sparkling life, full of rhythmic vitality and absolutely sure in the reproduction of his ideas. However, his imagination is that of an improvisator rather than the fantasy of a creator. It is rich and fresh, flowing and unrestrained rather than concentrated and forcefully formative.

Shostakovitch has the genuine talent of a fabulist which today is no longer found so often. In the present era one is more likely to come upon it among the composers of popular music forms, such as Johann Strauss and Offenbach, than among symphonic composers.

Stravinsky is no fabulist, he is a former; Schoenberg is a visionary. Shostakovitch does not belong in this class of musicians who portray in tones an inner world of unusual emotions and forms never before seen. His music does not move in new spheres, nor does it change anything in the spiritual possessions of the world.

It gives pleasure, creates interest, fascinates, but it does not enrich the present with music that unites the present with the future. The beauty and spirit of Shostakovitch music contains nothing that opens up a view into the future. It is all present, enjoyable and stimulating present.

Listening to the Gustav Mahler symphonies, one's interest is always directed to the man Mahler, to the fighting, struggling individual who has visions like an old prophet. Tschaikowsky symphonies fill the listener with the melancholia and mortal fear of the composer. In the symphonies of Sibelius the nordic nature with which the music is united is of rocklike hardiness.

Despite all intelligence and all technical invention, this human and personal quality is not very great in the symphonies of Shostakovitch. One senses too strongly the ease of invention that "shakes music out of its sleeve," and not sufficiently the strength of experience from which the music is derived. Even the greatest formal constructions of Shostakovitch, the most complicated rhythms and the most liberal harmony motions are masterful engineering art and elegant mathematical formulas rather than profound and serious experience. In the music is more spirit of a technical age than poetic, emotional and expressive power.

One has to admire the hand, so light and so sure, that wrote these scores, more than the head that coined the ideas; it is a delicate, elegant hand with flexible joints. According to his personal disposition Shostakovitch is the born scherzo composer, as is every clever and not very profound composer. He is never more brilliant and dazzling than in his lively rhythms with bold figures and splotches of witty harmonies. His humor never becomes grotesque as it does in more profound natures who feel grief when they are supposed to laugh—and the humor of Schoenberg, Bartok and Stravinsky is of the latter type—his wit is that of a temperamental virtuoso, of a man of sparkling esprit whose pen draws pert lines on the paper much as a cartoonist does.

The symphony type that Shostakovitch created with masterly application of modern harmonic and orchestral elements as the musical form of his clever fantasy acquired a popular quality with the sixth symphony. The symphony becomes a kind of epos, it narrates like a rhapsodist. The musical thoughts are not bound with strong logical force but are loosely connected and drift along the shining stream of fantasy in which are reflected the light of the sun, the clouds in the sky, the forests and the villages lining the shore.

The ability of Shostakovitch to retain moods and to describe them with masterful means, clearly and expansively, is considerable. He does not possess the intrinsic strength of Sibelius, whose fantasy has been hardened by a dismal nature and by loneliness. Nor is there any mythical mood in his imagination such as was evoked in Sibelius by ancient sagas and heroic legends. In him we find absolute brightness of forming, lucidity of contours, distinctness of lines. Figures and fates of the communist state inspire him.

In his sixth symphony he portrays Lenin with an elegy in the first movement which is immediately comprehensible with its long trills, its weeping woodwinds, its chord screams and with the transfigured harp ending in consoling major key. The scherzo is forceful movement, robust work; the final movement a gayly stepping march music that sings like folk choruses.

All this is clear, plastically shaped music; and with all its wealth of modern lines that strike one another with force, and that go on side by side, and of modern harmonies, it is music with popular mood, ballad-like, rhapsodic. It is music without real depth from which a new form might emerge, but it is beautiful, resounding, interesting music.

The Seventh Symphony, too, which became the musical sensation of the war period, has its timely material: the invasion of the Hitler army into Russia. For the portrayal of the German war machine Shostakovitch borrowed the model of the Ravel tone gradation in "Bolero," but he employed it independently. There is symbolic greatness in this swelling of the orchestral timbre and in the portrayal of the war machine that comes ever closer, waxes larger and more and more brutally mows down every living thing. The grand enhancements of the ending also contain the mood of events during the war, of tragedy and triumph.

All this is gripping, colorful, impressively narrated music. There is nothing cheap about it as is so often the case in works written for patriotic occasions. The music is genuine and alive. The experiences of the war period and the reactions thereto are reproduced in pathetic pictures that bring to mind the popular greatness of the descriptions in Tolstoi's "War and Peace."

The portrayals are broad and detailed, like in the poems of popular narrators. But I would not even call this music really profound. It has too much intellect, too much technical virtuosity, too much brilliancy of performance; all of which are qualities that characterize the shimmering of a shining surface rather than a mystic light from the deep. Mussorgsky was never brilliant, while Shostakovitch always is. Mussorgsky was not light and flexible, but heavy and massive. He was clumsy, not bright. But he was bound to the innermost of the Russian earth as Stravinsky was in his great moments. He was gigantic, not agile.

The depth of great art does not exist for one moment in the work of Shostakovitch, only the spirit, the colored robe and the sparkling flexibility of virtuosity.

Shostakovitch belongs to those artists whose imagination is easily set in motion and who do not require much time to work up their inner experiences. That too, as well as his technical agility gives him the appearance of an improviser. Oftentimes shining compositions emerge from this improvising. The Trio that Shostakovitch started to compose in 1944 and that was dedicated to the memory of a dead friend, has as its background the atrocities of a concentration camp. The fourth movement is a tragic Jewish dance, a touchingly grotesque danse macabre. The third movement, a plaintive Chaconne, also is associated with the event that inspired this opus, and is a lament for the victims of bestiality. The Eighth Symphony too is a death lament.

Thus the war provided a strong impetus for the work of Shostakovitch and made him a forceful interpreter of the moods of his country and his people during the war. His preponderantly technical, masterful and intelligent talent, placed upon such a monumental pedestal, appears greater than it originally is. His rich talent, his light hand, his ingenuity in forming, almost assumed the traits of a genius in the glare of advertising spotlights that fell upon his Seventh Symphony.

After 1917 a great deal of good, interesting, talented music was written in Soviet Russia by such composers as Shostakovitch, Kabalevsky, Katschaturian, Shaporin, Knipper and many others, and the expansion of music life across all parts of the Russian state and to all classes of the population is of a certainty a cultural accomplishment of the first order. Russia not only remained the great music country it had become since the early nineteenth century; it contributed to common culture music in a greater measure than had hitherto been the case.

True, Russia's isolation from the world and the development of a special world and art conception removed Russian music life from Europe. Russian music which had been part of a uniform European musical cultural sphere since Glinka and Dargomysky to Rimsky-Korsakoff, Borodin, Tschaikowsky and Mussorgski—a music sphere that was influenced a great deal by musicians such as Tschaikowsky and Mussorgski—had now become an isolated sphere of culture. The intellectual purport and the social aims of the Soviet Union made a music land of the huge country that developed behind its high walls independent of Europe and the rest of the world and that was much more conservative in the essentials of music creation than France or America.

Despite all musical talent and all fostering of music, the country that undertook the greatest experiment in world history in the economic field has accomplished practically nothing for the advancement of music that could be compared with the efficacy of Debussy and Satie, Schoenberg, Bartok and Stravinsky. The situation is explained most clearly by the fact that Stravinsky, the great Russian, remained abroad and that Arthur Lurie, a searching, modern mind, left the country, disappointed.

Of course, we are only at the start of a new historical development in which the ideas and economic patterns, the political and spiritual purports of the Russian state will play an important part. This development has already gone so far today that Russia's isolation from Europe and the rest of the world can no longer be maintained. European ideas and Soviet principles will battle one another. The historical contrast between the West, which was civilized from Rome, and the East, which was civilized by Byzantium and the near Orient, will govern the future history of Europe in new forms. All this means: spiritual battles (in addition to the political struggles) and conflicts of art principles. The ideas and forms of art life in Russia will affect western Europe and America, but the ideas, art forms and art principles of the western hemisphere will retaliate in Russia.

The music of Russia will be in closer contact with the music of the west and, in competition with the music of western Europe and with progressive America, will have to develop new forms and new techniques of music. The formal conservatism of Russian music of today will undergo a change under the influence of western music.

The new era with its strong political contrasts, its social struggles, its new elevation of economy, its new social, economical, philosophical and religious transformations will withdraw with its music further and further from old forms. Russia will no longer be isolated from this evolution and will no longer be able to regulate with such ease her strong musical energies according to the wishes of those who are in power and are accustomed to exercising this power.

In a Russia that distrustfully retired from the world the music of a planned administration could also be subdued. In a Russia that has become great and powerful through the second world war, that extends her influence to the west and southeast of Europe, to Central Asia and to East Asia, and that is in constant contact with the western powers, musical ideas will flow from east to west and from west to east, and the former isolation will not be able to impede it. A new era will present new problems to Russian music also and the old music forms will no longer suffice.

14

Between Two Wars

I

THE RUSSIAN revolution of 1917 was the first flaming sign in the skies that had proclaimed the collapse of the old world order. In 1918, after four years of bloody war, Europe collapsed like a card house. Austria, Turkey and Bulgaria capitulated in October, and on November 11, 1918 the armistice was signed in the woods of Compiègne. Germany, like Russia and Austria, became a republic. The Czar was dethroned. The last of the Hapsburgs signed his abdication. Kaiser Wilhelm, the theatrical Hohenzollern, fled. The German noblemen were blown out of their palaces by the world tempest.

The age of emperors and kings, noblemen, princes and courts which had extended into the new era of machines and factories with all the pomp of the middle ages, seemed to have come to an end. Actually, it was the mediaeval Europe of feudal domination and feudal society that collapsed. The victors were the big democracies.

Despite all these political and social upheavals, the problems that produced the war were not solved by the great conflict. The old tensions that had indicated that the economic and social apparatus was not functioning properly not only continued to exist, but it soon became evident that they had become more acute. The fever line climbed higher and higher, and its irregular pattern indicated a serious disease. All Europe, the countries of the victors as well as those of the vanquished, were drawn into upheavals that, with irregular jolts, rocked the foundations of the social structure.

From out of the devastation and the blood bath of the big war
emerged the revolution, the critical acceleration of all contrasts,
struggles and tensions of administration and of social classification.
Revolutionary movements pervaded Germany whose romantic-
mediaeval structure had been destroyed and she did not have a
firm hold on the ideas of the new age. The old powers: feudal
society, the army, the masters of the banks and industries, the
magnets of the steel, coal and electric trusts, remained the economic
and political masters of Germany.

The democratic forms were weak and were not filled with
living spirit by convictions of the people. Modern minds such as
Rathenau were murdered. Armed organizations warred at the
German borders, or in the interior, or they intimidated. In Berlin
the revolt of radical socialists was suppressed by violence; in
Munich communism came to power for a while.

Hungary also had a communistic rule. In the industrial regions
of Italy labor was fermenting. On the other side of the barricades
fascism, attempting to solve the social problems of the time with
force and suppression, was gathering its auxiliary troops, its unions
and its private militia.

To combat the danger of a forcible domination of financial and
industrial groups in the state which felt themselves threatened
since the revolution in Russia, liberal, socialistic and communistic
parties joined forces in many European countries. In France and
in Spain "People's Fronts" were formed from all democratic
parties and in all European countries the social and political conflicts became increasingly bitter. In the industrial regions in the
north of Italy and in the country riots broke out from 1920 on and
were aggravated by a railway strike and finally by a general strike.

From out of these riots there emerged in Italy the first dictator,
and rose to power. On October 22, 1922 Mussolini marched at the
head of his black shirts into the ancient Rome of the Caesars and
of Cola di Rienzi; he destroyed the workmen's unions, the leader
of which, Mateotti, was brutally murdered; proclaimed the battle
against socialism and communism, and yelled martial watchwords
into the world from the balcony of the Palazzo Venezia.

In Germany another gloomy dictator was fascinating the masses with uniforms and parades, with military music and flags; and the German generals and the German industrialists soon recognized in him,—the man who yelled his hatred of the Jews and the socialists with hysterical screaming and threatening gestures into the masses, —a useful tool for their purposes.

All over the world fascism was bolstered as helper and as soldier of jeopardized capitalistic society. In Spain the third dictator thrust the poor, feverish country into a civil war in which the great states, backing the fighting Spaniards, participated: Germany and Italy on one side, Russia on the other. In all the states ruled by dictatorship—which were joined by Hungary and Austria— violence and the suppression of political freedom were considered the best means of eliminating the social tensions and the economic contrasts of society which had become menacing. As though it were possible to repair a machine that does not function properly by destroying important wheels. The fact of the matter was that the world's economic apparatus had become diseased and that the world had no means of peaceably regulating the mightily increased production process and making it balance with the needs of the masses.

The equality of production and consumption had been still more intensified through the political, economic and social devastations of the postwar period, and Russia's gigantic experiment increased the difficulties for the time being. By tearing her economic structure away from the economy of Europe and isolating herself behind high walls, Russia excluded one sixth of the world from general commerce.

At the sick-bed of European society the dictators were the charlatans in martial attire. Their primitive curative methods were the same everywhere. They destroyed the organizations of the workmen that raised the living standards of the laborers and created better working conditions. They fed the big industries with war deliveries. They enslaved political, spiritual and cultural life. They ridiculed the peaceful, unadorned democracies and threatened the democratic powers of society. They gave nationalism new banners, the police new prisons; they gave new power to social retrogression, and a free hand to bestiality and brutality. Finally, since none of their methods could improve conditions in the countries, they drove to war everywhere.

The years between 1918 and 1938, during which the attempt was made to forcibly remove the social difficulties, the economic contrasts and social conflicts of the time, were years of unrest and increasing spiritual tension. The contrasts that had piled up in the world and had evoked a continuous series of revolutions expressed themselves in the intellectual field as dissatisfaction and unrest, as agitation and discord.

In all the arts there is evidence of a revolutionary, tempestuous state of mind. No great harmonic art production originated during this period.

In none of the musical works that were created between the two world wars is the inner purport of the age comprised in great forms as, for instance, the purport of the epoch of the French Revolution was comprised in Beethoven's symphony. The torn, suffering, self-destructive era that staggered from the crisis of the first world war into the inflation crisis and then into the epoch of social revolutions, sought a new form and solidity in music; but the intrinsic contrasts had become too great to carry big arcs in musical works of art.

All the art trends after 1918 were agreed in only one thing: in the rejection of the real world, in their hatred against reality, in the resistance against rationalism. Out of a revolt against logic and sense "surrealism" emerged in 1924; its spiritual fathers were a philosopher, Henri Bergson, and a psychiatrist, Siegmund Freud. From Bergson comes the glorification of anti-rationalism, the deification of intuitive perception of things, transformation of the inner being of objects into motion and change, and the flowing of world phenomena upon the waves of "Élan Vitale" ("l'Evolution creatrice," 1907). From Freud is descended the analysis of the subconscious soul, of the night of emotions out of which arise thoughts and sentiments, and the underworld of the illogical and uncontrolled beneath the surface of the soul.

Writers like Jules Romain and Gide employed the Freudian methods for character analysis. Proust, whose influence grew strong after 1919, developed Bergson's ideas in his novels. Art fled to the unrational and to the unreal from a period, the values of which were no longer considered reliable and which were contemplated skeptically. The materialistic world philosophy, the exact science constructed by modern civilization, natural scientific observation were depreciated in the war, for with the war elemental and sur-rational qualities had invaded the modern world of technique and sane analysis. The houses that were considered solid shook as in an earthquake, and so did the ground upon which the houses stood.

The subjective emotion of the individual which took on form and shape in classic and romantic art production also became questionable and began to be distrusted. According to the formulation by Jules Romain, man was not just an individual but a part of a social group. One should describe not individual characters but the large stream of mankind, and art is to be the portrayal of general experiences, of the struggles between groups and groups or individuals consumed by groups who, like Verhaeren and Walt Whitman are representatives of common sentiments. According to Jules Romain the path of art led from the individual to the universal, from the single person to the mass, from subjectivity to objectivity.

The individual artist was no longer proud of his particular and unique personality as Lord Byron and Goethe, Richard Wagner and Hector Berlioz, Rousseau and Victor Hugo had been; he sought emotional support in mystical union with the universal and irrational beyond reality. The automatic became the higher power to which all reality was subjugated.

No artist of the post-war period executed this turn with as much intellectual energy as did Igor Stravinsky after 1918. The same artist who, in works like "Petruschka," "Spring Rites" or the "Story of the Soldier" was united with the primitive forces of the Russian earth which flowed through melody and rhythmics like the sap of the soil in a wheat field—this artist changes into a European who now only speaks a universal language that has no home any more.

From something that is alive with extreme strength and colorful fullness, music changes to something mechanical of strongest spirit. Rhythm turns from a force of life to something automatic. The tone motions are quasi-motor driven. The timbre becomes rigid, harsh, noisy, objective tone. The wind instruments come to the fore.

In 1920 Stravinsky wrote his "Symphonies for Wind Instruments," dedicated to the memory of Debussy, in which the tone of the wind instruments already has that abstract timbre that Stravinsky in later years prefers to the expressive tone. In the "Octet for Wind Instruments" (1923) and in the "Concerto for Piano and Wind Instruments" (1923–24) we find the same tone of an ideal mechanical organ, the same metamorphosis of the tones into stony figure and the same inanimation of the tone. One gets the impression that music has been transformed into the ice era by a global revolution where vegetation freezes.

The tone form that Stravinsky could consider ideal can be attained only by mechanical instruments, for which the composer at that time evinced special interest. In 1917 Stravinsky composed his "Etude for Pianola," and in 1922 his works were arranged for Playel's mechanical piano. I have already pointed out, that originally Stravinsky had composed "Les Noces" (1914) for accompaniment with mechanical piano and electric organ.

He was a fanatic about the objectivization of music and the exclusion of everything that was subjective, of all personal feeling, all moodiness. He abhorred every personal interpretation of his music. "Interpretation," he writes in his memoirs, "is a thing I have a horror of . . . this is an absurdity in music and for the interpreter it is a source of vanity inevitably leading to the most ridiculous megalomania."

The man who records his works is the ideal interpreter of his music, not the most famous conductor who out of his own personality gives new shape to his music. A conductor should merely pull the rope to which a bell is attached. What goes on at the other end is no concern of his. The bells will take care of that.

The mechanization of the tone is accompanied by the mechanization of the tone motion. Music becomes a rolling of tone figures. It is an ideal machine with turning wheels. In the Piano Sonate (1924) the music is a cylinder that rotates, whirls and rolls. We find the same thing in the Serenade for Piano (1925). Here the music has lost all color, even the gray, and has shrunk down to a line. The voices are harsh. Dry staccati invade the music. The chords are rigid.

During the time that the European world was tossing in a fever, Stravinsky's music had turned completely mechanical. This mechanism contained spirit, knowledge, technical talent and keen intellect; but the connection between music and life was disrupted, and the cries of the dying and the battle cries of those who fought for freedom did not resound in the music. Nor did the longing of prisoners for light, nor the jubilation of victory. The music lost everything that united it with life except the spirit. It has no home, no fatherland, no earth; it is merely precise, technically perfected, ingenious like every machine.

In the same period Stravinsky's good friend, the painter Picasso —who was alienated in Paris from his native Spain as Stravinsky was from the Russian earth—transformed the shapes of life into geometry, or he threw them into an apparatus where they were torn apart and their limbs distorted or intertwined. It seemed as though nature, life and reality had lost all meaning for the two great artists, and as though for themselves God had become a huge mechanism that crushes reality with its wheels.

The great classical work of Stravinsky's turning against reality is his opera oratorio "Oedipus Rex" (1926–27). This opus is not a tragedy, but the monument of a tragedy; a tragedy that has turned to marble. The ancient myth is not translated into a modern version, thereby obtaining life, as Girardoux did with "Elektra"; it is placed at a distance. The events in Cocteau's text stand still; the people are like statues. It seems as though a marble frieze would come to life for a few minutes, but its figures remain motionless.

A narrator who introduces the action transforms it into something that is not life, but abstract description. The Latin text of this opera, to use Stravinsky's expression, is "purely phonetic material for the composer" just as the Latin texts in churches which the Latin text prevents "from falling into sentimentalism and consequently into individualism." The Latin text lends majesty and monumentality to the ancient action. The stage scene should not be naturalistic: every profundity should be lacking, and the Akropolis should only be lightly indicated in chalk.

The scenery of the first act is blue with white curtains. In the second act, where tragic fate strikes, the background should be black. The actors may move only head and arms so that they resemble statues. In the second act King Oedipus is to appear with a new tragic mask. Thus the performance assumes the inflexibility and import of a symbol.

The music gives this sacred theatre style seriousness and depth. The declamation is a kind of ecclesiastical sculpture. It awakens memories of recitatives in Byzantine churches, and has the solemn gestures of priests in their vestments. Other parts recall Greek scales. Everything sounds strange, majestic, inert.

If figures out of Byzantine mosaics were to climb down upon the stage, they would have to sing similarly. The king and the queen sing coloraturas that are just as strange and archaic as everything else. The dark male choruses frame the action. They too are inflexible and like caryatids. From their singing sounds fate. The hammering of the piano, the harps and the drums that accompany their singing sounds like the stamping steps of tragedy. Archaic and torpid chords resound like a threat by superior powers.

Mechanical beats of drum and kettledrum, crashing fanfares of wind instruments, fugue-like choruses, harmonies that are like stone proclaim the might of fate that elevates man and also destroys man. The tragic destiny has the inflexibility of a machine. Here again one comes across Stravinsky's fatalistic and pessimistic disposition which changed his music from something human to something mechanical. However, never before did the belief in powers of a world beyond, that move life as with iron levers and pistons, find such magnificent artistic expression as in "Oedipus Rex."

In the ballet "Apollo Musagetes" (1927) Stravinsky attempted once again to shape the idea of a mechanized theatrical work. The ballet was to be an abstract play of pure forms. The dancing Apollo became a dancing automat that executed angular, constructive motions. The music was archaically traditional. Forms of Lulli, Scarlatti and Rameau, of French and Italian baroque give the impression of lifeless, playful motion. The tone of the string orchestra that accompanies the dances is bereft of all breath ordinarily expired by the violins. Abstract stage space is filled by abstract movements and abstract tones.

The idea of such an ancient ballet machine in crystal clear air and in cold light is certainly a literary idea rather than that of a musician. The spiritual influence of Jean Cocteau in this period of Stravinsky creative work was very strong. Later on the influence of Andre Gide, too, affected Stravinsky; Gide wrote the text to Stravinsky's ballet "Persephone" in 1933, adopting it from the Demeter hymn of an Homerian.

The mechanization of music is an idea that originated in the macadam pavement of Paris, not in Russian peasant soil. It is the idea of a European intellectualist who had become confused by the destroyed, devastated European world that was writhing in convulsions, and who searched for something solid to hold on to, even if it were only a rigid, lifeless form.

II

Just such a solid form and pattern as Stravinsky sought with all his intellect in Paris after the war, the musicians in other parts of Europe were seeking after 1918. That was the purport of the renaissance of Haendel's music and other baroque music which started out from the little German university town of Goettingen in 1922. Here the art historian Dr. Hagen, and the stage director Niedecken-Gebhard had revived Haendel's opera "Rodelinde" after it had been in oblivion for 200 years; they revived it not as a learned experiment but as a piece of the present. As an opera of grand style, but free of romantic exuberance; a psychological soul portrayal in big melodic lines; as an opera of majesty and human dignity, but not with naturalistic passion and nervous expression.

Haendel's opera with its static structure of recitatives and arias appeared as the counterpart of Wagner's dynamic opera and thereby in affinity with modern sentiment, which had turned from the Wagner opera. The stony form of "Oedipus Rex" by Stravinsky was also much closer to the form of baroque opera than to the Wagnerian music drama.

The incitation given in Goettingen was accepted by big opera houses in Germany. There originated a trend as though Haendel had become a member of the "International Society for Modern Music." One Haendel opera after the other was rediscovered, decorated by modern theatrical painters and staged by modern directors who had learned from Meierhold and Tairoff.

The mighty baroque periwig of Haendel was illuminated by modern stage lights. In 1922 he had become the opera composer of the day, and with Haendel the whole instrumental music of the baroque age came to modern life. Between 1918 and 1920 Diaghileff, founder of the Russian Ballet, had sensed with his flair for modern trends that baroque music was en route. He had commissioned Tomasini for a Scarlatti ballet, Respighi for a Cimarosa ballet and Stravinsky for a Pergolesi ballet. The latter, entitled "Pulcinella" was premiered in 1920 with decorations by Picasso; intelligent music, in which the mandolins of the south sound and harlequins joke. Between the instrumental pieces, in which Pergolesi's melodies blend with Stravinsky chords and counterparts, Pergolesi's arias are sung, and menuets and toccatas, buffo arias and tarantellas resound in the clear air which Stravinsky's orchestra sets in vibration.

The orchestral music of Corelli, Vivaldi and the other baroque musicians had a strong effect upon all composers of the post-war era. This music had a kindred element: it was not loaded with sentiment. Playful tone movement formed the greatest part of the concert, chamber and orchestra music of the eighteenth century. In the fast movements there was that purring, whirring motoric quality that delighted the composers of the twentieth century. The music of the eighteenth century seemed to be a forerunner of music in the Stravinsky age.

All this music, which was more play of moving forms than expression of passion or emotion and mood, was possessed of noble style.

In his novel "Fuoco" D'Annunzio describes the performance of a symphony by the Venetian ballet master Benedetto Marcello, in which the "figured movement immediately revealed a character of grand style. A thought that was full, clear and strong like a living personality developed with increasing fullness of power."

This great style of music by Corelli and Vivaldi, that played with its themes was studied and copied by Johann Sebastian Bach in Weimar. Young composers 200 years later tried to learn from this style, and Hindemith and Krenek. Even Stravinsky (in his "Capriccio," 1929) Bela Bartok and Ravel wrote music in the form of the Baroque concerto; in particular they favored the form of the concerto grosso which in all parts is filled with motion, motoric life and mechanical energy and in which the full orchestra alternates with groups of instruments.

In Italy the appreciation of the Italian baroque music as model for modern music creation joined with the national enthusiasm which was glorified by D'Annunzio with tuneful phrases. D'Annunzio edited a collection of Italian music from the seventeenth and eighteenth centuries which was to proclaim the greatness of the age of Cesti, Carissimi, Scarletti and Corelli: "Raccoltà Nazionale." Collaborating on this collection were the composers who gathered in D'Annunzio's villa on Lake Garda under pines and lemon bushes, among them Malipiero, Perinello and Pizzetti, who also all belonged to the circle of Alfredo Casella.

They all wanted to unite the lucidity of old Italian music with modern musical technique, just as Casella himself wanted to. After an age of symbolism that mixed precious and selected tones, and of impressionism that dissolved the Italian landscape into fragrance and color in works of Pizzetti and Malipiero, music as tone play was desired, as it was found in Italian baroque music.

Casella's "Partita" for orchestra gives a good conception of what the Italian composers of the D'Annunzio circle were striving for. Their patterns: the "Sinfonia" as first movement and the "Passacaglia" as second movement are the favorite forms of Italian music in the seventeenth century. The work is a "Chamber Sonata" come to life again. The orchestral instrumentation itself is soloistic: several wind instruments, piano and strings with three kettledrums "concertize" * in the character of the seventeenth century; every instrument an individuality, every instrument like players on a

* concertare: to compete responsively; to wrangle with one another.

tennis court in full motion and tension, catching themes and throwing them back like balls. Thematics are stylized Corelli; harmonics simple diatonics with atonal middle voices. The solo instruments are fully active, they babble and gesticulate. Groups change with groups, lively figure work rolls off as from a player cylinder. The musical inclination is fresh, and the pale cheeks of philosophical thinkers or nervous dreamers have vanished. With the tumult and chatter of the Italian street, with the colorful activities of the carnival, with the melodic versions of the Italian folk song, with Rossinisms and fugatos from Verdi's "Falstaff" Stravinsky's free harmonics are blended.

Exactly the same unburdened, lively phonetic play that fills many voices with motion of every kind and that is so remote from romantic description and exuberance of mood is to be found in Hindemith's "Concerto for Orchestra" or—with strong constructive power—in Krenek's "Symphonic Music," in Bela Bartok's "Divertimento for String Orchestra," and in his magnificent Second Orchestra Suite. The "Divertimento for String Orchestra" is a genuine concerto grosso like the works of the eighteenth century, in which a group of solo instruments competes with the full orchestra.

All this music is "concert music" in the sense of the Italian baroque masters; orchestral music as rhythmically vivid motion of voices and tones. One is quite remote here from all romance, whether it be the poetic romance of Schumann or Chopin, the descriptive romanticism of Liszt and Richard Strauss or the Debussy romanticism of vibrating nerves. Music amuses itself in this kind of music with phonetic plays and combinations of tone figures. This is reality music, abounding with vitality, variety, nimbleness as orchestral and chamber music had been in the seventeenth and early eighteenth century; but this music had a tinge of sportful energy that belonged to the twentieth century.

Stravinsky himself contributed to the renewal of baroque music with his "Capriccio" for piano, concertizing quartet and full orchestra (1929). As in the Italian baroque concerti, the first and third movement are full of motion. Ornamental figures, short, garland-like tone thoughts, dancing tone movements, embellishments over plucked obstinate basses give the corner movements their substance. The form scheme is the three-part classical; the tone the Stravinsky-ish mechanized tone, created by the preponderance of the woodwinds in the orchestra.

The two movements, in which the musical play impulse spends itself in tones, are separated by a mystic Andante Rhapsodico, as in works by Corelli and other Italians of the eighteenth century.

When I told Stravinsky how very reminiscent of baroque concerti was the mixture of motoric music in the outside movements with the melancholy andante music in the inside movement, he replied proudly: "The first and third movements are quite cold, quite cold. Only the slow movement has feeling." Like Stravinsky, Ravel also contributed to the baroque spirit of music with his piano concerto in ingeniously refined manner.

The approach to baroque music was an important date in the history of modern music. It meant two things. First: complete liberation of music from all non-musical influences. Domination of the phonetic forces of music. Full release of the rhythmics. Detachment of music from ideologies. The composers of the twentieth century sometimes took odd detours to attain this goal and often used force, as Stravinsky did, to suppress everything that was emotional in music and to transform music to a mechanism so that the musical tone might be free of all literary, picturesque or poetic mood-inspiring influences.

Second: The return to baroque music also signified a new desire for form and figure after the living forces that effect growth and development of forms had vanished from the classic-romantic forms. It was not interest in antiques that led music in the twentieth century to baroque music, nor educational interests such as led Mendelssohn to Haendel in his oratorios, or Brahms in his "Deutsches Requiem" to the art of the Bach cantata.

The orchestral art of the eighteenth century was for musicians like Paul Hindemith, Stravinsky or Bartok the form they themselves sought, the music they wanted, the road they themselves took. Baroque music was nothing historical to them, it was alive.

It was the anti-romantic music which they aspired to, in a noble, grand form. It was the heritage of their fathers that had been admired by Johann Sebastian Bach and then fell into oblivion.

Bach music itself also took on a new meaning for the modern musicians. When the romantic musicians at the start of the nineteenth century re-discovered Bach's forgotten music, they found in Bach a romantic composer. Bach's polyphony had been Gothic mysticism for Mendelssohn and Schumann, just as the mighty pillars, the dark vaults and the pointed windows adorned with stone ornaments, of the Gothic domes had been. The fugues were romantic figures to them, and their interlaced voices as mysterious and symbolic as the window designs of the Gothic cathedrals.

The Wagner era discovered the dramatic in Bach's "Passion," in the mighty peoples choruses in the cries: "Crucify him!" Wagner's Lohengrin choruses have their model in the mass choruses of the Bach Passions. Here they learned the realistic confusion of voices, and later Wagner composed the thrashing scene in "Meistersinger von Nuernberg" in the pattern of the Bach fugue.

Thus every generation had heard in Bach music just what it felt and wanted itself. For the romanticists Bach was the greatest romanticist, for the dramatic Wagner he was the greatest dramatist. For the modern musicians of the twentieth century Bach became the greatest architect of music, and his fugues the greatest engineering art. Here structures were built solely out of tones and without any other admixture. Here was music that was just gigantic form. The many voices contained nothing but movement of tones that had rhythmic life.

Bach's polyphony was the greatest form of that polyphony with which all the composers of the twentieth century had replaced the classic and romantic homophony, and it belongs as much to the style of twentieth century music as free harmonics. Paul Hindemith's "Marienleben," opus 27, or his "Liederbuch fuer mehrere Singstimmen" opus 33 are composed in Gothic-polyphonous style, and Stravinsky's polyphony is austere and harsh just as Gothic polyphony always had been.

When Arnold Schoenberg completely dissolved classic-romantic harmonics, there was nothing left in his music but rhythmic tone lines that moved and united according to new laws in a tonal sphere hitherto unexplored. He thereby attained a new Gothic style that constructed music forms the way mediaeval architects built cathedrals and the way Bach, the last of the Gothics, had constructed fugues. Gothic in architecture meant: flowing lines in stone shape, straight lines, arches, circles. All Gothic patterns, with the exception of the demonic gargoyles, are geometric forms. The geometrical forms indicate a higher law, divine orbits, suns and planets, eternal being. They are symbols.

So, too, the Gothic fugue is a mathematical form. The starting points of the themes are regulated mathematically. Counterpoint has its mathematical law. Bach's last big work: the "Art of the Fugue" was the greatest accomplishment of abstract spirit in music. The theme that is employed in the 14 fugues and 4 canons of the "Art of the Fugue" has nothing florid as fugue themes of Bach usually do, but something commonplace. ("Barren and rigid, without color, without light, without motion," Schweitzer calls this musical world). A theme crystal is turned back and forth, a stony form. Bach entitled the fugues "Kontrapunkte" as though he had intended to write a theoretical work. Besides he only wrote these fugues in the score to show that they are musical lines that joined to form abstract constructions.

It is strange that Arnold Schoenberg, at the peak of his work, came to the same region where music changes to abstract constructions. After 1914, when he wrote his "Five Piano Pieces" opus 23, his "Serenade for Seven Instruments" and his "Suite for Piano" he could have called his music "Kontrapunkte." In all this music it is a matter of working out a fundamental idea which in manifold shape and turned around in various directions, in inversions from top to bottom and from back to front, forms the composition. From such basic ideas which are as universal as geometrical figures the Schoenberg music is constructed in strict lawfulness.

Horizontal musical lines and vertical tone groups emerge from the same forms. The six movements of the "Piano Suite" are all the re-formation of three tone figures; together they result in the twelve-tone scale which is the basis of the Schoenberg phonetic work. Whatever melodic and harmonic events appear in the "Piano Suite" come from these groups of three times four tones.

Like everything that is Gothic, the Schoenberg music of this period assumes architectuarl character. Like in Bach's "Art of the Fugue," the tone forms and tone lines that develop logically from a basic idea receive a universal quality such as figures of a superior world may have. The colorfulness and fullness of earthly reality is gone. From life, where nature produces thousandfold gay figures, and where mankind fights, loves and suffers, one has risen to higher regions in which magnificent abstractions of being hover in cold, clear air. The Gothic architect copies such abstractions in stone in their symbolic structures, and Arnold Schoenberg copies them in tones that form images possessing the uniformity of mathematical figures.

If, in compositions like the Sextet, "Verklaerte Nacht" and the "Gurrelieder" one has admired the abundance of color, and the intensity of emotional expression in compositions such as the F-Sharp Minor String Quartet, or "Pierrot Lunaire," then in the compositions of the later Schoenberg one must admire the logical power of abstract phonetic thinking. This logical forming had been foreshadowed in compositions such as the D-Minor Quartet, opus 7; in the "Chamber Symphony" and in the F-Sharp Minor String Quartet. It merely developed, intensified, free of earthly material and transformed into the purely spiritual.

All this architectural and constructive work is accomplished by Schoenberg in an unknown space in which there are none of the classic and romantic forms of music and none of the harmonies upon which classic music had been built. Here is nothing but the twelve tones of the chromatic scale from which Schoenberg takes the tone groups of his "basic figures"; out of these he develops his music. A dialectical rigor of a similar type as that used by Arnold Schoenberg to organize his music was employed by the scholars of the middle ages to construct the world in thoughts. Anyone who knows how the reflections of the Arabs and of the Jewish rabbinical schools in France affected this scholastic thinking also knows that Schoenberg's dialectics, which give strength, and clarity to his constructive ability, are a part of the dialectics of his people.

With a dialectical power similar to that with which Arnold Schoenberg created a music of abstractions and constructions, Marx analyzed society and economy and constructed a new society and economy, and Albert Einstein re-erected the physical foundations of the world scene.

Even as a spiritual accomplishment that which Shoenberg created in an uninterruptedly progressing evolution of logical powers can be compared only with the very greatest accomplishments of spiritual strength. He had already proven the greatness of his musical fantasy when as a young musician he had composed "Verklaerte Nacht," the "Gurrelieder" and "Pelléas and Mélisande." The greatness of his constructive thinking did not show until he wandered from the romantic night of magic into the dawn of a new day where no trail and no finger-post was visible.

III

Schoenbergism had been the performance of an individual. As soon as the new elements of Schoenberg's work began to take effect, it became the technique of a school of young composers. Each of these pupils had an individual personality, and each represented one side of Schoenberg's personality.

Anton Webern was attracted by Schoenberg's mysticism. He heard music, strange, fine sounds, gentle voices that faded rapidly, resounding lines that, like the threads of Indian summer, assumed peculiar shapes when they soared through the air—all this he heard in Schoenberg's four-dimensional sphere.

Egon Welles employed Schoenberg's doctrine as culture experiences in operas and ballet music. Hans Eisler borrowed from it the form for revolutionary choruses and film music in the style of "Begleitung zu einer Lichtspielzene" that Schoenberg had written in 1931.

But the heir of Schoenbergian constructivism was Alban Berg, born in Vienna in 1885. Berg grew up in Vienna in the Mahler era. Here the nervousness of a new age, the impressionistic color arts, the psychological Ibsen theatre, the new functional architecture produced a fermentation that a young artist like Alban Berg absorbed with special vigor and enthusiasm. At that time Berg was writing the piano score of Schoenberg's "Gurrelieder," the piano score of Schreker's "Ferner Klang" and that of the "Eighth Symphony" by Gustav Mahler. He was, therefore, in the midst of all the romantic colorful lights and magic tricks of orchestra blends.

A peculiar Viennese poet who held ecstatic speeches in front of drunken prostitutes in the night cafés of Vienna—speeches on Christ, love, nature and delicate feminine souls—Peter Altenberg, inspired Berg to his first composition. It was entitled "Ansichtskarten" (Illustrated Postcards) and was performed by maestro Arnold Schoenberg in the concert hall before a laughing, hissing, fuming audience. A slap was heard: some one had recognized a genius in the composer of these funny songs.

This was followed by lieder and a string quartet with a warm lyricism in the Schoenberg style. In Berg's music romanticism is concealed in the atonality; he was a Tristan of 1900 who had met Schoenberg.

The final movement of Berg's "Lyric Suite" even contains a Tristan quotation; not ironic as it is found in Debussy's "Children's Corner," but with all its longing and ecstasy. In this composition too we find Alban Berg's first great constructivistic accomplishment. The ghostly fast movement comes roaring along like an autumn storm, and subsidies again in reversed tone sequence. In this manner Alban Berg had made a poem of the Schoenberg technique of inversions.

Berg's constructivism becomes still more magnificent in the opera "Wozzeck" which was composed in 1922, in the period between the two world wars. Judging by the mood, this opera is a creation of expressionism which had filled the German theatre with revolutionary tempests between 1918 and 1925. Dissatisfaction with society, disappointment in the world that was driving toward chaos and self-destruction, and horror of the apocalyptic horsemen who rode over Europe's battlefields had torn the dramas to shreds. The pictures passed by like the scenes of a wild dream.

The world appeared deranged; the agitated soul of the poets saw matters only in the instant of ruin and dissolution.

George Buechner, from whose tragedy "Wozzeck" Alban Berg took the text for his opera, had been a forerunner of theatrical expressionism. Born in the same year as Richard Wagner, the romanticist, this tempestuous, wild German poet was a revolutionary who, in the fifteen scenes of his "Wozzeck" reproduces the fate of a confused, tortured soldier; scurrilously in one instant, visionary the next, then again tragically. "Man is an abyss: one gets dizzy looking down," Buechner proclaimed as the tenet of his tragedy.

Berg's music is condensed and compressed to the extreme with Schoenberg-like technique. The lyrical is given strongest intensity; the dreadful becomes eerie mood; gentle and sentimental qualities take on a soulful timbre; the grotesque and distorted characteristic sharpness. The world is pictured as it appears in Wozzeck's soul which, in its agitation, sees all figures distorted and hears military and dance music shrill and menacing. A sinister, increasingly swelling orchestral trill announces the catastrophe and at the end, after death has devoured the poor human creature, children dance their roundelays in bright sun light. All the tragic scenes of the piece, filled to the brim with dynamite, are bound by strong musical constructions. Individual scenes are compressed in closed musical forms, one being a variation, another a fugue and the third a symphony in five movements.

Paul Hindemith employed constructive forms of a different type in his opera "Cardillac," which appeared a year after Stravinsky's "Oedipus Rex" (1928) and adopted the objective style from that granite opera. The three-part musical form predominates in the scenic structure. Each scene is a musical unit. In addition the orchestra and singing voices are bound by polyphonic forms. A love scene is composed as a flute duet.

The forceful cinematic story of Goldschmied who attacks and kills the people who have bought jewelry from him is transformed by the closed musical forms and by the polyphonic orchestral treatment into a piece of music that is neither a realistic description nor a psychological analysis; it constructs musical forms according to laws of its own.

The inspiration given by Stravinsky's "Oedipus Rex" was put to use in different brilliant form by Darius Milhaud in his opera "Christophe Colomb" (1930) with a libretto by Paul Claudel. As in "Oedipus Rex," a narrator is engaged here and reads the story of the life of Columbus and the discovery of America out of a book while it is performed on the stage with cinema pictures. The chorus accompanies this narrative with exclamations, questions and discussions. Once Columbus stands on stage while simultaneously another Columbus stands with the chorus explaining the drama. With its 27 scenes, with 50 actors and with cinematic pictures it presents the life of Columbus and the fate of his discoveries following his death as a kind of mystery play.

IV

Stravinsky's "Oedipus Rex," Schoenberg's twelve-tone constructions, the European return to the baroque concerto and to Gothic polyphony, the increase in abstract forms in music—they all prove how great the need was in music between the two wars to attain solid forms.

The classic-romantic forms had been destroyed. Classic harmonics on which centuries had been building, had dissolved. The classic-romantic orchestra, having swelled to gigantic proportions, had reached the limit of its possibilities. However, since every genuine crisis is not just a crushing of old forms but a transition to new forms as well, aspiration to new syntheses in music was bound to become apparent. That this happened in the period between the first and the second world war proves, that all the tumult and all the battles of this period, all blood-shed and all revolutions, civil wars and social struggles were the labor pains of a new era which, in politics as in economy and society, had the old mother ground of the European world writhing in cramps.

The composers of this era, unlike the painters, were not satisfied with destroying world phenomena, with transforming them into rigid geometrical and stereometrical shapes and with blazing a trail with violence and despondent courage from this world to a Hereafter that would give meaning to unsatisfying life,—although Stravinsky was close to these painters with his music after the war. Nor were they content, as were the expressionistic poets and painters, to change the real world to hallucinations of an agitated fantasy, although there was a period in Schoenberg's work when he tried that too.

All important musicians between 1918 and 1938 felt the urge, to reorganize music that was free of romanticism, and to redevelop forms, tone, harmony, expression and technique from purely musical forces. True, the intensive occupation of musicians in this period with technical problems, the many experiments with musical style and technical media, the concentration of so much strong, dazzling spirit on forming, especially on the organization of phonetic material in scales and tone groups, had the disadvantage that music in the time between the two wars was remote from everything that filled mankind with sorrow, fury, bitterness and hope. Not in one musical work does one sense a reaction to the murdering that goes on in the war.

When the painter Heckel painted soldiers with bandaged limbs, or the engraver Beckmann set the convulsions of the wounded on the copper-plate, or corpses or the misery of the military hospitals; or when Ernest Barlach carved his wood relief "Hunger"; or when Emil Nolde or Roualt painted religious pictures out of a deep inner struggle, one is affected directly by the life of the era.

In stage plays by Ernest Toller or Kaiser, Goering or Hasenklever one finds the excited atmosphere of the epoch, the noise of its political battles and the resentment of its social needs.

In music of the same time there is no similar moment in which one might hear the cry from the depth of the era. Only Stravinsky's "Story of the Soldier," and much later Schoenberg's "Ode to Napoleon" were great musical works of art in which are echoed the problems of the serious crisis that filled the world with war, revolution and slaughter.

Lesser creations of the day such as Kurt Weill's "Dreigroschenoper" and his opera "Mahagonny" owe their success partly to the aggressive social satire of their ballad like music. They are acute and courageous in the popular style.

Almost all the music that was composed during and after the first world war sounds as though it were in a vacuum where no noise from the real world can penetrate.

This striking phenomenon is explained by the fact that the music of this period opposed every kind of naturalism and every kind of emotionalism. Detachment from reality and from everything that was mood, emotional expression and passion had become an historical necessity. Naturalistic portrayal and naturalistic effect were expressive forms for twentieth century music which it declined ardently because they belonged to an obsolete art.

From the energy with which an artist like Stravinsky threw himself upon mechanical and objective music one can sense how intrinsically he was bound to realism, which he fought within himself and which, in "Noces" broke through again so forcefully.

One senses equally in the emotional and spiritual energy with which Schoenberg barricades himself behind constructive forms how great is the capacity of his soul for reverie and emotion, which he tries to conceal. In all of these modern musicians a piece of romance is left which they try forcibly to keep incarcerated.

Their hearts bled when they tore themselves away from reality and life, but they went the predestined path and fought against every kind of romanticism, even the romanticism in their own soul.

Their historic task had been to liberate music from the poetic, from the philosophical, from the picturesque, and from the subjective sentiments of emotionalism, in order to construct pure forms of tone. In accomplishing such great spiritual work, they were not able to listen to the voices that sounded from the uprooted earth of the time; cries of battle, watchwords of political strife, cries of fear and despair, the wail of human suffering. All that would have only led back to a music which they were opposing violently. Only naturalistic music would have been capable of describing the conflicts of the epoch and of portraying life with all its contrasts and its wrestling. Only emotional music would have been able to express all the want and misery of mankind, all the hope and longing, all the horror and all the dreams.

Music was not an art like architecture that could construct only with abstract and geometrical forms and in which genuine material in practical form produced new forms of architectural beauty. Neither was music painting which—as "surrealism" had done—demolished world phenomena and disturbed their cohesion, yet was still able to preserve forms that recalled life, just as a dream is a re-formation of reality. Music as rolling mechanical motion of tones or as abstract play and music as phonetic figure in objective distance was removed from the living source of music. It no longer brought reality to mind, and even when there was spirit in it, it seemed to be technical spirit rather than living spirit.

Music without a background of nature and without the human heart as a center had an unreal character. This spiritualistic trait of modern music that changed to forms of abstract tone—forms that are more closely related to mathematics than to the motley figures of life—separated music from life of the present for a while. Still, the re-organization of phonetic material in music was a great creative accomplishment. It presupposed a keen understanding of the meaning and the necessity of the time; great emotional valour, an impressive neutrality. It was a positive constructive achievement that the twentieth century composers attained.

We are indebted to these composers for having prepared the material with which composers of the future will fuse in new ways the human and emotional purport of the time that was being shaped in a fiery furnace during the great crises of the twentieth century. It will not be the problem of future music to blend the technical, phonetic, harmonic and orchestral innovations of twentieth century music with ancient forms, as Shostakovitch does with dazzling talent and superficiality. Its mission will be to develop out of phonetic material that has been freed of all foreign admixtures new forms of pure musical vitality which will absorb the new humanity and its spiritual substances.

Great work by many important musicians had a part in this phonetic material. Richard Strauss first made the romantic tone hard and characteristic in the workroom of naturalism; he took the solemn ideology away from music and let the romantic gala cloak fall to the floor. Gustav Mahler gave nervous intensity to the tone, and new expression to the musical lines. Claude Debussy dissolved harmonics and transformed them into color. The French "Six" turned music into pure phonetic play.

In the midst of these developments that gave tone material new colors, new significance, new associations, Stravinsky and Schoenberg led music from the romantic period into a new era and with intellectual energy enhanced the pure musical forces.

The dissolution of old harmonics is in the background of this evolution, the destruction of classic triads by the ever increasing chromatics, the substitution of the seven-tone scale by the twelve-tone scale. With that is connected the dissolution of the homophonic composition upon which the classic form and classic music expression are based, and the development of a new polyphonous style of music. And beneath the visible surface of all these manifestations we find as real driving force: the turning from subjectivism, which had animated classic as well as romantic music, to objective form and the detachment from Rousseau-ish exuberance, from Byronism, from romantic nature and landscape description, from the colorful illusions of tone color, from the romantic blending of arts, from theatrical pathos and from external imitation and copying of the surface of things.

All these were great achievements that will endure. Music will remain phonetic form and a structure of tones and, as a distinct world, it will be motivated by forces that belong solely to this world. The substance of music will be the life of the tones, and not foreign or borrowed life. No blood transfusions from other arts will be necessary to inject music with vital strength. It will retain the dignity of a great symbol of tones, and will reproduce not subjective moods, but objective legality.

The great subjectivistic era that began with Beethoven, Goethe and Lord Byron, and closed with Liszt, Berlioz, Chopin and, finally, with Debussy and Scriabin, has ended. It was one of the grandest and proudest areas of human fantasy in which artistic greatness expressed itself boldly and colorfully. This epoch attained its highest peak in the art production of Beethoven and Richard Wagner— the zenith of the classics in Beethoven, the zenith of romanticism in Wagner. It was so great that many have forgotten that there were other styles in the history of music beside that created by classic and romantic subjectivism and which for many is the only music style they knew.

The big epoch of Dutch art in the fifteenth and sixteenth centuries built masses and motets as constructive works of art in the manner of cathedrals. The 36-part canon motet of Jean d'Ockghem, "Deo Gratias" and the 24-part motet "Qui Habitat" by Josquin Près stood at the end of an evolution of contrapuntally arched music that had begun with the "Krebskanon" of Guillaume de Machaulte in the fifteenth century.

All this music is more architecture than emotional expression. Its polyphony is as artistic as the arch system of a Gothic church. The polyphonic masses of that time are consolidated by Cantus firmus melodies as with buttresses. The religious moods of these compositions are not expression of a subjective religious inclination. In majestic, objective solemnity voices rise above voices as pure tone that mounts like incense. That is the case in Palestrina's music yet. Masses and motets by Palestrina have a sublimely solemn quality that admits the religiosity of the individual into universal religiosity. Not until the baroque age does the tone of passionate, fanatical devotion penetrate sacred music which no longer proclaims the Immanence of God with calm orbits, but the religious ecstasy of the individual. All sacred music of the classicists is such baroque music.

That it is possible to build and construct with tones, and to weld phonetic lines to objective form was almost forgotten by the age that began in the Renaissance epoch with the release of the subjective; this despite the fact that Bach fugues in the eighteenth century revealed the power of constructive music. Again it was a religious era which, as the middle ages did in motets and masses, arched in fugues, constructed vaults and connected pillars. Following an individualistic age, as the seventeenth century had been, music in the era of Bach again became timbre and form of universal religious feeling.

Just as a geometrist comprises lines, planes and curves in abstract and general formulas which are symbols of their lawfulness, so did all great masters of polyphonic music—the Gothic musicians,

Palestrina and Bach—regard tone lines as abstractions and as allegories of higher spheres. The strong geometric character of Gothic architecture, and the mathematical character of Bach's fugue counterpoint (play with inversions, enlargements and diminutions of themes, double counterpoint, the quint inserts of the fugues) display an intrinsic affinity that is no coincidence.

It appears that only an era in which man realizes his affinity to the universe and in which subjective feeling is consumed by common sentiment, is capable of creating objective and abstract music works. Eras of that kind were religious ages, such as the moyen âge and the era of Bach. Their musical form of expression was always the polyphony in music. Their technical medium that regulates the connection of phonetic lines was counterpoint.

When twentieth century composers sought universal expression instead of subjective expression in music, and a new polyphony instead of the classic music of individual emotion, they gave proof that the world was searching for a new mutuality of society. European society had fallen to pieces, it had been split by national and social contrasts, had been thrown into a blood bath by wars and had been forcibly brought to artificial unity by dictators. In a crisis within which all unsolved contrasts of the age turned into economic disorder, national hate, social suppression, into revolutions and war, mankind worked its way through to new forms of life, economy and society that were to form a new unity.

Such new entity and such a new joint form was what the composers of the twentieth century were seeking when they veered away from the subjective music of the classic-romantic era. In modern times religious feeling could no longer form such a unity. But social feeling had taken the place of religious sentiments of the middle ages. The great crisis of the twentieth century with which all music of this time was associated was, above all, a social crisis, and for a long while it will be the mission of history to construct a new, harmonic social substance of society.

The aspiration of composers to new objective forms; the detachment of tone from all subjective accessories and all subjective interpretations; the turn to abstract shapes; the destruction of all foundations of music as expression of individual sentiment; the neutralization of music: all served the same purpose, viz: the metamorphosis of music from an artistic medium of expressing battles, moods, dreams and fancies of the individual, to the resounding form for universal sentiments.

It was not easy to go straight ahead on a foundation that was shattered by earthquakes. Detours were necessary, intermediate solutions. Again and again the technique had to be renewed, again and again new problems solved. One has only to glance at the artistic work of Stravinsky or Schoenberg to realize how much spirit and energy it took to advance. But the goal was a noble one, and in the history of the spiritual battles in the twentieth century the great musicians of this era will occupy a glorious position—musicians who gave tone the dignity of a great symbol that spread the calm light of a higher law upon the struggling world.

15

Music in the United States After the Second World War

FROM OUT OF THE second world war, in which the crisis of the world had staggered into blood and destruction for a second time, the great democratic countries and Soviet Russia emerged as victors. Only the future will be able to answer the anxious question as to whether the era of world wars has been brought to an irrevocable close by this biggest and bloodiest of all wars, or whether mankind's powers of invention will prove their ability to destroy culture and human lives in the devastation of a new war. Who would not hope that the world may never again need to wade through ruins and oceans of blood in order to re-erect its society, its economy and its humanity?

Europe, where the artistic accomplishments analyzed in the foregoing chapters were achieved, is for the greatest part a heap of debris, a place of want, misery and worry. In the east the Soviet Union has enlarged its territory and increased its power; its huge body extends from islands in the Pacific to East Prussia and to the Carpathian Mountains. Its political influence in the south and southeast of the vast state extends beyond the borders to the Balkan states and to the Adriatic and Aegean seas; and Slavic nationalism in these regions is united with the economic ideas of the Russian state.

The old separation of Europe into a western Europe that is governed by Roman culture, and an eastern Europe that is dominated by Constantinople and Greek-Oriental culture, is revised in modern forms and, as in olden times, the borderline runs across Vienna and through Austria over to the Balkans where Croats sing the Roman masses in church, and the Serbs sing the Greek-Oriental masses in their churches. Since a cabinet of the labor party is ruling in England, the contrast between the west and the east of Europe has been intensified by the differences between democratic socialism and autocratic communism. The democratic ideas of socialism belong to the west as the autocratic ideas belong to the east, the old country of the Czars.

Accordingly, we find in Europe piled-up masses of political, social, historic and religious ideologies that are bound to provoke contrasts and conflicts; but these differences and battles of ideas are a part of Europe's personality. From these differences grew the artistic and scientific achievements of Europe; they changed to the wrestling of philosophical and religious ideas; they created greatness, progress, spiritual motion, but they also produced war and devastation.

Of all the European countries that made culture and whose technique, science and art were considered as models the world over, Germany today is destroyed, full of ruins and big cities bombed to rubble. She perpetrated grievous crimes, including murder, and must expiate her sins, committed by forsaking civilization—a civilization the humane greatness of which was proclaimed by Goethe, Kant, Beethoven and many hundreds of men acknowledged by science—and by turning to barbaric idols. Nobody today can say whether the soul conflicts resulting from the cognizance of downfall in crime will produce art that will mean something to the world. It could be possible that a new music might result from these emotional shocks; just as Bach music came forth in Germany after the Thirty Year War which robbed Germany of two-thirds of her population and demolished a large part of the German cities.

Germany's tradition that states and cities have to foster music, and that the support of opera houses and concert institutes is a duty of the public, will without a doubt continue to exist in a poor and powerless Germany. All over Europe spiritual and artistic forces in poor countries will have to assert themselves amidst want, unrest and social conflicts. This can give them strong coherence with the struggling, wrestling ideas of the time and can fill European music with great emotional and philosophical energy.

The artistic spirit in France obtained its strongest stimulation from political conflicts, and Auber's opera "La Muette de Portici" as well as Meyerbeer's and Halévy's operas came forth from eras of political strife that wanted to see history on the operatic stage. Moral struggles supplied the German music of Bach and Beethoven with substance. National battles created Czech music, and Hungarian art music was the result of political conflicts.

The strengthening of musical activity and work in Soviet Russia, and the effect of Soviet ideas upon the music; the close association of the workmen's society with the opera house, will enhance the organization of musical activity in all European countries. In this manner musical life in all European states will be set in motion, and the contrast of political ideas, the social conflicts and spiritual, moral and national struggles will give music a new purport.

Music as luxury and music as business on the pleasure market will be replaced more and more by music as a cultural obligation of society. The whole evolution which since 1830, in the prime of capitalistic economy in European countries, made music a branch of this economy with manager, agents and publicity as driving forces of theatrical and concert business, has already exceeded its climax. But the association of music with life, with the broad classes of the population and with the masses, intensified by the technical inventions of radio and television is making progress.

From among the great countries of the world, the United States of America emerged from the war as the mightiest, the wealthiest, and technically the best developed power. This country, from whose ports ships set sail for Europe and the Far East, is united with the whole world to greater extent than ever before. Her economy, her ways of life, her industrial and cultural achievements will have an increasingly powerful influence upon other countries. This development will also be of utmost importance for music; for the development of America to a great land of music is one of the grandest accomplishments of this country, and the expansion and augmentation of her musical forces one of the most important results of the spiritual work achieved here during the nineteenth century.

The evolution of America to one of the first music countries in the world does not comprise more than 200 years. In the middle of the eighteenth century the first music societies were founded, in Charleston (1762), in Boston (1786) and in New York (1773). In 1800 the Philharmonic Society gave its first concert in New York at the Tontine Hotel on Broadway. In 1843 New York had its first quartet evening. In 1831 Haendel's "Messiah" had its first New York performance by a choir of 47 members and an ochestra of 38.

In 1815 the famous Haendel and Haydn Society was founded in Boston, where prior to 1700 there had been few instruments. In 1818 this society performed the first "Messiah" and in 1819 the "Creation," also for the first time. In 1857 the first conservatory was established in Baltimore. And vocal classes did not begin to exist in New York, Cincinnati and Pittsburgh schools until 1835, nor music classes in Boston's municipal schools until 1837. The first music professor of an American university was appointed in 1875: Paine, at Harvard; and Yale University has a music department since 1894.

Opera in popular form was welcomed even before 1800 in cities in the east. English touring groups brought ballad-operas to Charleston, Williamsburg and Annapolis, and in 1739 and 1750 to the theatre in New York's Nassau Street.

French troupes traveled with French comic operas from New Orleans to New York. In 1813 New Orleans became the first important opera centre in America with performances of operas by Rossini, Mozart, Spontini, Mehul, Gretry, Gluck and others.

In 1826 Manuel Garcia came to the Park Theatre in New York with his opera troupe and played Rossini's "Barber of Seville" and Mozart operas; in 1833 the librettist of the Mozart operas "Nozze di Figaro," "Don Giovanni" and "Cosi Fan Tutte," Da Ponte, established his "Italian Opera House" in New York at Church and Leonard Streets, and in 1847 the "Astor Place" opera house in New York opened with a seating capacity of 1800. This was succeeded in 1833 by the Metropolitan which gave New York society the proper gilt frame.

Musicians from Europe's main countries built up music life in

America: the Puritan English musicians who sang their hymns in the white wood churches of New England; the preachers in the German Lutheran congregations; the Herrenhuter in Bethlehem— where Bach's "Hohe Messe" had its first festive performance in America in 1900; the German music teachers in all the towns who, after the Civil War, laid the foundations of classic harmony and classic music all over America; and the Italian opera singers.

The influence of German musicians who represented a great old music tradition was especially strong toward the close of the nineteenth century and, owing to the activities of Anton Seidel, Theodor Thomas, Kneisel, and Damrosch, important for the propagation of solid music cultivation and classical culture.

The serious American musicians went to Germany to study music at its source; Stephan Emery (1841–1891) studied under Richter and Hauptmann in Leipzig; John Knowles Paine (1839–1906) who educated whole generations of American musicians during forty-three years at Harvard studied organ under Haupt; George Whitefield Chadwick (born 1854), director of the New England Conservatory, studied with Jadassohn and Reinecke; Edward MacDowell, America's foremost composer, who gained the respect of Europe too by his genuineness and seriousness, studied with Raff in Frankfort; Horatio Parker (1863–1919) who instructed at Yale since 1893, studied with Rheinberger.

It was not until much later that French artists, such as Fauré, César Franck, Debussy and Ravel began to affect the American composers. They were joined by the Russians Scriabin and Rimsky-Korsakoff, and finally the modern trend, with Arnold Schoenberg and Stravinsky—which from its inception was a collective movement in Europe—inspired the young musicians of America to a solution of their new problems. Thus serious music in America was based on a broad foundation right from the start. The technical bases of America art music were created from material that had been prepared in all European countries and was used by American composers freely and expansively for the formation of their music.

The more serious and solid compositions the work of American musicians produced, the greater waxed the desire to employ the technical means of the present for artistically expressing the ideas and moods of America.

The landscape of the new continent with its gigantic spaces, its forests and canyons, its mountains and waterfalls, the fields of the middle west and the cotton plantations of the south; the east coast with its ports and warehouses; with its boats going out to sea for fishing, and its freighters; the west coast that looks out to the isles of the Pacific and to the Near East; where the primitive melodies of the South Sea islands can be heard, the bell orchestras of Samoa and the hymns from Chinese temples; the huge metropolitan cities with their skyscrapers and factories, with work, speculation, trade, pleasure and crime in the accelerated tempo of a new, energetic, active world: what a background for American music! A new atmosphere, new colors, a new tempo! A new vitality and new humanity.

As everywhere else, the desire to make a new country resound with music was awakened with the treatment of popular melodies. The melodies of the new world were artistically arranged in the "Indian Orchestra Suite" by Edward MacDowell; in the "Negro Rhapsody," the "Indian Sketches" and in the "Comedy Overture on Negro Themes" by Henry F. Gilbert (born 1868); in the "Rhapsody Negre" by John Powell, in the "Plantation Sketches" and "Prairie Sketches" of Cecil Burleigh (born 1885) and in the arrangements of Indian songs by Philipp Heinrich (1781–1861) and the arrangements of Indian and Negro melodies by Harvey Wirthington Coomis, and in many other compositions of American musicians.

Modern composers too, like Aaron Copeland, drew inspirations from small and big towns, from bars and dance halls. But all this is only the beginning and a more or less superficial solution of the problem of finding a new music for the new country.

Chadwick already goes a little further by transforming into orchestra music the fresh, energetic, optimistic American outlook on life in his "Vagrom Ballad" and in his orchestra scherzo "Tam O'Shanter." Or John Alden Carpenter (born 1876) in whose "Perambulator" suite one finds that kind of humor which, when one comes across it in good cartoons, is designated as American humor.

What could be termed an American personality in music which would distinguish this music from European music is not yet very marked in great art music of today. On the other hand it is quite strong in smaller, popular forms. It can be found in the Stephen Foster songs (1826–1864), the sentimentality and lively rhythms of which grew out of American soil and have become folk songs everywhere. The best of these songs contain a breath of landscape and its old people and young girls with blonde hair, its river and its little houses which Foster set to music so sentimentally.

The Negro spirituals too, in which naive souls on the southern plantations praise God and Heaven, belong to the permanent possessions of American music, just like the military marches of John Philip Sousa which made their way all through the world with their vigor and pert optimism. And finally, American dance rhythms conquered the entire world, and jazz was danced in hamlets and in towns, the mountain hotels in the Alps and on the luxury liners crossing the seven seas. Its vitality was sensed everywhere as new tone and new rhythm. All this music collectively is America in tone, melody and rhythm. But the great musician who could bring nature, life and humanity of the grand country into a music form that would win international recognition has yet to arrive. The great personality that would be as American as Verdi's melodies were Italian, or as the music of Bach's "Passions" and Wagner's "Meistersinger" was German has still to grow from the soil of the country; just as Poe, Emerson and Whitman grew out of American earth. The magnificent development of musical culture in America in comparatively short time has prepared the ground for that.

The expansion of musical activity and musical work from America's east coast to the Pacific coast is as grand a spectacle as the spread of the population to the seacoast, woods and prairies; the growth of cities, the increase in industrial activity, the junction of all parts of the country by railroads and the fusion of people of various nations into one great nation.

However, the land of modern industries and modern technics

not only became a new music country within a space of 200 years; the entire position of music in the total life of America has changed from what it used to be several decades ago. In the middle of the nineteenth century music was still an ornament on the surface of life, a luxury for spare time after having earned money and entertainment for the well-to-do class. Hardly two per cent of the population attended concerts. It took a Barnum, who advertised Jenny Lind all over the country with circus methods (1850); or a Johann Strauss who came to Boston to conduct 20,000 singers and orchestra players in a performance of the "Blue Danube" waltz, with the help of 100 auxiliary bands and the cannon shot signals at the beginning (1872) before larger circles became interested in music.

Music life belonged to the wealthy who had acquired fortunes at the Exchange or in oil or railroads and who let a minute part of their speculatory gains trickle down upon the music field. The greatest part of the population stilled its musical hunger with ballads and musical farces. They had no operas and no concerts and no music as serious art that gives life substance and purport.

All this has changed within the last few decades. Music has progressed from the shining exterior of life toward the middle of life. It has reached increasingly larger classes of the population and has expanded more and more to the depth and breadth of society.

While music in the middle of the nineteenth century still belonged to show business—an industry for the propertied classes with managers as the moneymaking agents; with huge working capital and million dollar earnings (Jenny Lind earned over three million dollars in America within one year); with publicity oiling the wheels of the music machine—it now began to merit the support of the large public. Slowly music changed from an industry to a cultural activity. The surface of music life was still the glittering occupation of music business and music market, driven by sensation and advertising, with booms of favorite artists and the exhibition of masterful talents. But underneath this surface of business, social vanity, snobbishness and exchange methods which exploited artists like stocks and products of industry, music life began to re-form.

Music flowed across the entire country from universities and colleges, from music school settlements and public concerts in libraries, museums, parks and school auditoriums; from community choirs and open-air operas, from the music divisions of public libraries and from foundations. All the big universities formed their orchestras, their glee clubs, their chamber music groups and madrigal groups and their bands, thus making musicians and music lovers of thousands and thousands of young people. In many parts of the country colleges became centres of musical activity by giving concerts in their concert auditoriums, or in their gymnasiums, or churches, and by promoting a musical education with music libraries, and lectures on music, with student orchestras and student choirs and music clubs.

Bethany College in Lindsborg, Kansas, that presents an annual music festival with teachers and pupils, and that since 1882 performs the "Messiah" every Easter and, since 1929, the "Mathaeus Passion" on Good Friday, is but one example of many. Once eighteen special trains were required to bring visitors to these music festivals.

In many sections of the country community choirs encompass the entire population in musical activity, as for instance in Bethlehem, Pa., Lindsborg, Kansas, or in the towns of the "Litchfield County Choral Union," Conn. In Rochester, N. Y., the community chorus consisting of almost 1000 members sings in parks and school auditoriums. In many cities municipal bands provide for free concerts in public parks. Since 1924 the Daniel and Florence Guggenheim Foundation supports the concerts by the Goldman Band in New York's parks. Since 1928 the summer concerts in Santa Barbara have been supported by Major Max C. Fleischmann.

The accomplishments of foundations and endowments in fostering music education and music enjoyment are great. At the head of all music promotion is the Carnegie Corporation. Besides providing 4000 churches in the United States with organs, it has most generously equipped colleges with piano scores, books on music, recordings and victrolas; by 1935 it had expended one million dollars for music. By 1931 the Presser Foundation had provided eight colleges with music buildings. Big sums were raised by individuals and corporations, by women's clubs and other societies for the establishment of fellowships and scholarships, for musical contests and concerts. The Elizabeth Sprague Coolidge Foundation in Washington not only built a beautiful concert hall for chamber music concerts, but, since 1925, has spent $30,000 annually for concerts, prizes and commissions for new compositions.

All these springs that converged from various directions and flowed over fertile music soil, have saturated the ground and caused the musical harvest to shoot richer blades. Propagation of serious music by phonograph and victrola, by player pianos and finally by radio—soon to be joined by television—was merely the last stage of this development by which music expanded more and more and reached new classes of the population.

Technical development brought music into every home, and the concerts of America's great orchestra's as well as concerts by virtuosos and chamber music societies and the performances of the Metropolitan and other opera houses are available to every one. The progressing democratization of music life is one of the greatest achievements of the new era, and its further development can not yet be estimated. It assures the United States, in addition to their increased political power and increased material and technical development an intensified spiritual and artistic evolution as well, and the metamorphosis from the biggest music market in the world to one of the greatest music countries of the world.

In Russia serious music had been bound to national life by the planned economy of the state which directs music life, organizes it and even influences it spiritually. Next to Russia the United States of America became the greatest music land which, after having established music life first as a business and an entertainment industry, was now bringing it into modern form as a cultural achievement of a free society. In both countries musical life and musical activity stretches across vast spaces and to new ranks in society which never before knew music history to be so great. In both countries, abounding with music, music life assumes a proportion and a depth for which the history of music has no measure of comparison.

One now enters a new era in music. For this new era the composers of the twentieth century have prepared the musical tools, and it is without a doubt of significance for the United States that all prominent exponents of this music, led by Schoenberg, Stravinsky, Bartok, Hindemith and Milhaud, fled from the invasion of barbarism in Europe to this free country and worked and taught here.

A new technique can be learned; what cannot be learned is a new spirit, new ideas, new sense of living. In Russia these new substances of music are given by the state which provided the socialistic idea world with reality. In the United States the new substances will obtain phonetic form from creative musicians in free competition; but in both countries it will ultimately be the strength and talent of national society from which strength and talent of the composers will come forth.

Only a narrow and limited nationalism, which often results from war eras, can stem this development. But it has been one of the greatest achievements of twentieth century composers that for them music was a universal language, not the particular tongue of one nation. In war time too, modern music was music of liberal character, music of a united world, music of a universal spiritual form. Modern musicians everywhere belonged among the best cosmopolites. They considered Europe a unity, and the world a superior unity. This same tendency was found in the suppression of romanticism, which gave all music a national tint, and in the attraction to abstract music, in the formation of figures from pure tone.

The affiliation of music with the earth, with country and with nation should not detract any of its free spirit and world greatness from music, and the more a country's music will be filled with such tendencies, the greater a music country it will be.

Name Index